CRANIOKLEPTY

CRANIOKLEPTY

GRAVE ROBBING
AND THE
SEARCH FOR GENIUS

COLIN DICKEY

UNBRIDLED BOOKS

Unbridled Books

Library of Congress Cataloging-in-Publication
Dickey, Colin.
Cranioklepty : grave robbing and the search for genius / Colin Dickey.
p. ; cm.
Includes bibliographical references.
ISBN 978-1-932961-86-7
1. Skull.   2. Grave robbing—History.   I. Title.
[DNLM: 1. Grave Robbing—history.   2. Famous Persons.   3. History,
19th Century.   4. History, 20th Century.   5. Phrenology—history.
6. Skull. WZ 320 D551c 2009]
QM105.D53 2009
612.7'5—dc22
2009018527

1   3   5   7   9   10   8   6   4   2

Book Design by SH • CV

First Printing

The end of the story isn't the end of the story at all. It's simply the opening shot in the next story: the necrological sequel, the story of the writer's after-life, the tale of the graveyard things to follow.

· MALCOLM BRADBURY, TO THE HERMITAGE ·

FOR ALEX, AUDREY, AND SHANE

Contents

NON OMNIS MORIAR

At 2 o'clock in the afternoon on October 30, 1820, workers disinterred the body of the composer Joseph Haydn from his grave in the Hundsthurmer Church in Vienna, preparing it for transit to the nearby city of Eisenstadt, home of his powerful patrons, the Esterhazy family. There it was to be reburied in a tomb more worthy of the great composer, who had lain for too long in such a modest setting.

But there was a problem with what the grave diggers found that day.

HAYDN HAD LIVED much of his life between the two great musical cities of Austria: Vienna and Eisenstadt. Twenty miles to the northeast of Vienna, Eisenstadt had been home to the Esterhazy family since 1648; in 1687 Paul Esterhazy was elevated from a baron to a prince of the Holy Roman Empire as a reward for his fierce loyalty to the emperor. Paul was also an amateur composer;

played the piano, flute, and lute; and passed down to his progeny not just his title but also his love of music. Prince Paul's son, Paul Anton, was the first Esterhazy to hire Joseph Haydn as a *Kapellmeister* (a post whose duties included, primarily, composer-in-residence and artistic director of the orchestra). Except for a brief sojourn in London in the 1790s, Haydn would serve the Esterhazy family in that capacity until his death in 1809 at the age of seventy-seven. Much of his fame and success were inextricably tied to their patronage, so it seemed fitting that Prince Nicholas II, Paul Anton's successor, honor the composer with a tomb on the Esterhazy estate worthy of his talent.

But history had gotten in the way. Haydn had died during the battle of Wagram, the largest battle yet fought during the Napoleonic Wars. As the French had marched in from the west, Austria had quickly abandoned Vienna. Haydn faced this invasion (the third in a decade) with resolve: As the cannonballs fell all around his home, he told his family, "Children, don't be frightened; where Haydn is, nothing can happen to you."[1] But three weeks into the occupation, the chaos and misery having taken their toll on the aging composer, Franz Joseph Haydn died from exhaustion.

In such a cataclysmic situation, the death of a composer—even the most famous composer of the day—could not receive

[1] Quoted in Karl Geiringer, *Haydn: A Creative Life in Music,* 3rd ed. (Berkeley: University of California Press, 1982), p. 189. Further information on Haydn's last days can be found in H. C. Robbins Landon, *Haydn: The Late Years, 1801–1809* (Bloomington: Indiana University Press, 1977), pp. 379–390.

the ceremony it deserved, so Haydn's was a simple burial in the Gumpendorf suburb of Vienna, in the Hundsthurmer Church. When the fighting was over, Nicholas applied for and received a permit to move the composer's body to Eisenstadt, but he never acted on it, and the body remained in the graveyard where it had originally been laid.

Five years later, one of Haydn's former pupils, Sigismund Neukomm, erected a small marble marker over his grave with the simple inscription *Non omnis moriar*. The line, from the end of Horace's odes, translates as "Not all of me shall die," which Neukomm obviously meant as a reference to the lasting musical genius of his mentor. Although the composer's genius and his music did indeed live on, his grave remained unmolested for the next six years.

IT WAS NOT until 1820, eleven years after Haydn's death, that Nicholas II was reminded of his obligation to the composer. That autumn he had held a gala celebration to honor a visiting dignitary, Adolfo Frederick, the duke of Cambridge. On the program for the evening was *The Creation*, Haydn's late oratorio, considered by many to be his masterpiece. Based on the Book of Genesis, *The Creation* had become a hallmark of the Romantic notion of "the sublime"—the sense of being so overpowered by art that the feeling verges on terror, where "the mind is so entirely filled with its object," in Edmund Burke's definition, "that it cannot entertain any other, nor by consequence reason on that object that employs it."[2] As Gustav Schilling would write thirty-five years after its premiere, "there is still no music of greater sublimity than the passage 'And There Was Light' which follows 'and God said' in Haydn's *Creation*."[3]

Nicholas II was not quite the lover of music that his forebears had been, but he recognized its effect on those around him and had employed Haydn and a large symphony as much to enhance his status as from any love of the composer's works. But even though he may have preferred simple church music, Nicholas knew the impact that *The Creation* could have on audiences, and when he wanted to impress foreign dignitaries such as Adolfo Frederick, it was a natural choice. It certainly did the trick. After the performance, Frederick, visibly moved, remarked, "How fortunate was the man who employed this Haydn in his lifetime and now possesses his mortal remains."[4]

Prince Esterhazy took the compliment graciously without letting on that he did not actually possess the body of the composer. The next day he began preparations to move the body to Eisenstadt, fearing the damage to his reputation should it come to light that he had accorded so little respect to Haydn's remains. The prince had to reapply to the Hapsburg emperor for permission to move the body and, once he received it, set about exhum-

[2] Edmund Burke, *A Philosophical Enquiry* (Oxford: Oxford University Press, 1990), p. 53.
[3] Quoted in James Webster, "*The Creation*, Haydn's Late Vocal Music, and the Musical Sublime," in Elaine Sisman, ed., *Haydn and His World* (Princeton, NJ: Princeton University Press, 1997), pp. 65.
[4] Geiringer, p. 191.

ing and transporting Haydn's corpse. Only then did he discover, on that cold afternoon in late October, that someone had beaten him to it. When the grave was opened, the grave diggers found the body intact, but all that was left of the composer's head was the wig it had been buried in.

ESTERHAZY WAS OUTRAGED. He immediately notified the president of the supreme office of police, Count Joseph von Sedlintzky, demanding an investigation. The Viennese police were generally held in high regard and were known for being efficient, cordial, and fair. In order to do their job more effectively, the police employed a wide network of informants known as *mouches*—the French word for "flies." Penetrating all layers of society, *les mouches* were always looking for information that could be converted into ready money. When Sedlintzky's men came to them for information, they did not disappoint—but then again, the owner of Haydn's head had not been particularly discreet. After two weeks the investigators, aided by this network of informants, found someone who seemed to know something.

On November 13, a pharmacist named Joseph Schwinner told them that he had once seen a skull in the possession of a man named Johann Nepomuk Peter. "At the period during which Peter was still the administrator of the tallow works, I was often in his garden," Schwinner told the police. "On the occasion of such a visit approximately ten years ago, he showed me and other close friends . . . a skull from which the flesh had been completely removed." Peter was proud of his trophy, Schwinner explained, and made no attempt to hide its origin. "He remarked that it was the head of the recently deceased composer of music, Haydn." Schwinner never inquired as to how Peter had come by the skull, but he did see the head again five years later. "Peter," he concluded, "mentioned each time that the head was Haydn's."[5]

Peter himself seemed perfectly forthcoming when the police questioned him the next day. If he was nervous, he didn't show it. He claimed that a certain Dr. Leopold Eckhart, a physician at the Vienna General Hospital, "with whom I had a close personal relationship and who also knew of my interest in the Gall system, gave me an already macerated head purported to be that of the composer of music, Haydn."

The "Gall system" Peter spoke of was "cranioscopy," or "phrenology," as it would come to be called. Invented by Franz Joseph Gall, it had swept Europe, in particular Vienna, as a means by which one could divine the workings of the brain from bumps and indentations on the skull. Gall had collected hundreds of human skulls in his quest to substantiate his ideas, and his theories had sparked an interest in the skull as a collector's object. "I bleached it in my garden and then mounted it on a velvet cushion in a small case," Peter told the authorities. "During the bleaching process and later, I showed the skull to my friends as Haydn's head."

---

[5] Joseph Carl Rosenbaum, *The Haydn Yearbook V: The Diaries of Joseph Carl Rosenbaum*, edited by Else Radant, translated by Eugene Hartzell (Vienna: Theodore Presser Company, 1968), p. 156.

But Peter went on to suggest that the skull Schwinner had seen was not in fact Haydn's. The identity of the skull was called into question, he told them, "first and foremost by the clerk to Count Esterhazy," Joseph Carl Rosenbaum, "a very close friend and former schoolfellow of mine." As a result of Rosenbaum's skepticism, Peter claimed, he lost interest in the skull: "So it happened," he said, "that my wife had several skulls removed to the graveyard, and the aforementioned Rosenbaum received three as a present; he himself chose the ones he wanted, among them the head alleged to be Haydn's."

Peter had no idea that Eckhart had come by the skull through any illegal means, and had he known, he told the police, he would have returned it long before. When he had first heard of the investigation, he quickly added, he had returned to Rosenbaum and asked for the head back. He now had the head again and was prepared to give it to the authorities. At this point Peter handed over a skull to the police, swearing that "it is the same head Eckhart gave me as Haydn's and which I showed to my friends as such."[6]

Thinking they had now recovered the skull, the police went to Rosenbaum the following day to corroborate the story. Rosenbaum had a much higher social standing than his longtime friend Herr Peter: A court secretary, he was married to one of the two most famous sopranos in Vienna and had been a personal friend of Haydn's—not to mention dozens of other noteworthy com-

[6] Ibid., p. 157.

posers and musicians. He was well liked and respected throughout Viennese society. He had just celebrated his fiftieth birthday and had treated the two hundred guests in attendance to a cantata composed in his honor by the current *Kapellmeister* Kinsky, followed by a fireworks display.

Rosenbaum's story meshed perfectly with Peter's. "I am a childhood friend of Herr Peter's," he said, and explained that Peter, as a passionate admirer of the Gall system, had received several skulls from the then senior physician at the Vienna General Hospital, Dr. Leopold Eckhart. Among them was one that Peter had passed off as Haydn's. "However," Rosenbaum informed them, "Peter later discontinued that hobby." At the time, none of the investigators made note of the fact that the language Rosenbaum used was nearly identical to Peter's—almost as if the two men had rehearsed their stories together. "And so it happened that I received three of the skulls from Peter as gifts, but not at the same time. Among them was the head alleged to be Haydn's." Rosenbaum concluded his story by affirming that, a few days earlier, "Peter urgently demanded that the head be returned," and that Rosenbaum had complied, to Peter's "great relief."[7]

Peter and Rosenbaum had both known Leopold Eckhart for years; he had been personal physician to both men. Having died, the doctor was in no position to rebut Peter and Rosenbaum's implication that it was he who had stolen the skull. But there were

---

[7] Ibid.

problems with the story nonetheless. The first skull they handed over turned out to be from a much younger body; a cursory inspection revealed that its owner had likely been in his twenties when he had died, not in his seventies.

The police went back to Rosenbaum and insisted on searching his premises for the right skull; Rosenbaum had no choice but to let them in. They searched the entire house and found nothing out of the ordinary, except that when they came to the bedroom they found his wife, Therese, lying awkwardly in bed. This was a bit unusual, since it was the middle of the day and she didn't appear to be ill, but it would have been inappropriate to ask the lady to allow them to search her bed, or even to ask her to stand up. The police left empty-handed.

PRINCE NICHOLAS FOLLOWED these events with increasing agitation. After learning that Rosenbaum was involved, he was doubly incensed. Rosenbaum had worked for the prince over twenty years earlier but had resigned following a contentious falling-out. The idea of having anything more to do with this man was deeply distasteful to the prince, but as word continued to spread that he had lost track of his composer's skull, it became increasingly important simply to get it back, no matter the cost. Convinced that Rosenbaum knew more than he was letting on, the prince resorted to bribery, offering a substantial amount to Rosenbaum if he could cause the head to reappear by whatever means necessary.

And so a few days later Rosenbaum turned over another skull. It had clearly belonged to an older man and seemed to match Haydn's physique in other regards, so it was made ready to be reburied with the rest of the composer's remains. The prince, however, did not bother to honor his promise of a bribe; having secured the head, he summarily dismissed Rosenbaum.

Haydn's headless body was in Eisenstadt by this time, and the prince had to forward the head "that was purloined by malicious persons but which has been recovered by the civil authorities."[8] On December 4, over a month after the theft was first discovered, the provost of the Esterhazy crypt interred the skull with the rest of the body. The prince had ordered that the bodily reunion be done in secret to avoid public humiliation. There had already been a fair amount of laughter at the prince's expense over his inability to keep track of his favorite composer's remains, and he was not anxious for the people in Eisenstadt to learn what too many in Vienna already knew. And so the provost entered the crypt under the pretense of affixing a small nameplate to the coffin; alone, he unscrewed and removed the coffin lid, then placed the skull in its proper position before resealing the coffin and affixing the nameplate.

And that would have been that. But as Haydn's pupil Sigismund Neukomm had inadvertently foreseen, at least a part of Haydn was to live on for quite some time. It did not come to light until much later—what neither the police chief or the prince

---

[8] Ibid.

himself could have known—that the head enshrined with the composer's remains was not in fact Haydn's. It was just as well, then, that the prince had reneged on his offer of payment to Rosenbaum since the clerk had delivered the wrong head to the authorities. Had they thought to ask Therese Rosenbaum to get out of bed, or had they simply checked the mattress on which she was lying, they would have found what they were looking for: the head of Franz Joseph Haydn, which Peter and Rosenbaum had brazenly stolen eleven years before, less than a week after Haydn was buried. It would be over a century before that skull found its way back into the ground.

PART ONE

A

MOST VALUABLE

RELIC

Poor skull, thy fingers set ablaze,

With silver Saint in golden rays,

The holy missal. Thou didst craze

'Mid bead and spangle,

While others passed their idle days,

In coil and wrangle.

· JOHN KEATS AND CHARLES BROWN,

"Stanzas on Some Skulls in

Beauly Abbey, near Inverness"

CHAPTER ONE

MAPPING THE
INVISIBLE

The theft of Franz Joseph Haydn's skull in 1809 was by no means an isolated incident. From the 1790s to the mid–nineteenth century, interest in phrenology sparked a bizarre and intense fascination with the human skull, and in particular with the skulls of great men. Just as phrenologists looked to the heads of criminals and the insane for proof of pathological deficiencies, they also sought out the heads of artists and philosophers for proof of genius and intelligence. Often they could investigate the heads of great men by taking plaster casts, but sometimes other means were necessary.

Francisco Goya had died in exile in Bordeaux in 1828 and lost his skull sometime before 1898, when the Spanish government exhumed his remains to return them to his home country. Upon discovering the theft, the Spanish consul dispatched a telegram to Madrid: "Goya skeleton without a head. Please instruct me." The response came back immediately: "Send Goya, with or without head."[9]

---

[9] Carlos Fuentes, *The Buried Mirror* (New York: Mariner Books, 1999) p. 230.

Emanuel Swedenborg, the eighteenth-century Christian mystic and philosopher, suffered a similar postmortem fate. During his life he wrote of spirits that had invaded his "cerebral chambers" and caused him great pain. "I spoke with them," he wrote, "and they were compelled to confess whence, who, and of what quality they were." These cranial spirits told Swedenborg that "they dwelt in dark woods, and were there of deformed aspect, having ferine faces and shaggy hair, and roaming about like wild beasts."[10] Having expelled these cranial spirits in life, he was less successful after his death in 1772, when his head was endangered once more—this time not by shaggy spirits in dark woods but by naval officers.

And then there was the English doctor and philosopher Sir Thomas Browne, who died in 1682 and stands as something of an icon in the history of cranioklepty because of the anxiety he seemed to express about the desecration of his own final resting place. Sir Thomas wrote in 1658, "But who knows the fate of his bones, or how often he is to be buried? Who hath the oracles of his ashes, or whither they are to be scattered?" Browne went on: "To be gnawed out of our graves, to have our skulls made drinking-bowls, and our bones turned into pipes to delight and sport our enemies, are tragical abominations."[11] Because of statements like these, Browne might be considered the patron saint of

[10] Emanuel Swedenborg, *The Spiritual Diary of Emanuel Swedenborg*, in five volumes, translated by George Bush and John H. Smithson (London: James Speirs, 1883), volume II, pp. 68-69.
[11] Thomas Browne, *Religio Medici, Hydrotaphia, and the Garden of Cyrus*, edited by R. H. A. Robbins (Oxford: Clarendon Press, 1972) pp. 91, 117.

stolen skulls, speaking for the collective indignity of all those whose heads were shuffled between museums, collectors, and anatomists throughout the nineteenth century. Browne's own "tragical abomination" occurred in 1840 when his coffin in St. Peter Mancroft Church, Norfolk, was inadvertently disturbed while a vault was being dug next to his plot. His stolen skull would ultimately find itself the focal point of an extended battle between science and religion.

Such thefts as these happened throughout Europe, thefts both brazen and surreptitious, reverent and sacrilegious. Motivated by curiosity, by money, by a morbid fascination that seems inexplicable today, cranioklepts subtly and stealthily helped to change how we view the grave and the corpse, and how we view the great artists and thinkers who come to define an age.

In the wake of the scientific revolutions of the Age of Enlightenment, the body became a site of conflict between several warring factions—the religious, the scientific, the mystical. And at the center of this dispute was the skull: twenty-two discrete bones that fuse together in the first months of life. The skull has always been a central symbol for the human psyche, representing the enigma of life and the unavoidability of death. But by the dawn of the nineteenth century it had begun to assume a new meaning and significance. This was due almost entirely to the popular work of one man, Franz Joseph Gall.

Gall was born March 9, 1757, in the small town of Tiefenbrum in Baden, Germany. His parents wanted him to enter the priesthood, as was the custom for second sons, but as he would later explain, his "natural dispositions were opposed to" religion.[12] Instead, Gall found he had a deep and abiding scientific curiosity, and in 1781 he went to Vienna to study medicine.

THE VIENNA WHERE Gall found himself in 1781 was a city of dust, a city of wonder, and a city of music. The dust came from the cobblestones that were ground into powder by carriage wheels and lifted by the wind. It hung in blooms like smog, especially in summer, so thick that many first-floor rooms kept candles burning throughout the day for light. One visitor to the city called it "one of Vienna's great plagues." The mortality rate due to tuberculosis, pneumonia, phthisis, and other respiratory ailments was incredibly high in Vienna, especially among coachmen, runners, soldiers, and anyone else who had the misfortune of a job that involved running a lot of errands. One man who recorded its effect was Johann Pezzl, a monk who came to Vienna in 1786 and wrote a series of journalistic reports on all aspects of the city. "If you leave your house at eight o'clock on a Sunday evening after a lovely warm day, it is like entering a fog," Pezzl wrote; "one can only make out the lanterns flickering through the dust; and if one leaves by one of the city gates, a dense dust-cloud covers the whole Esplanade. In a few minutes, one's shoes, clothes and hat are covered with dust. The wheels of sixteen thousand carriages

[12] Nahum Capen, "Biography of the Author," in J. G. Spurzheim, *Phrenology: In Connexion with the Study of Physiognomy* (Boston: Marsh, Capen & Lyon, 1834), p. 13.

and their horses' hooves, plus an army of more than two hundred thousand pedestrians, have covered Vienna in fog." It was so thick in summer that buildings couldn't be seen on the far side of the city's parks and plazas, and even the closest suburbs seemed to recede into some distant landscape. "The worst situation," Pezzl concluded, "occurs when, after several warm days, a strong wing springs up . . . the dust penetrates the mouth, nose and ears . . . and one's eyes weep."[13]

Nonetheless, people of all kinds flocked to the city, and visitors to Vienna noticed how cosmopolitan it was in comparison to Europe's other metropolises. Situated on the western edge of the Hapsburg Empire, where Eastern Europe met the West, its streets were thronged not just by Austrians but by Hungarians, Poles, Serbs and Greeks, Muslims and Jews—each with their own peculiarities of dress and style. It was a place where one could sample the world's riches—chocolate from Milan, oysters from Istria, wine from Tokay. "Works of art and music from Italy, France's fashions, Germany's books," Pezzl wrote, "appear at his purse's command, as if by rubbing Aladdin's lamp."[14]

It was a tightly packed city, seething with energy—a city of 270,000 people with only about 5,500 houses. Land was expensive, so buildings shot upward, and Vienna was known for its five-story townhouses crammed along narrow streets that allowed little natural light. Whereas in London there was an average of

---

[13] Johann Pezzl, *Sketch of Vienna*, in *Mozart and Vienna*, edited by H. C. Robbins Landon (New York: Schirmer Books, 1991), p. 55.
[14] Ibid., p. 62.

nine inhabitants for each house within the city limits, in Vienna that number was closer to forty-seven people. Houses were known not just by their street numbers and locations but also by such colorful monikers as "At the Green Wreath," "At the Three Green Trees," "Blue Lord God," "Eternal Light," or "At the Golden Bed." One house in the Bognergasse was known simply as "At the Skull."

It was also a city of wonder. At the north end of the Leopold-stadt was the Augarten, where the emperor released a massive flock of nightingales every year. And the Prater, a "pleasure garden," was home to one of the largest annual fireworks displays in Europe. In those days of revolution and enlightenment, Vienna was a place where one could still believe in miracles. In August 1784, a Swiss named Boden plastered the city with placards announcing that he would cross the Danube on foot. A massive crowd turned out to see him stagger out onto the water on oversized shoes made of cork. After two attempts ended in Boden plunging headfirst into the river, the assembled crowd was so enraged at his ineptitude that the police had to hold them back from attacking him.

Among the other wonders and pleasures that Vienna displayed was Angelo Soliman, or at least, what was left of him. Born in Nigeria around 1721, Soliman had been enslaved as a young child and bought by the Austrian governor of Sicily, Prince Johann Georg Christian Lobkowitz. In the service of Lobkowitz, Soliman distinguished himself as a companion and a soldier, and his fame and stature grew as he accompanied the governor on a number of military expeditions. After Lobkowitz's death,

Soliman went into the service of Prince Wenzel von Lichtenstein in Vienna. There he became a court favorite—he was fluent in six languages and was widely admired for his erudition and wit. He became a Mason in the same lodge as Haydn and Mozart.

Despite this prestige, when he died of natural causes in 1796, the Hapsburg emperor, Franz II, did not see fit to accord him the same rite of burial that any other Mason would have been granted. After Soliman's death the emperor had him skinned, and his skin was fitted onto a wooden frame and put on display in Franz II's "Imperial and Royal Physical Astronomical Art and Nature and Animal Cabinet." Wonder cabinets had been around for over a century, so when Franz II opened his in 1797, he wanted something special. In life Soliman had dressed in the latest fashions and proved himself equal to the greatest minds of Europe; in death he was decked in a loincloth and headdress made of ostrich feathers, perched alongside the birds of paradise.[15] He was the highlight of the cabinet.

But above all, what made Viennese culture singular was its obsession with music, which was elevated above all other forms of artistic expression. E. T. A. Hoffman, who spent years as a music critic before writing gothic tales like "The Sandman," wrote, "Music is the most romantic of all the arts; one might even say that it alone is purely romantic."[16] The English and the French

[15] More information on Angelo Soliman can be found in Philipp Blom, *To Have and to Hold* (Woodstock: Overlook Press, 2003) pp. 98–108.
[16] Quoted in David Gramit, *Cultivating Music: The Aspirations, Interests, and Limits of German Musical Culture, 1770-1848* (Berkeley: University of California Press, 2002), p. 3.

had their playwrights and their poets, the Dutch and the Italians their painters, but in Germany and Austria there were first and foremost the composers.

The Viennese believed in music as more than just a distraction or recreation. By the end of the eighteenth century Austrians had begun to regard symphonic music as a fundamental component of civilized society. As one music critic explained, "when it is appropriately practiced and employed," music can "soften manners, ennoble feelings, spread joy and sociability among the people, and in general have a great influence on the cultivation of the moral character." This could be doubted, he concluded, only "by those who have never had occasion to reflect on the essence and effects of this art, or by those who have still not discerned that the culture of a nation promotes its happiness." Another writer went so far as to say, "I am convinced that music is not to be recommended to youth simply as a means to develop taste, as a noble form of entertainment, etc; it is infinitely more important (especially song) as the most excellent means of education, in order to develop a pure and noble spirit, to weave love of the good and beautiful in general, and of virtue and religion, deeply and intimately into our being, so that they remain forever inseparable."[17] It was expected that all members of the Austrian nobility and upper class be well versed in music, regularly attend performances, and patronize the many performers and composers who flocked to Vienna.

[17] Ibid., pp. 16.

LE Dᴿ FRANC.-JOS. GALL.

Franz Joseph Gall.

IT WAS TO this city of contradictions and manic excitement that Franz Joseph Gall came in 1781. Ambling with his awkward gait through the city, Gall kept mostly to himself, taking in everything. As he began his medical studies, he found himself to be a mediocre student. Struggling to keep up and envious of those around him, he began to fixate on students who excelled at memorization, staring at them across lecture halls and dissection theaters with admiration and frustration. How was it possible, Gall wanted to know, that these men could so easily keep track of that which bedeviled him? It seemed to him as if their brains must be structured differently. Over time Gall became convinced that there was something peculiar about these men, something worthy of attention. He started to notice that these men all seemed to have unusually large eyes. The longer he thought about it, the more he came to believe that this was not a random occurrence— the large eyes, he concluded, were somehow related to the faculty for memorization.

Convinced of this causal connection, Gall began to look for other correlations between mental attributes and physical appearance. "Proceeding from reflection to reflection," he would later write, "from observation to observation, it occurred to me that, if memory were made evident by external signs, it might be so likewise with other talents or intellectual faculties."[18]

This simple observation became the core of Gall's system, one that he would refine in the coming years. What he came to call "organology" had four main principles: (1) The moral and intellectual faculties are innate and determined from birth; (2) the manifestation of these qualities depends on their organization; (3) the brain is the exclusive seat of the mind; and (4) each faculty of the mind corresponds to a different independent section of the brain. Though it may seem dubious to draw such sweeping con-

[18] Franz Joseph Gall, *On the Origin of the Moral Qualities and Intellectual Faculties of Man, and the Conditions of Their Manifestation*, translated by Winslow Lewis (Boston: Marsh, Capen & Lyon, 1835), p. 59.

clusions from an arbitrary connection between memory and eye size, it is worth noting that contemporary neuroscience supports many of these same principles, albeit in modified forms. Indeed, it was ultimately the third proposition, the least controversial from a modern perspective, that would get Gall in the most trouble.

Gall's fundamental discovery was *localization*, the idea that different parts of the brain control different elements of our mind and body. Even two centuries later, with phrenology thoroughly discredited, most anatomists still recognize this concept as Gall's fundamental contribution to the study of the mind. Granted, Gall had no evidence for this belief and little way of proving or disproving it, but it was nevertheless to be a watershed moment on the road to modern neurology.

Armed with this simple principle, Gall set out looking for other correspondences between physical appearance and personality. "From this time," he would later write, "all the individuals who were distinguished by any quality or faculty, became the object of my special attention, and of systematic study as to the form of the head."

The question was how to go about this systematic study. What Gall needed was a way of mapping the brain and its functions. The brain's workings are invisible and silent. It doesn't work like other organs. Take the heart: Cut open a body and there it sits, at the center of the human world. You can trace its veins and arteries threading out in every direction, in order to understand its networks. If you cut open a still living body, you can see it going about its bloody work.

The brain is a different matter. It sits removed; it keeps its secrets to itself. When the Egyptians embalmed a body, they placed each organ in a separate urn; each was sacred, each was worthy of reverence—except the brain. It works not with blood or food but with its own electricity, and it keeps its own counsel. The Egyptians didn't know what it was for, so they threw it away. By the eighteenth century, anatomists knew more about the brain and its networks, but it still remained remarkably aloof.

IT WAS A few years before Gall hit upon his concept, but in the end his assertion was quite simple, even elegant. His discovery was a process he called "cranioscopy," what became colloquially known as "bump reading" and his pupil Johann Spurzheim would rechristen "phrenology." It was predicated on a few simple principles. First, Gall theorized that, all other things being equal, size determines propensity: A bigger brain implies a higher capacity for intelligence. This was, Gall asserted, equally true of different parts of the brain—if the segment of the brain devoted to memory was larger in one individual than in another, then it stood to reason that the former would have a higher capacity for memory. Second, it was well known that the skull, like all bones, is initially malleable upon birth, only gradually becoming more rigid. So it stood to reason, Gall theorized, that the ridges and folds of the brain might imprint themselves on the bone when it was still pliable and that one could come to know the brain by understanding these imprints.

From this apparent insight Gall began to explore the possibility that the brain's workings might be made visible by the patterns it made on the skull. This is the motivation that drives phrenology: a quest for the visible. From a contemporary vantage point, it is easy to dismiss it as quackery, but it made a good deal of sense at the time, given the prevailing intellectual climate. The Enlightenment was a time when people were obsessed with sight and metaphors of vision—you can see the obsession in the name itself, an age of illumination. To see a thing was to know it. The metaphoric connection between sight and knowledge drove much of Enlightenment thought, from Jean-Jacques Rousseau's desire in 1761 to become "a living eye" to Ralph Waldo Emerson, ninety years later, becoming a "transparent eyeball" in moments of transcendence. As one modern commentator points out, the Enlightenment conceptualized a reasoning mind whose "processes appear to have been closely akin to those of the seeing eye."[19] Gall was ultimately a man of his age, who sought knowledge in sight and did his best to bring the study of the brain into an era in which only sight mattered. Maybe he can be forgiven if in trying just a little too hard to solve this problem he created one of the most egregious pseudosciences of the nineteenth century.

Two hundred years earlier, Rene Descartes had written, "All the management of our lives depends on the senses, and since that of sight is the most comprehensive and the noblest of these, there

[19] Jean Starobinski, *The Invention of Liberty: 1700-1789*, translated by Bernard C. Swift (Geneva: Skira, 1964) p. 210.

is no doubt that the inventions which serve to augment its power are among the most useful that there can be."[20] He was speaking of telescopes and microscopes, but cranioscopy would soon find its place as just one more such lens, opening up what was hitherto invisible to the eye. As if a weirdly organic precursor to the phonograph, the skull appeared to phrenologists as something like a recording device, a malleable surface onto which a record of the ineffable could be printed. The etymology of the terms is telling: whereas "phrenology" means "mind-knowing," Gall's own term, "cranioscopy," means "skull-seeing." The skull, Gall reasoned, was a lens through which one could see greater things.

Even at the beginning, this line of inquiry was not without its detractors. While some people found Gall's attempt to see the mind stimulating, others thought it deeply offensive. Napoleon, for one, was utterly contemptuous of phrenology. "Nature does not reveal herself by external forms," he said; "she hides and does not express her secrets. To pretend to seize and penetrate human character by so slight an index is the part of a dupe or an imposter. . . . The only way of knowing our fellow creatures is to see them, to associate with them frequently, and to submit them to proof."[21] Napoleon would on his deathbed claim that his attempt to block phrenology in France was the best decision he ever made.

[20] René Descartes, *Discourse on Method, Optics, Geometry, and Meteorology*, translated by Paul J. Olscamp (Indianapolis: Hackett, 2001) p. 65.
[21] Quoted in Brian Burrell, *Postcards from the Brain Museum* (New York: Broadway Books, 2004) p. 49.

But Napoleon's view wasn't the popular one. Gall began lecturing on his findings in 1796 and was an instant hit. His public lectures drew large crowds to whom he espoused his ideas that the brain—rather than some ineffable, immortal soul—was the home of the mind and that the strengths and tendencies of this brain could be read through the skull. His lectures were scandalous in part because they were open to the general public, including women, though he claimed that women were never present when he discussed sexual proclivities and reproduction.

Gall worked largely by induction. He would identify a principle of the mind and then find someone whose personality demonstrated this principle. From there it was just a matter of finding something equally noteworthy about this person's head. Sometimes such connections were formed from only one or two examples. Aaron Burr, for example, had fathered a child out of wedlock and had a large ridge on the back of his head— thus, Gall reasoned, that portion of the brain must be where "love of offspring" was located, a faculty particularly excessive in Burr's case.

But even with such a lax methodology, he needed a body of evidence. He needed heads—lots of them. And so Gall quickly amassed a huge collection of skulls and plaster casts of heads. By his own estimate, this collection cost 7,000 gulden; on top of that was another 15,000 guldens' worth of preparations, a sum equal to forty times the average salary of a middle-class Viennese and over twice the value of Haydn's entire estate.

For the most part, Gall acquired his skulls from executed criminals and asylum graveyards; if he wanted the head of someone important for his collection, he would take a plaster cast. But that didn't stop his detractors from imputing darker motives. Pierre Flourens, a rival anatomist and one of Gall's many antagonists, would later claim that

> at one time everybody in Vienna was trembling for his head, and fearing that after his death it would be put in requisition to enrich Dr. Gall's cabinet. . . . Too many people were led to suppose themselves the objects of the doctor's regards, and imagined their heads to be especially longed for by him as a specimen of the utmost importance to the success of his experiments. Some very curious stories were told on this point. Old M. Denis, the Emperor's librarian, inserted a special clause in his will, intended to save his cranium from M. Gall's scalpel.[22]

This was mostly invention on Flourens's part, as Gall, it turns out, had some trouble acquiring skulls other than those of criminals and the insane. "Men," he wrote in a letter, "unhappily, have such an opinion of themselves, that each one believes that I am watching for his head, as one of the most important objects of my collection. Nevertheless, I have not been able to collect more than twenty in the space of three years, if I ex-

[22] Quoted in ibid., pp. 47–48.

cept those that I have taken in the hospitals, or in the asylum for idiots."[23]

But it wasn't for lack of trying. "If you could arrange it that any kind of genius would make me the heir of his skull, I would promise to build a splendid building within ten years," he wrote in 1898. "Certainly it would be dangerous for Kästner, Kant, or Wieland, if I had David's killing angel at my disposal." As late as 1827 his desperation for the heads of geniuses was evident; after receiving a bust of the head of Goethe as a gift, he replied that, should Goethe die, "I implore you to bribe the relatives of this unique genius to preserve his head in nature for the world."[24]

For the general public, this was the most disturbing by-product of Gall's new system, and it tapped into a larger fear that had begun to surface long before, when modern anatomists had first started to turn to the corpse as a means of understanding the body. There was a widespread belief, especially in Catholic areas like Austria, that one's intact and naturally decomposed remains were vital for resurrection. Dissection or dismemberment represented a fate far worse than death, and it was for this reason that only executed criminals were turned over to anatomists—dissection was seen as the final form of punishment. To have one's body cut open for science implied the damnation of one's soul. A particularly horrific cartoon from the early nineteenth

[23] Quoted in David George Goyder, *My Battle for Life: The Autobiography of a Phrenologist* (London: Simpkin, Marshall, and Co., 1857), p. 138.
[24] Quoted in Michael Hagner, "Skulls, Brains, and Memorial Culture: On Cerebral Biographies of Scientists in the Nineteenth Century," *Science in Context*, Vol. 16, Nos. 1 & 2 (2003), pp. 200–201.

century showed a dissection lab on the day of the Last Judgment, with dismembered arms and legs reanimated and moving about, desperately seeking the rest of their bodies.

But what Catholics saw in Gall's skull collection was something far more sinister than the doctor could have meant. Gall's contention that the brain was the sole organ of the mind suggested a dangerous form of heresy—"materialism"—that went counter to centuries of church doctrine. The implication inherent in phrenology was that one need not consider the immortal soul because everything of consequence could be located in the brain. It was this notion that led the Austrian government, motivated by the Catholic Church, to ban all public lectures by Gall on January 9, 1802.

Gall attempted to defend himself in a lengthy retort against this and other accusations. He wrote,

It has occasioned to me infinite distress, that his Majesty has been led to entertain the unfounded apprehension, that my theory appears to lead to materialism, and consequently to militate against the first principles of morals and religion. In all ages, it has happened that truths entirely new, or even truths only better demonstrated, have appeared to threaten the existence of all previously established principles. But experience has uniformly proved, that old and new truths soon cordially combine, and mutually support each other, that opposition to them is only pernicious, and, especially, that obstacles thrown in their way tend only to promote their advancement.

He went on to argue that he did not actually believe one could determine a subject's personality solely by looking at the bumps of a skull: It was impossible, he claimed, to distinguish the worthless from the virtuous solely through the skull "because moral, social, civil, and religious conduct, is the result of many and different concomitant causes, and especially of many powerful external influences; for instance, education, example, habits, laws, religion, age, society, climate, food, health, and so forth."[25]

Ultimately, though, Gall saw the writing on the wall and was forced to leave Austria for France. He could not afford to transport his extensive skull collection, which was subsequently lost. Eventually Gall and Spurzheim made it to Paris, where they were instantly popular, having among their many clients notables such as Prince Metternich. Austria, it would seem, was free of its dangerous heretic.

But Gall's subversive ideas had already begun to have an impact. Enterprising phrenologists quickly understood that if they were going to know the mind, they needed the skulls not just of prostitutes and murderers but of greater men and women—and, more important, that these skulls might be worth something.

Around the same time Gall began lecturing on the properties of the skull, the sexton of Vienna's St. Marx Church, Joseph Rothmayer, undertook a rather unorthodox mission. A few years earlier he had been present when Wolfgang Amadeus Mozart had

---

[25] Franz Joseph Gall, *On the Functions of the Cerebellum*, translated by George Combe (Edinburgh: Maclachlan & Stewart, 1838), p. 328.

been buried there, and, sensing the potential value of the composer's skull, he had wrapped a metal wire around the corpse's neck before it had been unceremoniously dumped into the mass grave. Now, in what Peter J. Davies has aptly described as "a moment of animated musical enthusiasm," he dug up the communal grave and picked through the pile of remains until he found the skeleton with the wire around its neck. He removed Mozart's head and saved it from destruction.[26]

[26] Peter J. Davies, *Mozart in Person: His Character and Health* (New York: Greenwood Press, 1989), p. 171

CHAPTER TWO

THE MUSIC
LOVER

Gall's banishment from Vienna was the talk of the town. A
month after the prohibition was first issued, a group of
middle-class gentlemen gathered to discuss the events of the
day. Among them was one of the few Viennese unfamiliar with
Gall. Later that night the gentleman wrote, "At mid-day, Csis-
kowsky (the steward of the Cobenzl Berg), Eckhart and Klimbke
lunched with us. We talked a great deal about Schall's theory of
phrenology."[27] It's unclear why he got the name wrong in his
diary; he may have just misheard it, or perhaps he'd conflated
the doctor's name with the German word *"Schädel,"* meaning
"skull." The man's name was Joseph Carl Rosenbaum, and in the
seven years between Gall's banishment from Vienna and Haydn's
death, Rosenbaum's relationship to phrenology would change
dramatically.

---

[27] Rosenbaum, *The Diary of Carl Joseph Rosenbaum,* p. 99.

JOSEPH CARL ROSENBAUM was born in 1770. His father was a house steward for the Esterhazy family, and so, although he had been born in Vienna, Joseph grew up in Eisenstadt. As was the custom, he followed his father's footsteps by entering Esterhazy service at the age of twenty and in 1797 came back to Vienna as the controller of the accounts of the vast Esterhazy stables.

Rosenbaum was, by any measure, a capable and successful accountant and a kind and generous friend. Above all, though, he was a lover of music. He rarely went a day without attending the theater—indeed, scholars have long turned to his diaries for precise information on the dates of performances of important operas or symphonies as well as a detailed record of the major performers and the quality of their performances. He was well known throughout the musical world and was on friendly terms with Haydn and less-well-known composers such as Johann Fuchs as well as with people such as the painter Francesco Casanova (brother of the more famous Giacomo) and Constanze Mozart, the widow of the composer whose head had lately been rescued.

Shortly after arriving in Vienna, Rosenbaum was introduced to two sisters, also from Eisenstadt, who had come to Vienna to begin a career on the stage, primarily singing Haydn's masses. Their names were Maria Anna and Therese Josepha Gassman. Almost immediately, Therese, the younger, caught Rosenbaum's eye.

The Gassmans' father, Florian, had been a court composer, and the family was well known in the musical society of Austria. To commemorate Therese's birth, Haydn had given the family a specially designed cuckoo clock that played original melodies he had composed. Both Therese and her sister were destined for music before they were even born. Just before Therese's birth in 1774, Florian died unexpectedly, and the girls' musical education was turned over to their godfather, Antonio Salieri. While Maria Anna's talents were never more than adequate, Therese became one of the most celebrated singers in Vienna, in particular for her success in the difficult role of the Queen of the Night in Mozart's *The Magic Flute*. One newspaper commented that "the purity, modulation, and unusual range of her voice are certainly a most admirable and rare gift of nature." She was a personal favorite of the Hapsburg empress, Maria Therese (daughter of Maria Theresia), who once confided to her, "You sing confoundedly high, I am often frightened when you sing so high and often tremble."[28]

With such a pedigree, Therese's mother had high hopes for both of her daughters. It seemed well within the realm of possibility that the girls might marry into nobility, and with titles (not to mention money), the family's legacy would be secured.

Rosenbaum began to pay regular visits to the Gassman household and made a point of seeing Therese whenever she performed. Her singing enthralled him; at the theater it was Therese alone who "made the hours pleasant" for him. Five months after

[28] Ibid., p. 113.

their first meeting he made the decision to propose to her. It turned out to be a fateful decision—one that would lead to two years of dashed hopes and frustration, nearly ruin his career, threaten to ruin hers as well, and make the prince a permanent enemy.

AT FIRST THINGS seemed quite promising. Rosenbaum began his courtship by taking Therese to the ballet and the opera and to all the sights and pleasures of the city. They traded coquettish love letters, acting like giddy teenagers. But despite Therese's obvious affection for Rosenbaum, her mother, Theresia, had not given up on the idea of a title for her daughter, and she saw that she had to take action lest her grand plan be derailed. She began to circulate all manner of rumors about Rosenbaum's character and prospects, repeatedly trying to wreck Therese's impression of him; in one pointed exchange Theresia told Rosenbaum loudly in Therese's presence that he should not bother to buy the girl any more presents because once he lost his job he would have to ask for them all back. But the suitor was not deterred, and mother Gassman soon saw that her whisper campaign was not enough. She needed someone powerful to break this attraction, and so for the second time in her life she went to royalty on behalf of her daughter.

It was well known that the Esterhazy princes generally preferred not to have their employees married, fearing divided loyalties; anyone in the service of the prince needed his permission before he or she could marry. So when Therese's mother decided that she needed to stop the marriage, it was to the prince that she went. She explained her dilemma, telling the prince that there was simply no way that one of the brightest stars on the Viennese stage—who might yet be courted by counts and barons—could be allowed to marry a midlevel clerk. The prince was swayed and made it clear to the young Rosenbaum that he was not likely to approve any marriage anytime soon.

What had seemed a sure thing was quickly slipping from Rosenbaum's grasp, and he turned to his friends for aid. He asked for advice and support, called in all the favors to which he had a claim, even requested that the dowager princess put in a good word for him. And then he turned to Joseph Haydn.

Rosenbaum and Haydn, both members of the court staff, saw each other regularly—Rosenbaum often came to the composer on business matters and stayed to discuss Haydn's latest work or theatrical gossip. Haydn liked the young man for his earnestness and palpable love of music. Rosenbaum had an unerring sense of taste, and his enthusiasm and sensitivity naturally endeared him to musicians like Haydn, whom Rosenbaum recognized as of a special distinction. Only a few weeks after Therese's mother began her intrigues, Rosenbaum and Therese made separate entreaties to Haydn for his assistance and asked him to intercede; this, Rosenbaum happily reported, Haydn "faithfully promised to do."[29]

---

[29] Ibid., p. 37.

Haydn was of course a great asset in one's corner. With the court's cultural and moral investment in symphonic music, the composer had become something like a saint in Vienna. E. T. A. Hoffman is one of many writers who singled Haydn out as the most romantic of artists in the most romantic of arts: "His symphonies lead us into a boundless, green glade amid a lively, jovial throng of happy people," Hoffman wrote. "Young men and women swing past in round dances, and laughing children, eavesdropping behind trees and rose bushes, throw flowers teasingly at one another."[30] But even such a saint did not succeed on Rosenbaum's behalf. On numerous occasions Haydn tried to convince the prince not to listen to the vicious rumors circulating about Rosenbaum and to persuade him of the young man's worth. But to no avail.

For two years this courtship dragged on. Despite all the rumors and obstacles, Rosenbaum continued to court Therese, spending as much time as he could with her. A year after they first met he took her to Franz II's wonder cabinet. Rosenbaum noted in his diary, "There are so many pretty things that one could entertain oneself very interestingly for weeks." One exhibit in particular stood out for him: "I especially liked Angelo Soliman who stands there stuffed, next to a Moorish girl of 8."[31] There was something captivating about Soliman, this taxidermied man in a room of frozen nature. He had lived beyond death, been brought

---

[30] Quoted in Gramit, *Cultivating Music*, p. 87.
[31] Rosenbaum, *The Diary of Carl Joseph Rosenbaum*, p. 53.

back from decay to defy time. It was an idea that would stay with Rosenbaum and grow in him in the years to come.

It's not entirely surprising that someone like Rosenbaum would be drawn to this stuffed man. Soliman's figure was special in part because the process of taxidermy was still in its infancy— it wouldn't come into high demand until later in the nineteenth century, when European colonialists needed a reliable way to transport hunting trophies and zoological specimens back home. In particular, very few taxidermists had found a way to stuff a human in a realistic manner. "All the efforts of man to restore the skin of his fellow creature to its natural form and beauty, have hitherto been fruitless," Sarah Bowditch wrote in her taxidermy manual in 1820. "The trials which have been made have only produced mis-shapen hideous objects, and so unlike nature, that they have never found a place in our collections. We have only some parts of man, either dried or preserved in spirits of wine, sufficiently entire to be recognized."[32]

Either she was unaware of Soliman or judged him to be one of those "mis-shapen hideous objects" because the lone exception that Bowditch mentioned is the work of Frederick Ruysch, who was well known for his exotic and groundbreaking preparations. A hundred years earlier Ruysch had found a way to preserve "wet" specimens using a mixture of mercury oxide, blue pigment, and clotted pig's blood, and in 1717 he sold his unique

---

[32] Sarah Bowditch, *Taxidermy: or, the Art of Collecting, Preparing, and Mounting Objects of Natural History* (London: Longman, Hurst, Rees, Orme, and Brown, 1820), pp. 20-21.

specimens to Peter the Great, who built an elaborate wonder cabinet around them. Ruysch was so famous that in 1824 the poet Giacomo Leopardi composed an operetta about him titled *Dialogue between Frederick Ruysch and His Mummies*, in which Ruysch's specimens come to life for a single night to explain the mysteries of death. "What were we?" the mummies sing,

What was the bitter point called life?
Stupendous mystery is today
Life to our minds, and such
As to the minds of the living
Unknown death appears. As when living
From it death fled, now flees
From vital flame
Our naked nature
Not joyous but secure;
For to be happy
Is denied to mortals and denied the dead by Fate.[33]

Ruysch's mummies, Bowditch noted, were an exception, "and since the bony part of our body is the only one which we are able to preserve entire and in its natural position," Bowditch recommended that the best way to preserve a human was by cleaning and displaying the skull.

[33] Giacomo Leopardi, *Operette Morali: Essays and Dialogues,* Translated by Givanni Cecchetti (Berkeley: University of California Press, 1982), p. 271.

ROSENBAUM'S ATTEMPTS TO gain permission to wed were stymied at every turn. Gradually his description of the city he loved gave way to bleakness. "No day can be lived to the end without there being something distressing about it," he wrote after a particularly bitter row with Therese's mother. The day he turned twenty-eight years old he summed up his life thus far: "We torment and vex ourselves, and do not know why; we drag ourselves along in the chains of misery—to the grave."[34]

Though he was constantly beset by depression, his love for Therese never wavered, and if anything he felt the most pain at having caused her so much grief. "May she become my wife soon," he wrote at one point, "so that I may make recompense, through fidelity and love, for her having suffered so much."[35] At no point did he think of dropping his pursuit. His only choice was to persevere and hope that his fortunes would change. But the tensions continued to mount. The longer the courtship was prolonged, the more his loathing for her mother grew, as did his enmity for the prince.

By December 1799 Rosenbaum had grown increasingly impatient and, sensing that the time was right, finally brought the prince the marriage license for his signature. The prince took the document, ominously muttering that he would "attend to it."

[34] Rosenbaum, *The Diary of Carl Joseph Rosenbaum*, p. 47.
[35] Ibid., p. 60.

Rosenbaum was not sure what to make of this comment, but when he asked about it again three days later, on Christmas morning, the prince tore up the marriage proposal in front of him and, "with great hue and cry," threw the shreds at Rosenbaum's feet, saying that he wanted to hear nothing more about marriage.[36]

It was a crushing blow, nearly devastating the young man, but it led to a moment of clarity. All this time the impediment had been the prince who held such power over him. Rosenbaum had worked for the Esterhazy family for ten years, but if he were free of the prince's control, there would be nothing left to stand in the way of his marriage—the prince had no control over the lives of private citizens. Shortly after the Christmas incident, Rosenbaum raised that point with the prince, and on January 30 he received a curt letter that stated, "The supplicant's petition to marry is hereby dropped; he is free, however, to conclude the preparations already made by proceeding directly to marry, which step will have as a consequence his immediate dismissal from service."[37]

It was not a great time to take such a risk. Since the heady days of the 1780s and '90s Vienna had become a different place, an apocalyptic city. Rosenbaum was giving up one of the few secure jobs to be had in an increasingly unstable Austria, risking financial ruin and ridicule not just for himself but for Therese as well. Should her mother's worst fears come to pass, one of the city's most promising sopranos and one of its most eligible

---

[36] Ibid., p. 72.
[37] Ibid., p. 73.

women would be doomed to folly and disgrace. But to Rosenbaum and Therese, their love was worth the chance. Rosenbaum resigned his post, and on June 11, 1800, he and Therese were finally married.

ROSENBAUM AND HIS new wife woke up from their private misery to find that the Vienna around them had changed. The city was under massive strain, keeping up a thin pretense of prosperity as dark clouds threatened to the west. The year they were married, Vienna celebrated the millennial anniversary of the coronation of Charlemagne, the symbolic founding of the Hapsburg Empire. "It would be an affront to the inhabitants of the Imperial capital," read the proclamation posted everywhere in the city, "to doubt that patriots of all stations will be present at this so rare observance."[38]

Meanwhile, a different sort of millennium was coming from France. The letters in the words *"l'empereur Bonaparte,"* as Pierre Bezukhov discovers in *War and Peace,* can be converted into numbers that add up to "666," and it was Napoleon's apocalyptic army that bore down on Vienna the night of its grand celebration. On Christmas Day, exactly a year after the prince had torn up his marriage petition, Rosenbaum spent the day watching frantic defense preparations along the outer walls of the city and then went to the millennial celebration in the evening. "It was

[38] Ibid., p. 87.

quite full," he noted, and Therese "sang with rare art . . . during the cantata people were talking of a defeat."[39]

It was the inauspicious beginning of a dark decade for Vienna. The splendor and gleam that had typified the city only a few years before were gone, replaced by the endless threat of war, high unemployment, and out-of-control inflation. Bread riots broke out, and bakeries were ransacked; the imperial guard had to be called out on numerous occasions to brutally suppress popular uprisings. In 1807 a freak hurricane destroyed the famous Augustinian Church, rolling up its massive iron clock dial like a sheet of paper. And for several days afterward a comet with a long tail was visible in the night sky.

IMPROBABLY, THROUGHOUT ALL of this Rosenbaum and Therese prospered. Their marriage flourished—in part because of his business acumen, in part because of her talent and stardom, and not least because of their love for each other. For all her mother's fears, Therese was provided a comfortable middle-class life. The couple remained devoted to one another for the rest of their lives. But Rosenbaum never forgot the anguish the prince had put them through.

Haydn remained close to the young couple. Forty years their senior, he nonetheless visited and dined with them often, particularly in the few years immediately after their marriage. In 1801

[39] Ibid.

46

they came to Eisenstadt for two weeks and saw Haydn nearly every day. He entertained them, showered Therese with compliments, drove them around in his carriage, and treated them to carousing dinners that lasted late into the night. As his health declined he saw them less, but in 1803 he steadfastly assured them both of his affection.

Despite this close connection among the three of them, Rosenbaum would always remain the odd man out: the greatest composer of his day, the most-sought-after soprano in Vienna, and the accountant. At dinner together they talked of Therese's art, of the reasons her voice was superior, and of how she might mentor other young singers. They talked of Haydn's new compositions, of the medal he had received from the Paris Opera. They did not spend much time talking about Rosenbaum's work.

During this time Rosenbaum began to develop another, more controversial interest. In the six years since he had first heard of Gall's theories, he had grown steadily more fascinated with the principles of phrenology. He began to spend more time with people like his childhood friend Johann Nepomuk Peter, who had a similar interest in studying the brain's machinations, and who liked to refer to the founder of phrenology by the diminutive nickname "Gallschen." Together they discussed the latest discoveries, differences between Gall's system and that of his pupil Spurzheim, and the ways in which the Austrian penal system might be improved if phrenological reforms were instituted. This new science of the brain, both were convinced, was the way of progress and the future.

47

There was a great deal about this new science that would appeal to someone like Rosenbaum. He was essentially a man of numbers who worked in a world of quantifiable facts and known outcomes. He knew at all times what he was worth and kept meticulous records of what he was owed. He had gotten this far in life through analytic rationality. And yet the world he loved was one of ineffable beauty, spectacular excess, and musical genius.

According to Immanuel Kant, genius is something that can be identified but not defined: A genius is "a talent," Kant wrote, "for producing that for which no definite rule can be given." For Kant, the genius "does not know himself how he has come by his ideas; and he has not the power to devise the like at pleasure, or in accordance with a plan, [or] to communicate it to others in precepts that will enable them to produce similar products."[40] At the same time that Gall was working out his theories, Kant was explaining genius as an invisible force that drives the engine of progress, as a thing whose products can be seen but which itself remains elusive.

It was in this sense that phrenology—alone of all the sciences—might be useful, in giving one a tool for understanding genius. With phrenology, it seemed, one could map the unknown and invisible territories of the brain. And this was perhaps its most appealing aspect: Just as it could decode and explain pathol-

[40] Immanuel Kant, *Critique of Judgement*, translated James Creed Meredith (Oxford: Oxford University Press, 2007) p. 137.

ogy, it could also reveal the truth about genius in a way that even the genius him- or herself could not. The discussion surrounding the physical location of genius in the brain and its manifestation on the skull became a recurrent source of debate. For phrenologists, the only true way to know for sure was through exact measurements of the actual heads.

It was the promise of understanding something as ineffable as creative genius that resonated most strongly with Rosenbaum. Even as he dutifully recorded in his diary exactly what Therese's performances earned her—how many people attended each performance, the admission prices, and her percentage—there was no way to put a price on a voice so high and trembling that it terrified the empress. He could gather every known fact on Haydn and weigh each available datum and still never understand why one's spirits soared almost to the point of terror when the chorus sang, "And there was light."

It was phrenology, Rosenbaum came to understand, that could bridge these two worlds.

ON MARCH 27, 1808, a tribute was held in Haydn's honor. The seventy-six-year-old composer at first did not think he was up to attending but in the end was cajoled into it. He donned his Paris medal, and servants carried him into the hall on an ornate armchair. To universal applause he was welcomed by the prince; his fellow composers Salieri and Beethoven knelt and kissed his hand. By the end of the first half of the concert, the strain was too much and he had to leave. But he stood and bade his farewell to the musical society of Vienna, greatly moved.

That night Rosenbaum noted in his diary, "Thus Haydn was, after all, honored during his lifetime."[41] He knew the composer was dying and knew he might soon be given the chance of a life-time: to know the mind of the greatest composer the world had yet seen! To be able to get the exact measurement and propor-tions of his head, to quantify each segment of that magnificent mind. What alchemy! To convert those adagios and crescendos into centimeters and grams, to assemble a picture of the man in terms not of art but of science. Haydn would live for another year, but Rosenbaum was already making preparations.

It's not clear at what point he decided to steal Haydn's skull, but he began planning the theft long before the actual death. He knew in advance how difficult it would be, and he decided to take a practice run.

[41] Rosenbaum, *The Diary of Carl Joseph Rosenbaum*, p. 142.

CHAPTER THREE

"So Was She, So She Is Now"

T he subject of Joseph Carl Rosenbaum's first foray into cranioklepty was the actress Elizabeth Roose, who died in childbirth in October 1808. Roose was from a family of actors; she, her father, and her husband had all come to Vienna in 1798 and had made a huge impression on the theatergoing public. Of Elizabeth, a reviewer noted that she had a "magnificent head and an expressive face," and it was this magnificent head that Rosenbaum and his conspirators would cut from her corpse a week after her death, this same expressive face that they would cut away with a scalpel and burn off with lime.[42]

WHEN ROSENBAUM REMOVED Betty Roose's head from her body in November 1808, he joined a long line of body snatchers

---

[42] On the impact and influence of Roose on Viennese theater, see Rosenbaum, *The Diary of Carl Joseph Rosenbaum*, p. 143.

in a practice that had grown rampant over the past several hundred years. As doctors began to abandon the model of the four humors in favor of direct observation of the workings of the body, the corpse became the primary site of education. Anatomists were free to dissect the bodies of executed criminals, who had forfeited their souls, but as demand outpaced supply, doctors and schools increasingly turned to grave robbers, known as "resurrectionists."

By the eighteenth century a thriving trade in grave robbing had taken root. In 1728 the anonymous author of a pamphlet titled "A View of London and Westminster" noted that the Corporation of Corpse Stealers "support themselves and Families very comfortably; and that no-one should be surprised at the Nature of Such a Society, the late Resurrectionists in St Saviours, St Giles's and St Pancras' Churchyards, are memorable Instances of this laudable Profession."[43]

This desire for corpses was to last well into the nineteenth century. As late as 1890, for example, the Kentucky School of Medicine was accused of plundering various graveyards, including that of the Asylum for the Insane in Anchorage, Kentucky. The school was unapologetic: "Yes, the party was sent by us," a school official told the press. "We must have bodies, and if the State won't give them to us we must steal them. The winter classes were large and used up so many subjects that there are none for

---

[43] Quoted in Ruth Richardson, *Death, Dissection and the Destitute* (London: Phoenix Press, 2001) p. 55.

the spring classes. The Asylum Cemetery has been robbed for years, and I doubt if there is a corpse in it. I tell you we must have bodies. You cannot make doctors without them, and the public must understand it. If we can't get them any other way we will arm the students with Winchester rifles and send them to protect the body-snatchers on their raids."[44]

This was only ten years before the turn of the twentieth century.

This extensive history of grave robbing had gone a long way to divest the gravesite of its sanctity—despite religious prohibitions, men of learning and progressive thought could believe that grave robbing in the name of science, while not quite legal, was morally acceptable, even laudable. This change in belief helps to explain why Rosenbaum and his friends were able to speak so openly about their actions and why they thought nothing of displaying their trophies in glass cases in their living rooms.

Among those who fell victim to the resurrectionists was Laurence Sterne, author of *Tristram Shandy*. When he died of tuberculosis in 1768, Sterne, who had often gone by the nickname "Yorick," was insolvent, and buried in a pauper's grave. As such he was easy pickings: A few days later his body was stolen by grave robbers and turned up on a dissection table. It was only by chance that he was recognized by the doctor who received his body and was quickly returned to the ground. Sterne's situation

---

[44] Quoted in Erik Larson, *The Devil in the White City: Murder, Magic, and Madness at the Fair that Changed America* (New York: Vintage, 2003), pp. 150–151.

was unfortunate, but it highlights the difference between an average resurrectionist and a cranioklept such as Rosenbaum. Sterne's was just one fresh body among many, his genius and wit inconsequential. In contrast, the cranioklepts were looking for something specific. Whereas the anatomist wanted the whole body, the cranioklept wanted only the head—cleaned, bleached, impervious to time and radiating its mystery. The skull, for men like Rosenbaum, was something like a scientific fetish, a secular relic.

In this regard men like Joseph Carl Rosenbaum had much earlier antecedents. The ancient Christian cult of relics had long since put a premium on the remains of the dead, and in particular of dead saints. Their tombs were privileged places where Heaven and Earth met; the bones of the saints were the physical evidence of the coming resurrection, a tangible proof of Christ's promise in the form of the undecayed corpse.

But that didn't mean one couldn't steal them. Relic theft had long been an accepted practice in medieval Christianity. Indeed, such actions were not considered thefts at all—the term for this process was simply "translation," and it was almost universally praised and considered an act of Christian virtue. As Patrick J. Geary explained, "A real conviction that the relic was the saint, that the relic was a person and not a thing, undoubtedly helped mitigate the more blatantly immoral aspects of stealing. Paralleling the customs of ritual 'kidnappings' of brides by their prospective husbands, the theft of relics was at once a kidnapping and a seduction; overcome by the force of the thief's ardor and devotion, the saint allowed himself to be swept away to a new life in a new family."[45] This attitude captures the motives of men like Rosenbaum much more closely than the pure-profit motive of the typical resurrectionist. The stealing of Haydn's skull was in many ways an act of love: reverence by way of defilement. Why hide such a worthy skull out of the sight of humankind when it could be proudly displayed, a testament for centuries to come?

Any piece of a saint might be potent and valuable, but by the end of the Middle Ages the skull in particular had developed an iconic exceptionality. Associated with the trope of *vanitas*, or *memento mori*, the skull embodied a complicated union of ideas and themes, from bodily decay and physical death to penance and ultimately salvation. As Thomas Browne himself wrote, "In these moral acceptions, the way to be immortal is to die daily: nor can I think I have the true Theory of death, when I contemplate a skull . . . with those vulgar imaginations it casts upon us; I have therefore enlarged that common *Memento mori* [Remember you must die], into a more Christian memorandum, *Memento quatuor Novissima* [Remember the four last things], those four inevitable points of us all, Death, Judgement, Heaven, and Hell."[46] By the time Browne's own skull was put on display, it was perhaps contemplated for different reasons, but certainly phrenology and cranioklepty contain the echoes of this much earlier legacy.

Perhaps because of this tradition, it would seem that to possess another's skull allowed for a unique connection that could

---

[45] Patrick J. Geary, *Furta Sacra: Thefts of Relics in the Central Middle Ages* (Princeton: Princeton University Press, 1990), pp. 132–133.

[46] Browne, *Religio Medici, Hydrotaphia, and the Garden of Cyrus*, p. 47.

last beyond death. Saint Francis of Assisi, who himself would come to be iconically associated with skulls, recorded the lament of a Brother Julius, who, upon the loss of a close friend and fellow monk, cried, "Alas, woe is me; for there is no good left me now, and all the world is darkened to me by the death of my sweet and most loving brother Amazialbene! Were it not that I should have no peace from the brethren, I would go to his grave and take out his head, and out of his skull I would make me two vessels; from the one I would always eat, in memory of him, for my own devotion, and from the other I would drink when I was thirsty."[47]

Many of the more prominent thinkers of the Enlightenment, of course, had tried to put an end to this kind of sentimental attachment to human remains. Voltaire decried the worshipping of relics as a "superstition" left over from "our ages of barbarity," when they had appealed to "the vulgar: feudal lords and their imbecile wives, and their brutish vassals."[48]

But even so rational a thinker as G. W. F. Hegel, from whom so much of modern philosophy derives, was susceptible to the aura of the skull. In 1807 he published his opus *The Phenomenology of Spirit*, which included a lengthy section on phrenology. Although he ultimately concluded that phrenology as a science was dubious at best, he nonetheless recognized the cultural importance of the skull: "The skull-bone does have in general the

[47] Raphael Brown (ed.), *The Little Flowers of St. Francis of Assisi* (New York: Doubleday, 1958) p. 236.
[48] Quoted in Anneli Rufus, *Magnificent Corpses* (New York: Marlowe & Company, 1999) p. 5.

significance of being the immediate actuality of Spirit. . . . If now the brain and spinal cord together constitute that corporal *being-for-self* of Spirit, the skull and vertebral column for the other extreme to it, an extreme which is separated off, viz., the solid, inert Thing. When, however, anyone thinks of the proper location of Spirit's outer existence, it is not the back that comes to mind but only the head."[49]

THE THEATER WORLD in Vienna was small, and if the Rosenbaums did not know Elizabeth Roose directly, they certainly had many friends in common with the actress. Her unexpected death during childbirth was a tragedy for her family and a blow to the theatrical world, but Rosenbaum saw it as an opportunity. He was clearly not thinking of the possibility of stealing her skull before her death, and he made no mention of her in his diary before the "dull, melancholy" day of her burial on October 26, 1808. But when he heard the news of her death, something clicked in him, and he quickly saw that she was the perfect specimen.

Roose was in many ways an ideal subject for phrenological study. When her family had come to Vienna (both her husband and father were also well-known actors), they brought with them a new style of acting. A contemporary reviewer wrote that "with the appearance of this family a proper conversational tone came

---

[49] G. W. F. Hegel, *The Phenomenology of Spirit*, translated by A. V. Miller (Oxford: Oxford University Press, 1977), pp. 200, 197.

to the theatre, and naturalness replaced the stilted, strutting style of play-acting."[50] And while Betty's father was known for his awkward gait, his stout frame and gangly limbs, her own genius was largely in her face and expressions.

The night after her burial, Rosenbaum and Peter discussed their plan to liberate Roose's head, discussing what possible correlations might be found between her appearance and her character once they could carry out exact phrenological measurements. There was something intoxicating in the possibilities. To the phrenologist the skull had its own landscape, where valleys and ridges told a secret story, a hidden territory to be unearthed. Like a geologist reading the strata of rock, a phrenologist could unravel a decades-old history in the contours of a cleaned skull. Rosenbaum and Peter spent the long night talking of these possibilities, imagining what secrets Betty Roose's head might reveal about the actress and her genius. Therese was so revolted by their discussion that she left the room: "Her phantasy," Rosenbaum explained, "conjured up nothing but dreadful sights."[51]

It took Peter a few days to work out the details, but by the end of the month he came back to Rosenbaum with high hopes. Therese already asleep, Peter sketched out the plan of first securing the head, cleaning the bone of as much flesh as they could, and then soaking it in limewater to bleach it fully. They decided they would need to have a glass vessel built so that they could

[50] Rosenbaum, *The Diary of Carl Joseph Rosenbaum*, p. 143.
[51] Ibid.

watch the bleaching process through the various stages of decay. That night Rosenbaum wrote in his diary, "It is of the greatest interest for me."[52]

By this point they were making no secret of their agenda; over the next few days friends occasionally dropped in to see whether Rosenbaum had yet found the means of liberating the actress's head, though he was careful to spare Therese any further discussion of his sudden preoccupation.

THE THEFT WAS planned for November 3, almost a week after the actress's death. On the 1st of the month Rosenbaum and Peter had driven out to the cemetery and met with the grave digger, Jakob Demuth, a "rather plump, tall, jovial man." He agreed to dig up the body and cut off the head for 25 gulden, plus gratuity. This was not an insubstantial sum, and certainly the money was not coming from Peter. But it was all Rosenbaum could think of in those days, and he wanted desperately to have his prize. As they waited for darkness, Peter and Rosenbaum went over their plans again, not just the dissection but also "the solemn burial of the brain, flesh and fat" in Peter's garden.[53]

The theft was delayed a night because when they arrived on the 3rd they found Demuth drunk and passed out. "We ultimately had to leave," Rosenbaum wrote that night, "after so

[52] Ibid.
[53] Ibid., p. 144.

many sacrifices, with nothing accomplished. . . . I returned home around 1 o'clock, greatly annoyed and exhausted."[54] A man of business, Rosenbaum worked diligently on his accounts nearly every day of his life, awake at 4 or 5 in the morning and at his desk by 6:30. These nocturnal forays would quickly take a toll on him, especially if he was to be repeatedly dragging himself to the cemetery past midnight only to be stood up.

The following night was more successful. Rosenbaum, accompanied by Peter, supervised Demuth as he unearthed Roose's coffin. Normally resurrectionists worked by digging down only over one end of the coffin; when the top was exposed, they pried off the lid, using the weight of the earth over the rest of the coffin as leverage and splitting the lid in half. But this was Demuth's cemetery, and as long as they were within its walls they could take their time without fear of discovery. "At 8 in the evening the great work began," Rosenbaum wrote that night. "By shortly after 10 o'clock the head had already been removed." Only after they had finally unearthed the body did the reality of what they were doing occur to Rosenbaum. Ten days after her death Roose's body was well into decomposition. "The foul smell beggars all description," he explained, "and we were actually concerned for the gravedigger's life. She had begun to decompose badly."[55]

Having finally achieved their goal, Rosenbaum and Peter were

[54] Ibid.
[55] Ibid.

faced with a dilemma: They had fantasized about the clean, anti-septic skull devoid of any trace of decay that they could study at their leisure, but neither had prepared himself for the great stench of a rotting and rancid head whose smell would be evident to any-one who came within fifty feet. Afraid that they'd be stopped by the police with such odoriferous cargo, they decided to keep the head in the cemetery. Demuth agreed to hide it under some old coffins that he kept in a shed, provided they return to fetch it the next day.

THE NEXT DAY dawned dark and cold, and early in the morn-ing Rosenbaum drove back to the graveyard. On the way to De-muth's shed, they passed Roose's gravesite: The soil was visibly disturbed, and anyone who cared to notice would have seen that something was amiss. But there was nothing to be done about that now. Demuth was eager to be rid of the head, though he agreed to conceal it under his cloak and carry it as far as the car-riage Rosenbaum had left waiting. They drove directly to Peter's house, and it was Rosenbaum's turn to hide his foul-smelling tro-phy under his coat as they brought it inside.

Once in the house they put it in the glass jar they had had built and immersed it in water, mainly to suppress the smell. The head submerged, they put a lid on the jar and let the room air out. Only then could they finally take stock of their prize. "The face was distinguishable," Rosenbaum commented. "The left side and part of the right were greenish black, the forehead green with black stripes, the right side yellowish white . . . the eyes were closed but bulged greatly, the mouth was slightly open so that the teeth could be seen."[56] It was an odd trophy, a grim and garish reminder of the reality of death and a far cry from the phrenological resource they had hoped to recover. Rosenbaum went home, leaving Peter to finalize the details for the dissection and cleaning.

Giddy with excitement, Rosenbaum told Therese of his plan and its success. He wanted her to share in this moment, to understand why it was important to him and why she should care about his triumph. But on some level, he also wanted absolution from her. With all the morbid illegality and sacrilege he'd lately engaged in, Rosenbaum was a bit uneasy about what they'd done, and he was eager to display the "solemnity" of his intentions (a term that he used frequently in his journal) as if to absolve himself of any crime. He assured Therese of his intention to bury the remains of Roose's head in a separate ceremony and invited her to participate in this private reburial. He also asked her to bring a few friends. With an audience of respectable ladies, it would be clear to all—including Rosenbaum—that this was not simple grave robbing but something more noble.

Therese was unsure. She was still deeply uncomfortable with what her husband had done, but she tried her best to fulfill the role of supportive wife. In the end she agreed to pass the invitation on to her friends, but she declined to come herself.

[56] Ibid.

The following day, November 6, they began the true work—the same day, as Rosenbaum grimly recorded, that both Roose's husband and father were back onstage, performing once again. Peter had recruited a young doctor named Weiss to handle the actual dissection. "The stench was simply inconceivable," Rosenbaum reported, "the most noisome odor was made by the brain which had become completely putrid." It was difficult to get too close to the head without getting nauseated. But Weiss was fearless, and Rosenbaum "had to admire the young man for the dexterity with which he cut everything away."[57] To combat the odor, they burned incense, so much that the smoke turned Weiss's face black. The young doctor cut away the skin and muscle, slowly scraping away the layers that made up Elizabeth's celebrated face until the bone was exposed. He broke through the occipital bone on the underside of the skull and scooped out the brain, collecting everything in a bucket. Curiously, Weiss left the jaw attached, and by the time he was finished there was still a great deal of ligament still intact. Perhaps the smell had started to get him, too.

Afterward they put the skull in limewater to bleach it out, then buried all that Weiss had cut away under a plum tree in the garden. As Peter, Rosenbaum, and Weiss concluded their "solemn actus," their audience arrived: Madames Geissler, Goldman, and Hocheder, all of whom had been invited to participate. Hocheder had been a close friend of the actress in life, and now Rosenbaum,

---

[57] Ibid., p. 145.

presiding over these improvised last rites, had her wave a funerary torch three times over the makeshift grave. This act of mourning completed, Rosenbaum led the women back to Peter's grotto and proudly showed them "the head stripped of all flesh."[58]

WHEN CALCIUM OXIDE—quicklime—is mixed with water, the resulting chemical reaction gives off a great amount of heat and quickly raises the temperature of the water to boiling. For this reason, limewater is ideal for cleaning bone—the heat boils off any remaining matter or viscera but leaves the bone relatively untouched, thus bleaching it white and clean. For a month they kept the skull in a solution of limewater, changing the solution every so often as it worked on the actress's skull. And slowly the head lost whatever traces it might have borne of a living woman, becoming instead a sterile death's-head perfect for study.

A month later the head was out of the lime; Rosenbaum and Peter uncovered it in its new state and stood looking at it for quite some time. Gone were the flashing eyes, the sly smile that could captivate an audience, and the dimpled cheeks. What was left of Betty Roose was a series of grooves and ridges, a map of her mind in the white bone that was all that remained beyond death. Finally Rosenbaum said, "So was she, so is she now."[59]

[58] Ibid.
[59] Ibid.

THE SKULL WAS to stay in limewater for the next four months in Peter's garden, where it would occasionally be shown to visitors. Four months turned out to be much longer than necessary. So long, in fact, that the lime burned off too much of the fat and necessary oils in the bone, and the skull became overly brittle. After a while, to make matters worse, the skull began to grow algae. On Easter 1809, Rosenbaum the resurrectionist noted that "the head is very spotted, wild and greenish."[60]

This was the last entry in Rosenbaum's diary that mentioned Elizabeth Roose. If he worked more on her skull, he didn't mention it. But by then other events had been set in motion. In May the French laid siege to Vienna, and shortly thereafter, amidst the chaos, the great and venerated Joseph Haydn died. The night he heard of Haydn's death, nearly oblivious to the massing armies around him, Rosenbaum "pondered Haydn's destiny."[61] The next day he went to work.

[60] Ibid., p. 146.
[61] Ibid., p. 148.

CHAPTER FOUR

THE
GOLDEN LYRE

While in London Haydn had begun working on an opera to be called *The Soul of a Philosopher*, a retelling of the story of Orpheus and Eurydice, which he never completed and was never staged in his lifetime. Of all the Greek and Roman myths, the tale of Orpheus and his beloved had special resonance for musicians: The poet and singer, whose lover dies tragically, is so overcome with grief that he descends to the underworld with his lyre and there plays a song so beautiful that even the Lord of the Dead is moved and allows Orpheus to return with Eurydice to the land of the living, so long as he doesn't look back at her while they ascend. It is a story about the power of music to transcend all boundaries, including death. There had been at least three other operas based on it, including works by Monteverdi and Gluck. When E. T. A. Hoffman made his case for the supremacy of music, he invoked Orpheus to prove his point: "Music is the most romantic of all the arts; one might even say that it alone is purely romantic. The lyre of Orpheus opened the gates of Orcus. Music unlocks for man an unfamiliar world having nothing in common with the one which surrounds him."[62]

In life Haydn would have been the natural choice to play Orpheus, but now it was Rosenbaum who prepared to assume the role, descending into the land of the dead to snatch back his beloved.

ON MAY 10 the French had taken up positions outside the city walls of Vienna, ensconced in the western suburbs. They demanded that the Archduke Maximilian surrender; he responded by opening fire. His bombardment was so intense that the hospitals and almshouses were draped with large black flags so they might be recognized and avoided by his cannoneers. Around 9 o'clock that night, the French returned the gesture. Throughout the night they hit Vienna with everything they had—literally. By 3 a.m. they had to stop shelling because they had run out of ammunition.

Citizens of Vienna, most of whom had spent a terrified night barricaded in their cellars, stepped out onto the street that frigid morning of May 11 to find that they could not walk for the broken glass that covered every inch of the ground. In addition, there were fires everywhere; Rosenbaum came out of his cellar that morning to find a fire racing down the block toward his building. He managed to save it only by a heroic effort organizing the neighbors into a bucket brigade.

[62] Quoted in Gramit, *Cultivating Music*, p. 3.

By then Maximilian's army had withdrawn to the far side of the Danube, burning bridges in its wake and leaving the city to the French. In the ensuing occupation Napoleon had an honor guard stationed at the door of Haydn's home to spare its owner from looting or further distress. But Haydn's strength was fading, his long life nearing its end. A few days before his death a French officer called on him and sang for him one of his own arias, from *The Creation*, "with so much truth of expression and real musical sentiment" that Haydn broke down in tears of joy.[63] Later that day he called his family to the piano one last time and played for them the Austrian hymn that he had composed for the emperor ten years before, an anthem for a country that now lay in ruins around him. He played it three times, building in intensity each time, and then retired. The next day he could not get out of bed, and on May 31 he passed peacefully into death.

ON THE DAY of Haydn's funeral the air was thick with "warm, choking dust"; breathing was difficult, and it exhausted the mourners. Haydn lay in state in his room, adorned with his medals of honor from Paris, Russia, Sweden, and Vienna. In the afternoon his coffin was carried to the Hundsthurmer Church in Gumpendorf, carried three times around the church, and then brought inside. It was a small ceremony, and after a short service

[63] Quoted in Geiringer, p. 189.

Haydn was buried in the Hundsthurmer cemetery. Buried next to him was a prominent artist named Löschenkohl, who had been known for his silhouette portraits and had once been the lover of Therese's friend Madame Geissler.

On the other side of Löschenkohl's plot was the violated grave of Elizabeth Roose.

As soon as the dusty funeral was over, Rosenbaum pulled aside the grave digger, Jakob Demuth. Since Rosenbaum had last seen Demuth, all his possessions had been plundered by the besieging French army, and he was certainly in the state of mind and economic position to accept another bribe from Rosenbaum. His financial straits quickly outweighed any concern he might have had over desecrating such a famous corpse. And so Demuth agreed to dig up the body the following night and remove the great man's head.

With the grave digger's help once again secured, there was only one loose end. Rosenbaum's descriptions of his first try at skull cleaning suggest that he had fouled Roose's skull by leaving it in limewater for so long, and he didn't want to make the same mistake with an infinitely more valuable head. As capable as he might have been with numbers, anatomy and chemistry seemed beyond him, so he decided that this time he would have to hire someone to clean the skull professionally. The question was who—Rosenbaum needed someone of both great skill and great discretion.

After Rosenbaum was finished at Gumpendorf he was exhausted, the dust in the air making it difficult to breathe, but he still dragged himself to Peter's to explain the details of the plan and secure his friend's support. But he found Peter to be on edge, frantic, suddenly uncooperative and erratic. The realization of their long-standing plan was finally at hand, and Peter was at moments wildly exuberant about the prospect. But then he would suddenly become paranoid, convinced that the theft of such a famous man's head would not go unnoticed. This was no up-and-coming but little-known actress. This was a significantly more serious undertaking.

Peter's nerves might also have been justifiably shaken by the cataclysmic battle going on all around them. But Rosenbaum knew the war to be a stroke of luck. Had Haydn died at any time other than in the middle of such a citywide catastrophe, he would have been given a lavish state funeral, and the theft they now contemplated would have been impossible.

THE NEXT DAY a small service for Haydn was held, with a requiem by his brother Michael. According to Rosenbaum, the music was "abominable," as was the attendance. Only a meager handful of people turned out, and none of the *Kapellmeister*s of Vienna bothered to attend. In fact, the only Viennese singer to perform was Therese herself. It was as if the city had already forgotten the composer.

After the dreadful mass, Rosenbaum drove to the cemetery to speak with Demuth, but the grave digger wasn't there. Rosenbaum regretted having to place so much faith in a compromised alcoholic, but what other sort of man could so readily be bribed into stealing the head of Franz Joseph Haydn?

On his way home Rosenbaum happened to run into Leopold Eckhart, his friend and doctor. Eckhart knew of Rosenbaum's interest in phrenology and had been present seven years earlier when they both had first heard Gall's name. He was the sort of man, Rosenbaum now saw, who not only could be trusted but also could prove quite useful. Rosenbaum revealed to him the plan to steal Haydn's head and the need for someone as skillful as Eckhart to carry out the dissection and maceration.

Eckhart readily agreed to help with the dissection., More important, like any doctor, he knew of the usefulness of cleaned skeletons for teaching and reference purposes. Like any good medical institution, he said, the Vienna General Hospital where he worked employed men whose job it was to clean and articulate skeletons professionally. He offered to put Rosenbaum in touch with the corpse bearers who worked at the hospital.

After meeting those men at the hospital morgue, Rosenbaum was doubtful. The cleaning of Haydn's head had to be done flawlessly, and he was unimpressed with the rough and grubby workers whom Eckhart brought him. It took a great deal of personal assurance on the part of the doctor to convince Rosenbaum of the quality of their work and to get him to agree to let them undertake the project. Finally Rosenbaum told them that he would have the head the following night, and they should be ready to receive it. The last piece had fallen into place. Now all that was needed was the head itself.

DURING THAT LONG week Rosenbaum's public persona continued to be that of a respectable member of the Viennese bourgeoisie. But throughout it all, his darker personal agenda continued. The night after meeting Eckhart—Friday, June 2—Rosenbaum drove to the cemetery to receive the head, but no one met him there. Rosenbaum waited in vain for some sign from Demuth before finally heading home, once again empty-handed. For a time his plans seemed on the verge of unraveling, and it was not at all clear to Rosenbaum that he would be able to pull off the theft. He had entered a subterranean economy with questionable associates—the notoriously unreliable Demuth, the increasingly erratic Peter, and Eckhart's too-earthy corpse bearers, who were to him an unknown quantity.

Rosenbaum had hoped to keep the head in his possession for a few nights before turning it over to be cleaned. Roose's head had always been on hand for inspection and meditation, but now that Rosenbaum had involved professionals, he was going to lose the head for over a month. Before that happened he wanted some time alone with it, stinking and rotting though he knew it would be. But he didn't get the chance. Saturday, for the second night in a row, Demuth failed to show. The reason, it turned out, was that he had been beaten the night before and was still recovering. Rosenbaum was forced to inform the corpse bearers at the hospital that it would be another night before the head would arrive.

Finally, on Sunday, June 4, Rosenbaum drove to the cemetery with Peter and a few other friends. They found that Demuth had already decapitated the body, and while the others waited in the carriage, Rosenbaum undertook the retrieval.

At the gates of the cemetery he felt himself transformed. He had become Orpheus—he had seen someone he loved taken by death and now stood on the precipice of the underworld. Through dedication and perseverance, he would venture into places unknown by the living. And so Rosenbaum strode forth to meet Demuth, who delivered, as promised, "the most valuable relic of Joseph Haydn."[64]

A MILLION THOUGHTS raced through Rosenbaum's mind: elation at having finally accomplished what he'd spent over a year planning, anxiety about the hurdles still to be overcome. But above all, like Orpheus, he was overcome by a desire to look, to gaze upon his prize. As he returned to the carriage, he peeled away the rags in which Demuth had wrapped the head and looked down at the now horrific face of his old friend. Haydn had died almost a week before, and this was Vienna in June. And so, upon entering into the carriage with the head, its stench now confined within the carriage's narrow walls, Rosenbaum did what anyone might have done: He threw up.

[64] Rosenbaum, *The Diary of Carl Joseph Rosenbaum*, p. 150.

Surrounded by friends, Rosenbaum struggled to regain his composure. He covered the head once more and had the driver deliver them to the hospital. Still feeling ill, Rosenbaum nevertheless understood that he had a duty to be present during the dissection.

Eckhart himself cleaned away the molding skin and muscle and divested the skull of its putrefying brain. "The sight made a life-long impression on me," Rosenbaum later wrote. "The dissection lasted for one hour; the brain, which was of large proportions, stank the most terribly of all. I endured it to the end."[65]

This time there was no solemn reburial of the remains in Peter's garden. Eckhart and his men were professionals and treated Haydn's remains as they would any medical waste, disposing of it unceremoniously in the hospital's furnaces.

Still nervous about the competence of the corpse bearers, Rosenbaum once again impressed upon them the need to take the utmost care with the skull. He was extremely reluctant to part with it, and Eckhart once again had to provide assurances of the quality of the work. And so, with "a thousand reminders of the diligence and precision with which this head is to be macerated and bleached," Rosenbaum finally relinquished the skull.[66]

Peter, meanwhile, had become bored during the dissection and wandered off; he now returned with an already cleaned skull he had found, asking whether he might buy it for his collection.

[65] Ibid.
[66] Ibid.

TEN DAYS LATER there was another requiem for Haydn, staged this time by the Friends of Music. It was a far more successful affair than the earlier performance. The requiem this time was Mozart's; the church and its pews were draped entirely in black; and in the center a *castrum doloris* had been erected, displaying Haydn's seven medals of honor. This time all of Viennese society appeared in mourning; it was "most solemn and worthy of Haydn," Rosenbaum wrote.[67]

Among those present was a contingent of French officers who had been granted leave to attend, including a young commissary named Henri Marie Beyle. Of all those present, Beyle would have been most sympathetic to Rosenbaum's project had he been aware of it. Like Rosenbaum, Beyle loved Haydn's music and would shortly publish a biography of the composer (which, it turned out, was largely plagiarized). He also had an abiding interest in phrenology, having been one of Gall's patients back in Paris.

But the affinities between the two men ran deeper, though they were never to know each other. Beyle was fascinated by the story of Marguerite de Navarre and her lover Boniface de la Mole: Boniface had been guillotined for high treason during the height of the French terror, and his head had been impaled on a spike as a warning to other dissidents. Marguerite had put herself

[67] Ibid., p. 151.

75

at some risk by taking down the head and then, according to legend, had had it embalmed and placed in an ornate jeweled case that she would show off to friends. In 1830, when Beyle was writing his masterpiece under the pseudonym "Stendhal," he would be reminded of the story of Marguerite and Boniface and would incorporate a version of it into the final scene of the book that was to become *The Red and the Black*. In that novel, after Julien Sorel's death, his lover Mathilde (whose family name, de la Mole, was itself an homage to Boniface) goes alone to his crypt the night before his burial and decapitates his corpse, spending a night alone with the head before interring it in a separate, private ceremony.

Paying his respects to Haydn that day, Beyle scarcely could have imagined that life was busy imitating art some twenty years in advance and that, while he and the other mourners had gathered to honor the composer, Haydn's head was soaking in lime-water at a nearby hospital.

WHILE NAPOLEON'S ARMY was massing all around him, preparing for the largest land battle Europe had ever seen, Rosenbaum waited for the corpse bearers to finish cleaning the skull of Joseph Haydn, all the while designing the display cabinet. In the surreal context of a city under siege and in the process of disintegration, the skull never left Rosenbaum's mind. In early July he wrote in his diary, "At 12 o'clock midnight the great and decisive battle began. May its outcome be favorable for us!" following this sentiment immediately with the line, "At Reimann's I altered our design of the case for Haydn's head."[68] At the end of the month he retrieved the head. True to their word, the corpse bearers had done an excellent job and delivered the clean, pristine skull of the world's greatest composer. After more than a year's worth of preparation and planning, considerable expense, and no small amount of risk, Rosenbaum at last had his prize.

It was an odd moment to be celebrating, given that the world around him was crumbling. On September 2 he gave the following description of Wagram, the site of Napoleon's last victory: "Of a population of 400 in the village, 2 to 3 die each day, because of the shortage of food and because so many people are cooped together in each house." A week later, in this same climate of famine and scarcity, Rosenbaum complained of having to spend the outrageous sum of 12 gulden on "taffeta and fringe" for Haydn's display case.[69]

It is during moments like these that it becomes most clear that there are two kinds of death. There is Death, the immortal and symbolic figure embodied in the skull, and then there is the other, messy death that was happening all around Rosenbaum, the death that came with the waste of battle, a dismembering and decapitating death, a death of putrefaction and unbearable smells. What Rosenbaum struggled with, even at his most audacious, was that alchemical transformation from one kind of death to the other, a

[68] Ibid.
[69] Ibid. pp. 153-154.

transformation that required more than just quicklime. The clean white skull that philosophers have long gazed at has an antiseptic quality, utterly inorganic and pure. But resurrectionism is dirty work, and a severed head is a long way from a skull. It is a reflection of the singular nature of those times that men like Rosenbaum could so clearly hold both attitudes toward the dead simultaneously, even if these attitudes contradicted one another.

THE DISPLAY CASE Rosenbaum designed for Haydn's skull was a simple, elegant black box with a glass front and a taffeta curtain. It was understated, mostly devoid of ornamentation save for one feature. Hanging above the skull inside the case was the symbol of Orpheus, a golden lyre. Orpheus, emblem of all great musicians, patron saint of the ones who descend into the underworld to retrieve that which is most precious.

The skull of Joseph Haydn,
in the case designed by Rosenbaum and Peter.

CHAPTER FIVE

"ALL THE FERRETS WERE SET IN MOTION"

In 1820 the young poet John Keats and his friend Charles Brown collaborated on a piece titled "Stanzas on Some Skulls in Beauly Abbey, near Inverness," riffing off each other and trading verses. The abbey in question had been ransacked by Protestant reformers, and the records of those buried in its catacombs had been destroyed; Keats and Brown's poem in turn offered an alternate way of telling the stories of the dead:

> Your chronicles no more exist,
> Since Knox, the revolutionist,
> Destroyed the work of every fist
>   That scrawled black letter.
> Well! I'm a craniologist
>   And may do better.

A parody of the graveyard scene in *Hamlet*, the poem offered a series of mock readings based on various skulls. The jocularity of the tone only thinly masks a certain disgust at a changing world, one in which Hamlet's great meditation on Yorick's death has been replaced by the schematic rationality of Gall's system. Phrenology had threatened the church by suggesting that the brain trumped the immortal soul, and it had threatened more reputable sciences by its lack of rigor or verifiability. Poets like Keats were perturbed by phrenology for yet another reason: It sought to denude the skull of its aura and its totemic power, reducing it to just one more scientific apparatus.

Men like Rosenbaum might have reassured Keats on this point. Motivated by phrenology, his appreciation of the skull as a relic nonetheless tapped into something deeper, a respect and awe for the uncanny and the unknown that was more akin to the Romantics than to the quacks who had begun to travel the globe offering personalized phrenological readings.

Enshrined in its velvet case beneath the lyre of Orpheus, the skull of Haydn straddled so many worlds.

AND THERE IT stayed for most of the next eleven years, in its elegant box, Peter and Rosenbaum trading off possession every so often. But while Peter may have kept the skull in his garden occasionally, there was no doubt to whom it belonged.

It was the last skull Rosenbaum was to pilfer by such spectacular means. The excitement over, he and his wife returned to their lives. Therese had to retire from performing in 1812, her voice unexpectedly failing. For fifteen brief years she had cut a path of brilliance across the Viennese stage; now she settled into the life of a housewife. The Rosenbaums continued to prosper: They owned a large estate in the suburbs of Vienna, with their own lavish gardens. Therese's mother, had she lived to see it, would have no doubt been amazed at the lifestyle this no-account clerk had provided for her daughter. By the year he turned fifty Rosenbaum had settled with Therese into the perfect image of middle-class respectability. And then the past caught up with him when, four months after his birthday, grave diggers unearthed a startling revelation in Gumpendorf.

ROSENBAUM WAS ALWAYS well aware that something like this might happen. He had heard rumors that the prince was finally going to honor his obligation to the dead composer, and he could easily have guessed the likely outcome. He was well connected and had enough friends still in the prince's employ that he could keep abreast of developments. Throughout the investigation his own network of *mouches* kept him updated. The afternoon Haydn's body was exhumed, Rosenbaum noted calmly the discovery of the theft and that the prince was "infuriated at the deed." He also learned that the prince had already launched an investigation, upon which Rosenbaum noted dryly, "All the ferrets were set in motion."[70]

At first he was not particularly worried by the investigation

[70] Rosenbaum, *The Diary of Carl Joseph Rosenbaum*, p. 155.

and treated the unfolding events with great levity. "We talked about the Prince sending Haydn's remains, minus the head, to Eisenstadt on Monday," he related in his diary, "and that everyone is having a good laugh at the Prince's expense."[71] Twenty years before, the prince had kept Rosenbaum from acquiring something that he dearly loved—now, in an unexpected turn of events, Rosenbaum had something precious that belonged to the prince. He was going to enjoy every minute of it.

But the weak link, Rosenbaum quickly saw, was Peter. Once Sedlintzsky's men heard the story from Schwinner, who had named Peter as the owner of the skull, Peter panicked. The next day he came to Rosenbaum "in a fright," "moaning and wailing" and threatening to divulge the whole story.[72] Rosenbaum was furious—the theft of Haydn's skull was his great triumph, and he had worked too hard to see it lost because of this man's lack of nerve.

He repeatedly threatened Peter, demanding that he not tell the police anything. But Peter would not be quieted. Rosenbaum saw that Peter could not be trusted to stonewall the investigators, so he shifted tactics. He left the room and returned with a skull, already working on a new story. The police were simpletons, he explained. They were looking for a skull, and to them any skull would do. The best thing to do was to put all of the blame on their dead friend Eckhart, who was certainly in no position to protest.

---

[71] Ibid.
[72] Ibid.

This worked much better than either man could have hoped—the police bought the story completely, accepted the head that Peter provided, and thanked him for his cooperation. All that was needed now was Rosenbaum's version of the events, merely as a matter of record. The next day they came to Rosenbaum, who told them the same story. As he realized that the police had bought it, he visibly relaxed, and his conversation with the investigators became "good natured." Amazed at their gullibility, he and Peter convened afterward and "spoke laughingly about the Prince's foul tricks."[73]

It was all a game, he saw, between him and the prince—the two of them alone moved around pawns such as Sedlintzky and Peter. Rosenbaum could easily stay two steps ahead of the prince, who, for all his money and power, would never be able to outwit this common accountant.

But due to carelessness or apathy, Rosenbaum had given Peter a skull that even a cursory inspection revealed was the wrong age. Realizing that they had been duped, the police came back to Rosenbaum's house before he had any time to prepare. While they waited impatiently downstairs, he frantically looked for a hiding place. Not knowing what to do with the head and fearing the imminent search, he hid it in the mattress and threw down some blankets. Seeing right away that this wouldn't work, he told his frightened wife to get in bed and cover the skull herself. Twelve years after she had fled the room to get away from his

[73] Ibid.

morbid project, he had finally enlisted her as an accomplice—as he had enlisted Peter, Demuth, Eckhart, and so many others into his singular passion.

ROSENBAUM HAD SAVED the composer, rescued him from the oblivion of burial, that wall of earth that hides our remains for eternity. In time, he hoped, all would be able to see the skull of the great composer and meditate on his genius.

Alone in his room, finally left in peace by the police, he could take out the skull of Joseph Haydn, turn it in his hand, like a Renaissance painting of Saint Jerome or Mary Magdalene, and ponder the skull's mysteries in the flickering candlelight.

PART TWO

THE

ALCHEMICAL

BODY

We have a very large collection of the skulls of

murderers, who have been executed, and of soldiers

killed on battle-fields, also of Indians, Africans,

Egyptians, Chinese, and Cannibals, but we have only a

few from the higher class of minds, such as Reformers,

Statesmen, Scholars, & c. Of these we have hundreds of

casts, and busts from living heads, but not their skulls.

What a treasure it would be if some plan could

be devised, by which these leading "types" could be

preserved as specimens, for scientific purposes.

· *The Phrenological Journal,* May 1855

CHAPTER SIX

"THE RIDDLE-FILLED BOOK OF DESTINY"

The comedy ended for Beethoven, finally, on March 26, 1827. Four months earlier he had traveled from Vienna to Bonn to care for his nephew after a failed suicide attempt, and on the way home he came down with a fever and a hacking cough after spending the night in a village inn without heat. When the attending physician, Andreas Wawruch, came to see him on December 5, he found the composer breathing hard and spitting blood. To Wawruch it looked like pneumonia, and he treated it accordingly. After a week Beethoven had improved and was walking around, but a quick relapse followed, this one far more serious.

Wawruch diagnosed him this time with dropsy (what is now termed edema, a condition that results in an imbalance of fluid buildup inside the body), and two weeks later close to eleven liters of fluid were drained from his abdomen; as water flowed from his body, Beethoven wryly commented,

"Professor, you remind me of Moses striking the rock with his staff."[74]

His sense of humor still intact, the maestro bore his illness well, but his condition continued to deteriorate. Over the next two months three more draining operations took place, each removing over ten liters of fluid from the composer's distended body. The writing was on the wall, and none saw it more clearly than Beethoven himself. When Wawruch tried to cheer him up that March, suggesting that the spring weather would hasten a recovery, Beethoven responded, "My work is done; if any doctor could still help, his name shall be called Wonderful!"[75] The reference was to Isaiah 9:6—a verse Handel had transformed into a joyous chorus in the *Messiah*. But no such messiah was forthcoming; on March 23 Beethoven signed the final codicil to his will, and the next day he received the last rites. Shortly thereafter he slipped into the coma from which he would not recover.

AMONG THOSE PRESENT during the maestro's final days was a young boy named Gerhard von Breuning whose father, Stephan, had been a childhood friend of the composer. Stephan and Beethoven's relationship had gone through rough patches,

---

[74] Quoted in Alexander Wheelock Thayer, *Thayer's Life of Beethoven*, revised and edited by Elliot Forbes (Princeton: Princeton University Press, 1964), p. 1023. Further information on Beethoven's last days can be found in Thayer, *Life of Beethoven*, pp. 973–1011, and in Peter J. Davies, *Beethoven in Person: His Deafness, Illnesses, and Death* (New York: Greenwood Press, 2001), pp. 71-99.
[75] Thayer, *Life of Beethoven*, p. 1038.

including a ten-year period during which they stopped speaking altogether. But in 1825 they had reconciled after Beethoven had sent Stephan a miniature portrait accompanied by a letter pledging absolute devotion: "I know, I have wounded *your heart*, but my own emotions, which you must certainly have noticed, have punished me enough. It was not *malice* towards you that was in my mind . . . it was passion *in you* and *in me*."[76] Shortly thereafter, the composer moved around the corner from the Breunings—to a house that had once been a monastery and was called Schwarzspanierhaus, "House of the Black-Robed Spaniards"—and their friendship had resumed as if without a hitch.

Gerhard, who was twelve at the time, struck up a fast friendship with the composer, who referred to the young boy affectionately as either "Trouserbutton" (because he stuck to Beethoven like a button to a garment) or "Ariel" (after the ephemeral spirit from Shakespeare's *The Tempest*). It was Gerhard who, in his own immature way, proved beyond a shadow of a doubt that Beethoven was stone-deaf and could not even hear music, as some had alleged: When Gerhard arrived early for his music lesson one day, Beethoven asked the boy to wait while he finished work on a quartet. Bored, Gerhard went to the piano, where Beethoven could not see him, and began to play lightly. "I kept looking in his direction to see whether he might be feeling bothered," Gerhard later recalled. "When I saw that he was com-

---

[76] Gerhard von Breuning, *From the House of the Black-Robed Spaniards*, translated by Henry Mins and Maynard Solomon (Cambridge: Cambridge University Press, 1992), p. 53.

pletely unaware of it, I played louder, and intentionally quite loudly—and I had no more doubts."[77]

In two short years Beethoven and Gerhard grew extremely fond of one another, and when the composer's health failed, Gerhard and his father were among those who kept constant vigil. Beethoven had designated Stephan as his executor, and it fell to Stephan to put his affairs in order. On the afternoon of Monday, March 26, Stephan went to see about securing a grave plot for Beethoven in the Währing cemetery—where his own family plot was, so that he could be close to his childhood friend in death— while Gerhard remained at the House of the Black-Robed Spaniards. "I had stayed in the room of the dying man with Beethoven's brother Johann and Sali the housekeeper," he later recalled.

It was between four and five o'clock; the dense clouds drifting together from every quarter increasingly obscured the daylight and, all of a sudden, a violent storm broke, with driving snow and hail. Just as in the immortal Fifth Symphony and the everlasting Ninth there are crashes that sound like a hammering on the portals of Fate, so the heavens seemed to be using their gigantic drums to signal the bitter blow they had just dealt the world of art. At about 5:15 I was called home to my teacher. The end could be expected any minute;

[77] Ibid., p. 72.

I left him alive, or at least still breathing, for the last time.[78]

A half hour later, the composer was dead. Fellow composer and friend, Anselm Hüttenbrenner was one of the few present at the moment of death, and described the scene even more poetically. After a loud crash of thunder, he wrote, "Beethoven opened his eyes, raised his right hand, and gazed fixedly upwards for some seconds, with clenched fist, and a solemn threatening expression, as if he would say: 'I defy you, ye adverse powers, Depart! God is with me.' Or his appearance may be described as that of a brave general, exclaiming to his fainting troops: 'Courage, soldiers! Forward! Trust in me! Victory is ours!'" Many saw portents in the thunderstorm that day; even Wawruch later asked, "Would a Roman augury not have concluded that the chance uproar of the elements was related to his apotheosis?"[79]

MYSTERIES SURROUND BEETHOVEN'S death, his final days, and his afterlife. Much of the confusion stems from Anton Schindler, an acquaintance of Beethoven who took it upon himself to write the first major biography of the composer. Peppering his work with exaggerations and outright fabrications, Schindler used his book to aggrandize himself and persecute his enemies, in

---

[78] Ibid., p. 104.
[79] Quoted in Davies, *Beethoven in Person*, pp. 87-88.

the process distorting much of the historical record regarding the composer. This biography, along with Beethoven's troubled and peculiar health throughout his life, the dizzying number of symptoms recorded by his doctors, and the mystifying way in which his body was handled after his death, has left a record of a life with so many gaps and inconsistencies that the truth about the composer may never be fully known.

There are unanswered questions surrounding the way he died. What caused the dramatic and sustained illnesses that Beethoven suffered in the final years of his life? Was there some root source—such as lead poisoning or treatment with mercury—that might account for the host of symptoms? What led to the fatal edema that caused his body to fill with fluid? Could Wawruch have done more for him? Was the original diagnosis of pneumonia a fatal error, and could more have been done if Wawruch had recognized the edema earlier?

There is the mystery of the composer's deafness. Like the deaths of Mozart and Napoleon, the source of Beethoven's deafness has been one of those enduring medical mysteries over which musicologists, doctors, and historians have puzzled for close to two centuries now without arriving at anything close to a definitive answer. In 1879 George Grove postulated that the composer's symptoms were "most probably the result of syphilitic affections at an early age in life."[80] Though only vague, circumstantial evidence exists for this idea, the hypothesis has stub-

[80] Ibid., p. 121.

bornly persisted—in the century since Grove's first suggestion, dozens of commentators have repeated the diagnosis. But over the past two centuries a host of other theories have been advocated to explain Beethoven's deafness, including alcoholism, amyloidosis, arteriosclerosis, brucellosis, cerebral congestion, drug-induced ototoxicity, otitis media, otosclerosis, Paget's disease of the skull, presbycusis, rheumatism, sarcoidosis, acoustic neuritis, tuberculosis, typhus fever, and Whipple's disease. Peter J. Davies assessed all these theories in 2001 and was unable to offer a final conclusion (though he was able to debunk a good number of them)—each diagnosis matched some symptoms, it seemed, but most were ruled out by others.[81]

There is also the mysterious lock of Beethoven's hair that appeared for sale after World War II. This memento (now known as the "Guevara Lock"), which became the subject of a book by Russell Martin, was clipped from the maestro's head by the composer Ferdinand Hiller while the body lay in state and was passed on to Hiller's son Paul in 1883. But in the tumult of the early twentieth century both Paul and the lock of hair disappeared. Improbably, the lock turned up in the Danish town of Gilleleje in 1943, in the hands of Kay Fremming, a doctor working to give safe passage to Jewish refugees as the Nazis occupied Denmark. But the circumstances of the lock's travels over the missing years remain obscured, despite Martin's extensive research. How it got

[81] Ibid., pp. 207-216.

to Gilleleje, who gave it to Fremming, and what happened to Paul Hiller may never be known.[82]

Finally there is the mystery of Beethoven's skull, which was broken into fragments during the initial autopsy. Over the next fifty years, several of these fragments were stolen. Who took them, and why? Why just these fragments and not the whole head? And where did they end up? So many questions unanswered, so much hidden in what Gerhard von Breuning called "the riddle-filled book of destiny."

MUCH OF THE mystery stems from the odd way the body was handled during the autopsy. The head surgeon was named Johann Wagner; Beethoven's primary physician, Dr. Andreas Wawruch, also attended. Wagner was assisted by a young doctor named Carl von Rokitansky. It remains unclear who authorized the autopsy, though as executor, Stephan von Breuning must certainly have been involved. That Beethoven wanted an autopsy could be inferred from his 1802 will: "As soon as I am dead and if Dr. Schmidt is still alive, ask him in my name to describe my malady, and attach this written document [to his account] of the history of my illness, so that at least as far as is possible the world may become reconciled to me after my death." Dr. Schmidt had died

---

[82] The story of the "Guevara" lock of Beethoven's Hair is chronicled in Russell Martin, *Beethoven's Hair* (New York: Broadway Books, 2000).

years earlier, so Stephan turned to Wagner and his young assistant Rokitansky.[83]

Wagner and Rokitansky found a body wracked with disease. "The body of the dead man showed intense wasting," Wagner wrote in the autopsy report; "the abdomen was distended and swollen with fluid and its skin was stretched." The report, in Latin, went on to note that the abdominal cavity "was filled with four measures of rust-colored fluid. The liver was reduced to half its normal size, was like leather, hard and in color slightly bluish-green and throughout its substance were nodes each about the size of a bean." In their report the doctors were careful to note the condition of the brain and the skull, which was no doubt useful for phrenologists eager to understand the composer and his genius. The sulci (the folds and convolutions of the brain) were, they noted, "twice as deep as usual and (much) more numerous than is usually seen," and the skull was abnormally thick.[84]

Such a discovery was fitting for Beethoven: After his brother Johann had sent him a New Year's greeting in 1823 signed "The Landowner," Beethoven had signed his reply "The Brainowner." Wagner's knife had finally proved the fitting nature of the epithet.[85]

In order to get access to the brain, Wagner had sawed apart

---

[83] Quoted in William Meredith, "The History of Beethoven's Skull Fragments," *The Beethoven Journal*, Vol. 20, Nos. 1 & 2 (Summer & Winter 2005), p. 1.
[84] Davies, *Beethoven in Person*, p. 103.
[85] Breuning, *From the House of the Black-Robed Spaniards*, p. 51.

the skull, cutting off the top and segmenting it into its individual bones. But either he had been in a hurry or he was simply careless because he butchered the job. Ideally, one cuts as close to the seams of the skull as possible, using a fine saw so that the head can be neatly reassembled after the autopsy. But Wagner was extremely rough with the composer's skull, shredding the bone as he cut it apart—bone splinters and fragments were irretrievably lost, and when the work was done the doctors could only loosely fit the remaining pieces back together.

Because of this, Beethoven's body was in sad shape when it was put on display in the days before his burial. His lower jaw jutted forward in a grotesque manner, and his temples were misshapen and lumpy, as if his face were falling in from the sides. The head was wreathed with a crown of white roses, most likely as a means of hiding the extreme indignity it had suffered under the hands of Wagner and Rokitansky.

But this still was Beethoven, and his corpse's aura remained for those who admired and loved him. The composer Franz von Hartmann later stated that there "was a celestial dignity about him, despite the disfiguration he was said to have suffered . . . that I could not look at him long enough." Hartmann could not help but notice that there was "already a strong cadaverous smell," but he was deeply moved nonetheless. So deeply, in fact, that he left Beethoven's rooms and was nearly to the street before he remembered his main purpose for coming: He wanted a souvenir of the maestro, specifically a lock of hair.

Hartmann returned up the stairs for a second viewing, tipping the caretaker hired to watch the body and begging him "for a few of Beethoven's hairs." The caretaker motioned for Hartmann to wait while the other spectators—three "fops" who stood there "tapping their swagger-sticks on their pantaloons while looking at the dead man"—to leave. He then silently cut a lock of hair and handed it to Hartmann, who left, he later wrote, with a feeling of "mournful joy."[86]

Hartmann was not alone. Mourners who came continually begged to take away bits of Beethoven's hair as a memento. Hüttenbrenner had been given a lock of the composer's hair by Beethoven's sister-in-law just after the maestro died, and numerous others bribed or cajoled his caretakers into handing over souvenirs. Among them was the composer Ferdinand Hiller, whose treasure would wend the strange 170-year journey described by Russell Martin.

Gerhard von Breuning, too, had hoped to take a lock of hair as a souvenir, but his father—now ill himself and still deeply distraught over the loss of his friend—forbade it. Gerhard later remembered, "Father had not allowed me to do this before the lying-in-state ended, in order not to spoil his appearance; but now we found that strangers had already cut off all his hair."[87] Gerhard found this truly galling. Who were these other men—Hiller and Hartmann and Hüttenbrenner and countless others? Only casual acquaintances, factotums, and treasure-

---

[86] Quoted in Meredith, "The History of Beethoven's Skull Fragments," pp. 2-3.
[87] Breuning, *From the House of the Black-Robed Spaniards*, pp. 107-108.

hunting strangers. Yet they all now had precious relics of the great Beethoven, while he, son of the maestro's closest friend, had nothing.

HAIR WAS ONE thing, but Stephan von Breuning soon began to hear much more disturbing rumors. Beethoven's funeral took place on March 29, with a swelling crowd of over twenty thousand mourners accompanying the cortege, but there were some in the crowd who wanted more than simply to pay their respects. Four days after the funeral Anton Schindler told Stephan that the grave digger had "visited us yesterday and told us that someone, in a note that he showed us, had offered him 1,000 guldens C. M. if he would deposit the head of Beethoven at a specified location."[88]

It was never made clear who this someone was. Joseph Carl Rosenbaum, now fifty-seven, still had Haydn's head, but his days of skull-stealing were over (he would be dead in less than two years). By this point there were certainly any number of relic-seekers who would have followed in Rosenbaum's footsteps if given the chance.

Schindler noted that the police were investigating, but Breuning knew he could not rely on them. It was in fact not the first he had heard of such a plot—the rumor that someone wanted to steal the skull of Beethoven had been circulating for days. So per-

[88] Quoted in Meredith, "The History of Beethoven's Skull Fragments," p. 3.

sistently, in fact, that Breuning had hired watchmen to guard the grave and had even considered burying the body in a reversed position so that the feet, not the head, would be closest to the cemetery's outer wall. As Gerhard later explained, "The idea was that, although the watchmen had been engaged for the first few nights, there was a good chance they might doze off and it would be possible to tunnel under the wall and reach the head."[89]

The fear of some desecration of the composer's corpse continued to prey on Stephan. He had already seen the terrible disfigurement of the body from the autopsy he had authorized, and the fact that relic-hunters had cut off all of the composer's hair while he lay in state only added insult to injury. While the plan to reverse the body was ultimately abandoned, Stephan had a massive layer of bricks laid over the coffin so as to deter any would-be cranioklepts.

Still, when Schindler told him that unknown persons were out for the skull, Stephan was not about to count on his brick wall to keep the body safe. His chief worry was the sexton, who would certainly have the time in the dead of night to break through any defense. Even though it was the sexton who had come forward to Schindler and Breuning with the anonymous note, Stephan was convinced it was a shakedown and that the sexton had had a hand in creating the ominous letter. Exhausted, Stephan gave in: He plaintively offered the grave digger a substantial sum of money and begged him to leave the body alone.

[89] Breuning, *From the House of the Black-Robed Spaniards,* p. 109.

But the grave digger of Währing turned out to be surprisingly ethical. Twenty years earlier Joseph Carl Rosenbaum had profited from a down-on-his-luck grave digger who'd lost everything in a tumultuous time, but Beethoven's remains benefited from far more stable circumstances. The sexton refused Stephan's money, assuring the gentleman that he had no intention of violating the body. He only wanted to do what was right, he said, and wanted Stephan to know that there might be forces out there stronger than either of them with designs on Beethoven's head. Stephan rehired the guards to stand watch and hoped for the best.

Meanwhile, he did his best to get his friend's estate in order. He organized an auction of Beethoven's furniture and effects, and though he himself was seriously ill and exhausted, he forced himself to oversee the auction to prevent any theft or dubious transactions. The sight of his friend's life broken into lots and manhandled by the auctioneers was too much for Stephan: "As a result of these distressing scenes at the auction in the room where Beethoven had died," Gerhard later recorded, "my father suffered a relapse, with an inflamed liver that soon confined him to his bed, and on June 4 of the same year . . . he followed his exalted friend into the beyond."[90]

Writing of this later in life, Gerhard did not dwell on the fact that he had been orphaned at fourteen. In his memoir, immediately after relating his father's passing, Gerhard wrote, "I was only fourteen and learned of the second auction, in November

[90] Ibid.

1827, of the intellectual effects of Beethoven only after it was over. And so I have none of all the valuable manuscripts and autographs that got into other hands, always at low prices, sometimes ridiculously cheap; and all the more so because my father had strictly forbidden me to take even the smallest scrap of what Beethoven, when alive, would have given me by the armful if it had entered my mind to ask him for it."[91]

"*PLAUDITE AMICA, FINITE est comedia*"—so Beethoven is supposed to have said after receiving the last rites—"Applaud, friends, the comedy is over." In his memoirs, Breuning ended his lengthy description of Beethoven's final days with a slightly altered version: "*Tragoedia finite erat*"—"The tragedy was finished." But there was still more of the story to be told, so he added, "Everything we now have to say no longer relates to the living Beethoven among us, but only to the heritage of his genius, his immortal creations."[92] To this musical heritage add the fate of his unfortunate remains, battered and picked apart by doctors, well-wishers, and phrenologists.

[91] Ibid.
[92] Ibid.

CHAPTER SEVEN

THE NEW
SCIENCE

By this time phrenology had gone from a dubious scientific theory to a worldwide cultural phenomenon. Unlike Gall's organology, the brand of phrenology advocated by his star pupil, Johann Spurzheim, focused not just on identifying the various mental functions of the brain but on the possibility of actual self-improvement through phrenology. Though the two doctors had been inseparable through the early nineteenth century, in 1814 this philosophical difference erupted: Gall accused Spurzheim of distorting the project of organology, of turning his science into pop philosophy, and denounced his former pupil, calling him a fraud and a plagiarist.

Unbowed, Spurzheim taught himself English in six months and moved to London in 1814 to lecture on "practical phrenology." Spurzheim's phrenology may indeed have been a perversion of Gall's ideas, but it was a necessary perversion. The body of scientific evidence was now fairly strong against organology, and certainly against the bump-reading aspects of cranioscopy. In order for phrenology to survive at all, it had to move beyond science and into popular culture. This was what Spurzheim set out to do, to bring it into the public sphere as something other than pure science. "Phrenology is one of a group of sciences, different from anatomy, and its truths are of a larger stature," one phrenologist later put it. "It belongs to the doctrine not of the human body, but of man."[93]

In England Spurzheim quickly befriended a number of prominent phrenologists, including the Swede Johan Didrik Holm. Holm had been a captain in the Royal Swedish Navy before embarking on a lucrative career in private shipping and settling in London in 1805. He had met Gall at Napoleon's coronation in 1804 and had subsequently developed a large phrenological library and a skull collection that included the head of Alexander Pope and other notables. His zeal for the New Science was such that he had reportedly tried to plunder his own father's grave for his collection. One visitor to his home described it as "a museum, filled with natural history specimens, works of art and curiosities. Books and pictures cover the walls together with a large number of heads, such as marble busts, plaster casts, and real skulls of deceased persons."[94] His prominence was such that when Spurzheim died, it was to Holm that he left his own collection.

Spurzheim traveled widely through the United Kingdom,

---

[93] Quoted in Goyder, *My Battle for Life*, p. 183.
[94] Quoted in Folke Henschen, *Emanuel Swedenborg's Cranium: A Critical Analysis* (Uppsala: Nova Acta Regiae Societatis Scientiarum Upsaliensis, Ser. IV, Vol. 17, No. 9. 1960), p. 14.

where his lectures and demonstrations were met with fascination and derision. He turned both to his advantage. After a scathing attack against him was published in June 1815 in the *Edinburgh Review*, Spurzheim began performing dissections with the article placed alongside the brain, inviting spectators to compare what they had read in the *Review* to what they saw with their own eyes.

Among those deeply impressed by such showmanship was a young Scottish lawyer named George Combe. Combe had come from miserable poverty and carried with him a deep loathing of the backward religious and educational institutions that had oppressed him as a child. As an adult he had dedicated himself to liberal reform. He had immersed himself in the philosophy of Locke, Hume, and Adam Smith, but after watching one of Spurzheim's dissections he had an epiphany. "I attained the conviction," he wrote in his memoirs, "that the faculties of the mind he had expounded bare [sic] a much greater resemblance to those which I had seen operating in active life, than did those which I had read about in the works of metaphysicians."[95]

Spurzheim spent another seven months in Edinburgh and stayed in constant contact with his new disciple, carefully cultivating Combe to continue his work after he had left England. With the publication of *Essays on Phrenology* in 1819, Combe had established himself as one of the foremost writers and thinkers of

---

[95] Quoted in Stephen Tomlinson, *Head Masters: Phrenology, Secular Education, and Nineteenth-Century Thought* (Tuscaloosa: University of Alabama Press, 2005) p. 106.

Johann Spurzheim.

the phrenological movement in the country. Combe saw phrenology as the key to humankind's inner consciousness and the means
to diagnosing and curing society's ills. "I plead guilty of being
known to the world only as a Phrenologist," he wrote in 1834.
"Believing, as I do, that the same Divine Wisdom which ordained
the universe, presided also at the endowment of the brain with its
functions; that the brain is the organ of the mind, and that mind is
the noblest work of GOD; convinced, also, that this discovery car-
ries in its train the most valuable improvements in education,

morals, and in civil and religious institutions."[96] In other words, for Combe the brain occupied the midpoint between God and progressive reform; the key to bringing about God's plan for social justice lay in phrenological understanding.

With such a cosmic mandate, the possibilities were limitless, and phrenologists like Spurzheim and Combe took Gall's original idea much further than the doctor had ever intended. Seeing himself as a serious scientist, Gall had been deliberately modest about the possibilities of phrenology. When he was accused by the Viennese authorities in 1802 of attempting to distinguish "the worthless and the useless from the virtuous" by the shape of their skulls, Gall replied that such a thing was impossible "because moral, social, civil, and religious conduct, is the result of many and different concomitant causes, and especially of many powerful external influences; for instance, education, example, habits, laws, religion, age, society, climate, food, health, and so forth." In his English translation of this document thirty years later, Combe added this footnote: "This was written in 1802. I consider it quite possible, in the present state of Phrenology, to distinguish the naturally worthless and useless from the virtuous by the shape of their skulls. See Combe's System, vol. ii. p. 695. 4th edition."[97]

By the 1830s phrenology had come a long way indeed.

[96] George Combe, *A System of Phrenology* (Boston: Marsh, Capen and Lyon, 1838), p. viii.
[97] Gall, *On the Functions of the Cerebellum*, p. 328.

PHRENOLOGY WAS EXTREMELY attractive to reformers because it suggested that one's innate mental powers—not birthright or class or the blessing of a religious institution—determined one's worth. As such, Combe drew all manner of British liberals and socialist reformers, including the young Marian Evans, who had been introduced to phrenology by the philanthropist Charles Bray. Evans took to the New Science immediately and had a phrenological bust of her head made in 1844 in tribute to Bray. When Combe later saw it, he mistook it for the head of a man, and when he finally met Evans and read her scalp, he pronounced her the "ablest woman I have seen" with a "very large brain." She would later confide to her friend Maria Lewis that "having had my propensities sentiments and intellect gauged a second time, I am pronounced to possess a large organ of 'adhesiveness,' a still larger one of 'firmness,' and as large of conscientiousness."[98] Whatever sexual ambiguity Combe had found in her head was something Evans would exploit when she adopted the nom de plume George Eliot and began to revolutionize the Victorian novel. In works such as *Adam Bede* and *Middlemarch* Eliot created a new mode of depicting the inner consciousness of everyday

[98] George Eliot, *The George Eliot Letters, Volume I,* edited by Gordon Sherman Haight (New Haven: Yale University Press, 1954), p. 126. For more information on George Eliot and phrenology see Hugh Witemeyer, *George Eliot and the Visual Arts* (New Haven: Yale University Press, 1979), pp. 44-71.

people. And, particularly in her earlier fiction, phrenology was an important tool for accessing that inner consciousness. In 1851 she would affirm to Bray, "I never believed more profoundly than I do now that character is based on organization. I never had a higher appreciation than I have now of the services which phrenology has rendered towards the science of man."[99] Those services included her own fiction, which is infused with phrenological descriptions. In the early *Scenes of Clerical Life*, we are introduced to Lawyer Dempster, who is "weighed down" by "a preponderant occiput and a bulging forehead, between which his closely clipped coronal surface lay like a flat and newly-mown table-lawn."[100] Astute phrenologists would have immediately recognized the selfishness of such a character, a "preponderant occiput" indicating an overdevelopment of the faculties of approbation and self-esteem. Likewise, his flat "coronal surface" would indicate a developed intellect but a lack of veneration, conscientiousness, and benevolence. By contrast, in Eliot's first major novel, *Adam Bede*, Seth Bede is described as having thin hair that allows one "to discern the exact contour of a coronal arch that predominates very decidedly over the brow." Unlike Dempster, Seth's moral faculties are extremely well developed at the cost of his intelligence, resulting in an "arch" rather than a more "well-rounded" blend of moral and intellectual.[101]

[99] George Eliot, *The George Eliot Letters, Volume II*, edited by Gordon Sherman Haight (New Haven: Yale University Press, 1954), p. 210.
[100] George Eliot, *Scenes from Clerical Life* (London: Penguin, 1998), p. 197.
[101] George Eliot, *Adam Bede* (London: Penguin, 2008), p. 10.

Phrenology also appeared in the works of Dickens, the Brontë sisters, and dozens of lesser novelists. French writers such as Balzac had relied heavily on physiognomy, the correlation between facial features and personality, as developed by the Swiss Johann Kaspar Lavater. But English and American writers found the key to their characters' personalities not in the face but in the skull.

IN 1832 SPURZHEIM went to the United States to spread the phrenological gospel further in the English-speaking world. He had planned a two-year tour and was especially interested in the heads of Native Americans and of slaves. At Yale he dazzled the audience with the dissection of the brain of a child who had died recently from hydrocephalus and continued to impress wherever he went with his seemingly impeccable phrenological readings.

But only seventy-one days into his journey he succumbed to a fever while lecturing at Harvard and died on October 30, 1832. And so the task of proselytizing for the New Science fell to Orson Fowler, who began lecturing on phrenology while still an undergraduate at Amherst, and his younger brother Lorenzo. Together the Fowler brothers would build a phrenological empire, and with their ubiquitous ceramic phrenology bust, their name would gradually become synonymous with the most dubious elements of Gall's science.

Like Combe, the Fowlers saw in phrenology not simply

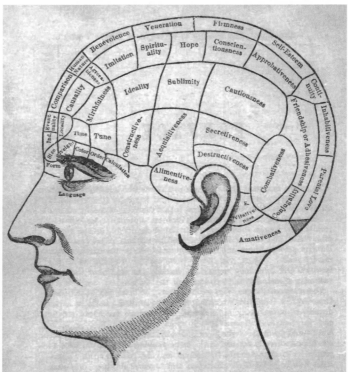

NUMBERING AND DEFINITION OF THE ORGANS.

1. AMATIVENESS, Love between the sexes.
A. CONJUGALITY, Matrimony—love of one. [etc.
2. PARENTAL LOVE, Regard for offspring, pets,
3. FRIENDSHIP, Adhesiveness—sociability.
4. INHABITIVENESS, Love of home.
5. CONTINUITY, One thing at a time.
E. VITATIVENESS, Love of life.
6. COMBATIVENESS, Resistance—defense.
7. DESTRUCTIVENESS, Executiveness—force.
8. ALIMENTIVENESS, Appetite—hunger.
9. ACQUISITIVENESS, Accumulation.
10. SECRETIVENESS, Policy—management.
11. CAUTIOUSNESS, Prudence—provision.
12. APPROBATIVENESS, Ambition—display.
13. SELF-ESTEEM, Self-respect—dignity.
14. FIRMNESS, Decision—perseverance.
15. CONSCIENTIOUSNESS, Justice. equity.
16. HOPE, Expectation—enterprise.
17. SPIRITUALITY, Intuition—faith—credulity.
18. VENERATION, Devotion—respect.
19. BENEVOLENCE, Kindness—goodness.

20. CONSTRUCTIVENESS, Mechanical ingenuity
21. IDEALITY, Refinement—taste—purity.
B. SUBLIMITY, Love of grandeur—infinitude.
22. IMITATION, Copying—patterning.
23. MIRTHFULNESS, Jocoseness—wit—fun.
24. INDIVIDUALITY, Observation.
25. FORM, Recollection of shape.
26. SIZE, Measuring by the eye.
27. WEIGHT, Balancing—climbing.
28. COLOR, Judgment of colors.
29. ORDER, Method—system—arrangement.
30. CALCULATION, Mental arithmetic.
31. LOCALITY, Recollection of places.
32. EVENTUALITY, Memory of facts.
33. TIME, Cognizance of duration.
34. TUNE, Sense of harmony and melody.
35. LANGUAGE, Expression of ideas.
36. CAUSALITY, Applying causes to effect. [tion.
37. COMPARISON, Inductive reasoning—illustra-
C. HUMAN NATURE, Perception of motives.
D. AGREEABLENESS, Pleasantness—suavity.

Phrenology Chart, by L. N. Fowler

the study of the mind but the key to the betterment of humanity. As it had in the British Isles, phrenology flourished by attaching itself to reform movements. The United States was being torn apart at the seams, the rift between North and South growing wider by the day. The division had become intractable, war was nearly a foregone conclusion, and everyone was looking for some kind of panacea to solve the nation's woes. Transcendentalists, abolitionists, hydrotherapy advocates, antilacing societies (against corsets: "Natural waists, or no wives!"), teetotalers, and vegetarians—all lined up to promote their causes; phrenology took them all in and made them part of its grand scheme. The Fowlers published tracts from all manner of reformers and idealists in their *Phrenological Journal*, aggregating every movement under the banner of bump reading. In the journal's tautological simplicity, all society's ills could be explained through the skull.

By the time the Fowler brothers opened their Phrenological Cabinet on Broadway in Manhattan, phrenology was a nationwide phenomenon, and people came from everywhere for readings with the famous Fowlers. Among those who came to the New York Golgotha to have their heads read was a young printer's devil named Walt Whitman. Whitman had already established himself as a phrenology convert. Three years before, in November 1846, as an editor of the *Brooklyn Eagle*, Whitman had written of phrenology, "Breasting the waves of detraction, as a ship dashes sea-waves, Phrenology, it must now be confessed by all men who have open eyes, has at last gained a position, and a firm one, among the sciences."[102]

And now he waited patiently in the lobby, paid the fee not just for the chart but for the full reading, and was examined by Lorenzo Fowler himself. Like most people who came to see the Fowlers, Whitman was told that on most counts, his skull was quite exceptional. He scored high in Amativeness, Philoprogenitiveness, Adhesiveness, Inhabitiveness, Alimentiveness, Self-Esteem, Firmness, Benevolence, and Sublimity, with lower readings in Concentrativeness, Acquisitiveness, Secretiveness, Approbativeness, and Marvelousness.[103]

Most of the chart, as can be expected, was composed of the sort of bland platitudes that were meant on the one hand to be reassuring, and on the other to be unverifiable: "You were blessed by nature with a good constitution and power to live to a good old age. You were undoubtedly descended from a long-lived family. . . . You are very firm in general and not easily driven from your position. Your sense of justice, of right and wrong is strong and you can see much that is unjust and inhuman in the present condition of society."

Some of it, in retrospect, seems fairly accurate with regard to the figure that Walt Whitman would become: "You choose to fight with tongue and pen rather than with your fist. . . . You are

[102] Quoted in Nathaniel Mackey, *Paracritical Hinge* (Madison: University of Wisconsin, 2005), p. 22.
[103] Whitman's chart can be found in Madeleine B. Stern, *Heads & Headlines: The Phrenological Fowlers* (Norman: University of Oklahoma Press, 1971), pp. 102–105.

no hypocrite but are plain spoken and are what you *appear* to be at all times. You are in fact most *too* open at times and have not always enough restraint in speech."

Some of it, on the other hand, was completely off the mark, given what we now know of the poet: "Your love and regard for woman as such are strong and you are for elevating and ameliorating the female character. You were inclined to marry at an early age. You could not well bear to be deprived of you[r] domestic privileges and enjoyments. . . . By practice you might make a good accountant."

In sum, the chart that Lorenzo Fowler produced for Whitman had the same measure of accuracy that any successful huckster could provide: a good snap judgment of character filled out by vague compliments and tautological nonsense.

Whitman ate it up.

The chart Lorenzo produced for him would go on to develop a life of its own—Whitman would publish it as a testament to his genius in the first three editions of *Leaves of Grass* and would keep it close throughout his life. When asked about his visit to Lorenzo in 1888, Whitman replied, "I guess most of my friends distrust it—but then you see I am very old fashioned—I probably have not got by the phrenology stage yet."[104]

The Fowlers, who were looking for a poetic genius with whom they could associate phrenology and further its cultural influences, saw in Whitman an opportunity. They carried his self-

[104] Ibid. p. 107.

published book of poetry in their storefront and advertised it in the *Phrenological Journal*. This was in many ways their most prescient act, the closest they came to anything like actual prophecy. Considering the dismal failure that *Leaves of Grass* was in its first edition (before Ralph Waldo Emerson's endorsement), the Fowlers' decision to back the young Whitman indicates a fair amount of poetic judgment.

It helped, of course, that Whitman had apotheosized phrenology in his work, going so far as to make it a central lynchpin in his poetry. In what would become a literary landmark, the voice that defined American poetry had constant recourse to phrenology; the New Science insinuated itself throughout. "The sailor and traveler," he wrote in the book's preface, "the anatomist chemist astronomer geologist phrenologist spiritualist mathematician historian and lexicographer are not poets, but they are the lawgivers of poets and their construction underlies the structure of every perfect poem." Whitman, a transcendentalist in the mode of Emerson, saw the world in terms of invisible connections and mystical threads that bound all things together; like the mathematician or the lexicographer, the phrenologist understood the secret laws of these invisible networks and offered the maps to traverse them. No skull-stealer himself, Whitman nonetheless shared with men like Rosenbaum a conviction that in phrenology creative genius could be understood, as it was one of the "lawgivers of poets."

As *Leaves of Grass* grew both in stature and in size, so did the bumps on Whitman's head. His phrenological chart was reprinted in subsequent editions, but Whitman felt free to edit it, and he increased the size of several of the bumps from the original measurements given by Lorenzo. By this point, of course, Whitman had become *the* American poet, and he saw himself as one of the few capable of speaking on the country's behalf. And the America that he spoke for was a phrenological one, as he wrote in "By Blue Ontario's Shore":

> *Who are you indeed who would talk or sing to America? Have you studied out the land, its idioms and men? Have you learn'd the physiology, phrenology, politics, geography, pride, freedom, friendship of the land? its substratums and objects?*

THIS WASN'T TO say, of course, that phrenology was without its detractors. Oliver Wendell Holmes lampooned the Fowlers in his newspaper column "The Autocrat at the Breakfast Table," where he described a trip to the offices of "Professors Bumpus and Crane," pillorying in particular phrenology's reputation for neologisms with his own string of nonsense words. "Feels of thorax and arm, and nuzzles round among muscles. . . . Mild champooing of head now commences. Extraordinary revelations! Cupidiphilous, 6! Hymeniphilous, 6+!, Paedipilous, 5! Deipniphilous, 6! Gelasmiphilous, 6! Musikiphilous, 5! Uraniphilous, 5! Glossiphilous, 8!! and so on. Meant for a linguist.—Invaluable information. Will invest in grammars and dictionaries immediately.—I have nothing against the grand total of my phrenological endowments."[105]

Perhaps most famously, Mark Twain conducted his own phrenological experiment, paying for a reading first as an ordinary, unpresuming citizen. "Fowler received me with indifference," Twain later recalled, "fingered my head in an uninterested way, and named and estimated my qualities in a bored and monotonous voice. He said I possessed amazing courage, and abnormal spirit of daring, a pluck, a stern will, a fearlessness that were without limit." The inordinate courage that Fowler found in Twain was negated, though, by a bump on the other side of his head, which Fowler identified as "caution": "This hump was so tall, so mountainous, that it reduced my courage-bump to a mere hillock by comparison, although the courage bump had been so prominent up to that time—according to his description of it— that it ought to have been a capable thing to hang my hat on; but it amounted to nothing, now in the presence of that Matterhorn which he called my Caution." This caution bump, Fowler explained to Twain, was why he hadn't been able to amount to much in life. Some time later the author returned, this time introducing himself as Mark Twain and wearing his now trademark white suit. The difference, as could be expected, was quite startling: "Once more he made a striking discovery—the cavity was gone, and in its place was a Mount Everest—figuratively speaking—

---

[105] Ibid., p. 132.

31,000 feet high, the loftiest bump of humor he had ever encountered in his life-long experience!"[106]

But it was Ambrose Bierce who perhaps put it most eloquently and succinctly in his *The Devil's Dictionary*: "Phrenology: n. The science of picking the pocket through the scalp. It consists of locating and exploiting the organ that one is a dupe with."[107]

The Fowlers took it all in stride. Phrenologists had always viewed this resistance to their creed as a badge of pride, proof that bump reading was so revolutionary that the institutions of science were unready for it. One was either predisposed to find truth in it or not. "Self-made or never made" was the Fowlers' favorite motto, and it could apply not just to their brand of reform and self-betterment but also to one's own view of phrenology—either you believed in it or you didn't. But in that dark decade leading up to the American Civil War, and in the bleak years that followed it, there were a lot of anxious souls looking for comfort, and for twenty-five cents one could be reassured not only of one's innate goodness and intelligence but also of one's capacity to better the world. It seemed a small price to pay.

PHRENOLOGY WAS A science for an uncertain time, and perhaps no one exemplified this better than the phrenologist and

---

[106] Mark Twain, *The Autobiography of Mark Twain*, edited by Charles Neider (New York: Harper Collins, 1959), pp. 85-87.

[107] Ambrose Bierce, *The Unabridged Devil's Dictionary*, edited David E. Schultz and S. T. Joshi (Athens: University of Georgia Press, 2000), p. 181.

revolutionary Gustav von Struve. The young Struve had come to Mannheim in Baden, Germany, to practice law, but his ambitions quickly grew. He began actively to promote both phrenology and radical reform, which he saw as inextricably linked.

Ever since Gall's expulsion from Vienna, German-speaking countries had lagged behind the rest of Europe when it came to phrenology. For Struve, this rejection accounted for Germany's lack of progress and why it still lay captive to oppressive religious and aristocratic regimes. He set out to remedy the problem, co-founding the German-language *Phrenological Journal* and advocating tirelessly for the New Science. Combe recognized the value of his contributions in his own *A System of Phrenology*, and the Fowlers regularly translated excerpts of his work in their own journal. His colleague Alexander Herzen claimed that Struve was so devoted to phrenology that he deliberately chose a wife who lacked a "passion" bump.[108]

Struve's own passion was for political and social reform. He argued for vegetarianism and temperance, against capital punishment. He set aside a portion of every day to meditate on the great secular heroes of revolution, from Washington and Lafayette to Rousseau and Robespierre. Contemporaries described Struve as having a face that "showed the moral rigidity of the fanatic . . . with uncombed beard and untroubled eyes," but he was sincere

---

[108] Information on Gustav Struve can be found in Priscilla Smith Robertson, *Revolutions of 1848: A Social History* (Princeton: Princeton University Press, 1968) pp. 145–149.

Gustav Struve.

in his desire for reform, and in 1847 he dropped the aristocratic "von" from his name in solidarity with the common man.

Mario Vargas Llosa, in his 1984 novel *The War at the End of the World*, would reincarnate this archetype of the revolutionary phrenologist and put him in South America. An amalgamation of Struve and Combe, Llosa's character, a Scotsman who takes the name Galileo Gall, comes to Brazil to foment revolution: "As other children grew up listening to fairy stories, he had grown up hearing that property is the origin of all social evils and that the poor will succeed in shattering the chains of exploitation and obscurantism only through the use of violence." Inextricable from this revolutionary fervor is a fervor for phrenology:

> Whereas for other followers of Gall's, this science was scarcely more than the belief that intellect, instinct, and feelings are organs located in the cerebral cortex and can be palpated and measured, for Galileo's father this discipline meant the death of religion, the empirical foundation of materialism, the proof that the mind was not what philosophical mumbo jumbo made it out to be, something imponderable and impalpable, but on the contrary a dimension of the body, like the senses, and hence equally capable of being studied and treated clinically.[109]

Galileo Gall thus operates from a simple precept: "Revolution will free society of its afflictions, while science will free the individual of his."

Something very similar was at work in the mind of Struve: a desire for a violent overthrow of oppressive regimes, which could in turn allow the democratic and progressive principles of phrenology to flourish. He was not alone in his democratic zeal: In 1848 democratic revolutions broke out all over Europe, starting in France and quickly engulfing the entire continent. The year Marx and Engels published *The Communist Manifesto*, all of Eu-

---

[109] Mario Vargas Llosa, *The War of the End of the World,* Translated by Helen R. Lane (New York: Farrar Straus Giroux, 1984), p. 14.

rope was ready for change, and men like Struve saw their chance. On March 31 of that year, German reformers gathered in a "Pre-Parliament" to discuss the establishment of a free, united German republic. During the discussion Struve read his fifteen-point plan to end the "subjugation, stultification, and bleeding dry of the people," which included the abolition of the standing army, all aristocratic privileges, and any connection between church and state and their replacement with laws that were based on "the spirit of our age," including phrenology.

The Pre-Parliament rejected Struve and his radical coalition in favor of a more moderate approach, and so the radicals decided to bring about emancipation by force. They raised a small army to march on the capital of Baden, but when they met the government's forces in the Black Forest they were severely routed, and Struve and the others were imprisoned. Freed the following year, the undaunted phrenologist once again joined another failed uprising against the government—one in which, it should be noted, his "passionless" wife fought with unmatched tenacity.

In Baden and elsewhere, these popular uprisings were brutally suppressed. In Vienna, for example, when dissidents took control of the center of the city, the royal response was swift and bloody, and the army savagely bombed the entire city. Among the casualties was the imperial zoological collection, which was hit by an errant cannonball, caught fire, and burned to the ground. Lost in the fire was the stuffed body of Angelo Soliman, who finally found his rest in the tumult of such an extraordinary time.

CHAPTER EIGHT

SKULDUGGERY

In such a climate, rare or significant skulls continued to be quite valuable. The "New York Golgotha" that was the Fowlers' storefront was filled with a wide variety of skulls, representing "saint . . . savage, and . . . sage," and (the *Phrenological Journal* reported) all "are represented in the mute eloquence of a thousand crania arranged and labeled among the walls of the building." The Fowlers were always looking to increase their collection: Any time a hanging was announced, they dispatched an agent to "attend the execution and take a cast of his head." They took anything, including alligator and deer skulls. But despite this plethora of crania, the skulls of the famous and the highly intelligent continued to elude the Fowlers. In 1854 the *Phrenological Journal* complained, "We have a very large collection of the skulls of murderers, who have been executed, and of soldiers killed on battle-fields, also of Indians, Africans, Egyptians, Chinese, and Cannibals, but we have only a few from the higher class of minds, such as Reformers, Statesmen,

Scholars, & c. Of these we have hundreds of casts, and busts from living heads, but not their skulls." In an era of hands-on, empirical science, busts and casts were simply not enough. "What a treasure it would be," the editorial concluded, "if some plan could be devised, by which these leading 'types' could be preserved as specimens, for scientific purposes."[110]

The phrenologists were not alone in this desire. As anatomical study came to be recognized as increasingly important in the preservation of life, an active campaign was mounted by burial reformers to change people's attitudes about what should be done with their bodies after death and to destigmatize dissection. If anyone, it was the scientists and burial reformers who would have to lead by example. A nameless French scholar in 1829 had delivered a lecture to the British Forum on the virtues of dissection, which concluded with a reading of his will, wherein he stipulated that his body should first be dissected, and then his skin tanned and made into a leather chair. In addition, his bones should be cleaned so that the head could go to the London Phrenological Society and the smaller bones could be made into "knife-handles, pin-cases, small boxes, buttons, etc."[111]

More famously, the Utilitarian philosopher Jeremy Bentham left his body to science, stuffed and arranged in what he called his "Auto-icon," the description of which he detailed in his will: a wooden box with a glass front in which his body could be seated

[110] Quoted in Stern, *Heads and Headlines*, pp. 127–128.
[111] Quoted in Richardson, *Death, Dissection and the Destitute*, pp. 168–169.

in a chair "usually occupied by me when living in the attitude in which I am sitting when engaged in thought." Bentham went so far as to stipulate that he be dressed "in one of the suits of black occasionally worn by me" and that he be made to hold his beloved walking stick, nicknamed "Dapple." His head was replaced with a wax replica (the original having been badly treated during the autopsy), and the "Auto-icon" was acquired in 1850 by University College London, which put it on display. For the 100th and 150th anniversaries of the college, the Auto-icon was wheeled into the meeting of the College Council, and when the roll was called, Bentham was listed as "present, but not voting" (though the college maintains that it is a myth the stuffed corpse has ever cast the deciding vote in the event of a tie).

Jeremy Bentham in his "Auto-Icon."

PHOTOGRAPH BY MICHAEL REEVE.

In 1875 the Anthropological Society of Paris founded a Society of Mutual Autopsy, not only to further the destigmatization of dissection but to recast autopsy as a form of immortality: Upon death a member would be immortalized in a detailed description of his body, particularly his brain—which would be added to the society's collection for all time.

But most people were not about to let their mortal remains be used as scientific toys or gothic mementoes. The fear of grave robbing was still strong through much of the nineteenth century, and new technologies arose to foil the resurrectionists. There was, for example, the "mortsafe," an iron grid that encased the coffin to prevent any molestation of one's remains, and in 1818 an Englishman named Edward Bridgman introduced the first device invented specifically to combat grave robbing: the "patent coffin," a cast- or wrought-iron coffin with spring catches hidden on the inside of the lid, configured in such a way that it was impossible to pry off the lid with a crowbar. The patent coffin was such a sensation that a man named Charles Dibden composed an ode to this "prince of coffin makers" and sold it as a broadsheet, an upbeat ditty that included the following choice verses:

> Each age has boasted curious selves,
> By patent notoriety,
> Whose inventions have enriched themselves,
> For advantage of society.
> I, an immortal artisan,
> Pray, gents, favour your scoffing,

Produce tonight, muse, sing the man
That made the patent coffin.

CHORUS:
Then toll the knell, each passing bell
Shall of the mighty name of this wondrous man be talking,
While foremost in the ranks of fame
His coffin shall be walking.

Resurrection men, your fate deplore,
Retire with sore vexation,
Your mystery's gone, your art's no more,
No more your occupation;
Surgeons, no more shall ye ransack
The grave, with feelings callous,
Tho' on the Old Bailey turn'd your back,
Your only hopes the gallows.[112]

That the inventor of a resurrection-proof coffin would be hailed as a national hero reveals the extent to which the general public still feared such a postmortem fate. Certainly the average citizen did not see the prospect of putting his or her skull on display as anything like a worthy tribute to a famous mind—after all, it was still primarily the case that if a skull was on display or under the eye of science, it had probably come from the gallows

[112] Ibid., p. 82.

or the insane asylum, and few wanted any such institutions associated with their own heads.

AND SO, AS expressed by that most basic tenet of capitalism,
the dearth of famous skulls coupled with increasing demand made
them that much more valuable, and their theft that much more
lucrative. In 1809 Joseph Carl Rosenbaum had to pay only 25
gulden to secure a grave digger's help; in 1827 those interested in
Beethoven's head were willing to go as high as 1,000 gulden.

A few rare skulls could be had through legal channels. When
the German poet and philosopher Friedrich Schiller's body was
exhumed in 1826, twenty-one years after his death, the Duke Carl
August had the skull mounted on a velvet cushion in a glass case
and displayed in his library. In order to keep the duke from being
confused with the religiously superstitious or macabre treasure
hunters, much was made of the fact that the skull was to be kept
in the library—the proper place for a skull of genius, which could
be read phrenologically, almost as if it were another book on the
shelf. As a private, special book, it was not for everyone. As the
director of the duke's library put it, the skull was to be made
available only to those "of whom one can be certain that their
steps are not governed by curiosity but by a feeling, a knowledge
of what that great man achieved for Germany, for Europe, and
for the whole civilized world."[113]

---

[113] Quoted in Hagner, "Skulls, Brains, and Memorial Culture," p. 205.

If anyone had that feeling, it was this librarian, no less than Johann Wolfgang von Goethe, who would become the bedrock on which much of Germanic literature was based. Either way, after a year the Duke got nervous about the skull and ordered it reinterred with the body. Respectable sources simply could not be relied on; if you wanted a skull, you had to steal it yourself.

SUCH WAS THE case with the head of the Swedish mystic Emanuel Swedenborg, which showed up for sale in England in 1816 or '17 (the reports varied). A polymath who had excelled in physics, geometry, and chemistry, Swedenborg turned to spiritual questions in his middle age and in the last thirty years of his life published over thirty books of spiritual revelations. In the years following his death a small but fervently devoted branch of Christianity was born.

Swedenborg stressed that the Second Coming was already upon us—not as a literal reappearance of Jesus Christ but his return in spirit, which affected all the world, ushering in a new age—what Swedenborg called the New Church. His writings depicted a parallel spiritual world which can be fully realized only in death, once we have left our mortal remains and when each of us is revealed as who we truly are.

Swedenborg was traveling in London in 1772 when he suffered a stroke and shortly thereafter was liberated from his own mortal remains. He was buried in the Swedish Church, which had been founded by his father to serve the small Swedish community of London and Swedish naval personnel passing through the port. Swedenborg was buried in the vault below the church, which was kept sealed and opened only occasionally to accept new occupants.

Swedenborg's coffin was first disturbed in 1790, though not by grave robbers. Rather it was an American Rosicrucian, traveling in England, who flatly refused to believe that Swedenborg had died and contended instead that he had discovered the secret to immortality, drunk an elixir of eternal youth, and then had a fake funeral performed so as to avoid discovery. After a heated discussion over dinner with friends one night, the American and his party resolved to settle the matter. Bribing the sexton, the American descended into the crypt with a small entourage, which included Gustav Broling and Robert Hindmarsh, who both later recounted the story. The coffin, it turned out, was airtight and had to be opened with the aid of a solderer called in to break the seal. Because no air or moisture had been able to aid in decomposition, Swedenborg's body was almost perfectly preserved—and smelled. Broling recalled how, upon opening the coffin, "there issued forth effluvia in such abundance and of such a sort that the candles went out, and all the observers were obliged to rush head over heels out of the burial vault in order not to be smothered." This was, finally, enough to satisfy the doubting American.[114]

---

[114] Broling's and Hindmarsh's accounts are both reprinted in Johan Vilh. Hultkrantz, *The Mortal Remains of Emanuel Swedenborg* (Uppsala: Nova Acta Regiae Societatis Scientiarum Upsaliensis, Ser. IV, Vol. 2, No. 9. 1910), pp. 3-10.

Once the vault was cleared out, they returned to find Swedenborg's body unchanged after eighteen years. "We all stood for a few minutes in silent astonishment," Hindmarsh wrote, "to observe the physiognomy of that material frame now prostrate in the hands of death, which had once been the organ of so much intellect." In awe, Hindmarsh placed his hand on the philosopher's face, triggering the sudden decomposition that had been postponed for so long: "The whole frame was speedily reduced to ashes, leaving only the bones to testify to future inspectors of the coffin that a man had once lived and died."

The coffin was never resealed, so anyone who happened to be in the vault might easily have had access to Swedenborg's remains. With phrenology spreading like wildfire through Great Britain, it was only a matter of time before curiosity got the better of someone.

The skull was stolen in either 1816 or 1817—the circumstances surrounding the theft were never very clear—but not much was made of the theft until 1823, when the *Times* of London ran a short notice on the skull's reunion with the rest of the philosopher's bones. The ensuing confusion regarding the circumstances and motives of the theft speaks volumes of the changing attitudes toward the dead body during this time. The *Times* article, which appeared on March 31, 1823, offered a particularly colorful version of the events. The newspaper related how a Swedish disciple of Swedenborg, "whether prompted by supernatural inspiration or by his own blind superstition," had in fact

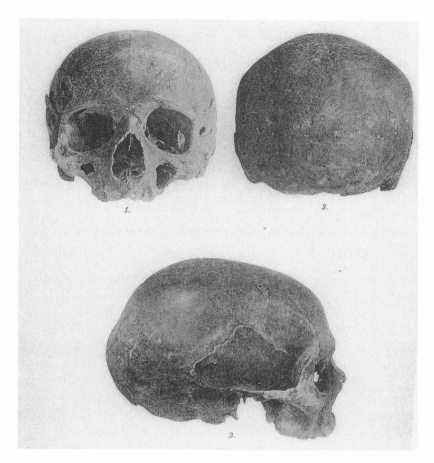

The skull of Emanuel Swedenborg.

contrived, by means of bribing the sexton or gravedigger, to gain admittance to the cemetery where his body was deposited. Here, in the silent hour of midnight (having previously supplied himself with the necessary implements) he broke open the coffin, and severed the head from the trunk of the departed saint, with the former of which he safely decamped to his own country. This *relic* he preserved with the greatest care and veneration till the day of his death, when it was discovered by his surviving relatives.

The writer went on to relate how the thief's friends, "alarmed at the consequences that might follow such an unhallowed violation of the tomb, and being desirous of atoning in some measure for the sins of him who had been guilty of so great a crime, caused the head to be forthwith transmitted" back to London so that it could be reunited with Swedenborg's body, "with due solemnity in the presence of the elders of the church."[115]

Alas, the story was almost entirely an invention of the *Times* writer. Oddly, it bore a striking similarity to the saga of Haydn and Rosenbaum: a devoted disciple motivated by a misguided passion and devotion, a midnight theft to retrieve a prized relic. Odd because at that time the story was not known at all beyond those few involved, many of whom (including Nicholas II) did not know the whole story. It was almost as if Rosenbaum's story had percolated into the collective unconscious of the age, as if from some common Romantic wellspring.

A series of letters quickly reached the *Times* to correct the erroneous account. The first of these, by one Reverend Samuel

---

[115] Quoted in Ibid., pp. 75-76.

Noble, was by far the most indignant. Noble was not only a minister in the New Church but was also the founder of the Society for Printing and Publishing the Writings of Swedenborg (now the Swedenborg Society) and editor of the leading Swedenborgian journal in Britain, the *Intellectual Repository*. To Noble, the *Times*'s account was "certainly sufficiently ridiculous, and calculated, with all who might believe it, to throw unmerited obloquy on the whole body of the admirers of [Swedenborg's] writings," and he had written to correct this miscarriage of justice. Yes, Noble confirmed, Swedenborg's head had been stolen, "but *it is not true* that the person who executed this singular robbery was *one of his disciples*." Rather than anyone connected with Swedenborgianism or the New Church, the thief was, Noble claimed, someone affiliated with phrenology, the New Science: "I understand that the motive which led him to obtain possession of this 'relic,' was the same as led Drs. Gall and Spurzheim to posses themselves of similar relics of other eminent men." The phrenologist, Noble explained, had been at the Swedish Church for the burial of Baroness von Nolcken, who had died in 1816, and after the funeral had been wandering in the tomb when he had noticed the opened coffin.

The reinterment, Noble went on, was carried out not by friends of this thief but by the Swedish Countess von Schwerin, who had heard of the situation and "requested an English gentleman of rank to wait upon the possessor, and request that he would allow the skull to be restored to its former situation." Most important for Noble were the motives for this reinterment: "*It is true*, then, that its re-interment took place; but *it is not true* that this was attended with any solemnity, or 'excited unbounded (or any) interest among his numerous followers.'"[116]

The erroneous claim that a Swedenborgian had done this was bad enough for Noble. But what was doubly insulting was any suggestion that the Swedenborgian community cared one way or another about the body: "Some of them knew that the skull had been taken away: but I believe that none of them (or not more than one) knew when it was restored; and I am sure that none of them cared anything about the matter."

Swedenborg in life had been a mystic, and those who valued his teachings above all valorized the spirit over the body. As David George Goyder, a phrenologist, Swedenborgian, and con- temporary of Noble, wrote, "Of all the different classes of Chris- tians, the Swedenborgians are the least accessible to relics of any kind, but more especially relics of the dead." As a temporary ves- sel, once the body has "fulfilled its use in this world, which use is principally to prepare the soul for heaven, it will be consigned 'to the earth as it was, while the spirit will return to God who gave it.'"[117] No matter who had taken the skull, he couldn't have been involved with Swedenborgianism.

In fact, Noble concluded, the sole motive of Countess von Schwerin was that

---

[116] Quoted in Ibid., p. 76.
[117] Goyder, *My Battle for Life*, p. 134.

the admirers of the writings of Swedenborg might not be charged with such stupidity as that of venerating the mortal remains of any man, which, Swedenborg maintains, are entirely unnecessary to the future existence of the soul, and will never be resumed; for she was aware, that if at any future period it should be discovered that the skull was gone, the robbery would be imputed to the admirers of his doctrines, and that misrepresentations of their sentiments, such as your anecdote contains, would be the result. Nothing, I assure you, can be more abhorrent to their principles, or to the doctrines of the New Jerusalem church, than any thing that can tend to the revival of *saint-craft*.[118]

And so, Noble believed, the skull had been stolen for phrenological purposes, not out of veneration for the dead. But another letter quickly arrived at the *Times* to clarify the matter further, and this writer, John Isaac Hawkins, not only knew more of the story but also identified the thief.

"Captain Ludvig Granholm of the Royal Navy of Sweden," he wrote, "called on me, near the end of the year 1817, invited me to his lodgings and showed me a skull, which he said was the skull of Swedenborg." Granholm had been in the chapel, not for von Nolcken's funeral but for the funeral of a fellow naval officer, when he noticed Swedenborg's coffin. Hawkins described how, "on observing that the coffin was loose, he was seized with the

---

[118] Quoted in Hultkrantz, pp. 76-77.

idea of making a large sum of money, by taking the skull, and selling it to one of Swedenborg's followers, who, he had heard,
amounted to many thousands in this country, and amongst whom,
he imagined, there would be much competition for the possession
of so valuable a relic. He watched his opportunity, lifted the lid of
the coffin, took out the skull, wrapped it in his pocket handker-
chief, and carried it out of the chapel unnoticed."

Hawkins himself had tried to set the captain straight: "I informed Captain Granholm, to his great disappointment, that the
members of the New Jerusalem Church reprobated the possession
of any religious relic, and more particularly a part of a dead body,
which, they believe, will never more come into use, the soul remaining, after death, a complete and active man in a spiritual body,
not to be again fettered with material flesh, blood, and bones."[119]

But did Hawkins have all his facts straight? A third writer,
who signed himself "Tertius Interveniens" (a legal term for one
who argues on another's behalf), wrote to clarify. This was Johan
Peter Wåhlin, who was pastor of the Swedish Church during this
time. Like Hawkins, he was intimately involved with the events
surrounding the theft. On his deathbed Granholm had summoned
Wåhlin and confessed to taking the skull, which Wåhlin took
away with him. Granholm may have not lived long enough to
find a buyer for the head, but after word got out that Wåhlin now
had the skull, someone offered him 500 pounds for it, which he
claimed to have declined somewhat indignantly.

[119] Quoted in Ibid., p. 77.

The Swedish Church council asked Wåhlin to keep the skull until the vault was opened again, "in order that it might not again come into unauthorized hands," but Wåhlin instead loaned it to Charles Tulk. Tulk was a member of Parliament and had helped Noble found the Swedenborg Society; he also was an avid believer in phrenology and had amassed a large private collection. Tulk displayed the skull in his museum until 1823, when Countess von Schwerin pushed for its reinterment; both Tulk and Wåhlin were on hand when the skull was finally reunited with the rest of the remains in the Swedish Church's vault.

Wåhlin's letter to the *Times* primarily concerned how the vault had been opened in the first place. Like Broling and Hindmarsh, he confirmed that a doubting Thomas from America had bribed the sexton to open the coffin, and that only when the lid was finally opened did "the mephitic vapours did at the same time expel the septic and his doubts upon the subject." These bizarre events in 1790, Wåhlin explained, had left the coffin unsealed and vulnerable to anyone who happened to wander into the crypt. Disagreeing with Hawkins's account, Wåhlin claimed that the theft had happened in 1816, not 1817; in addition, like Noble, Wåhlin claimed that it had been done not by a follower of Swedenborg or for profit but by a phrenologist "who expected to fix the *organ of imagination* beyond any doubt."[120]

The confusion that thus played out over a week in the *Times* was the question of what place the skull held in the world of the

[120] Quoted in Ibid., p. 78.

living. Was it a relic, something to be preserved with "the great-est care and veneration"? Was it a scientific instrument with which one might "fix the organ of imagination beyond any doubt"? Or was it, as Hawkins affirmed, simply an item of commerce?

It's too simplistic to say it was all three of these things at once. Rather, as the debate over Swedenborg's skull suggests, re-ligion and science were each in their own way trying to claim the skull as exclusively belonging to their respective realms. And men like Granholm understood quickly that there was money to be made in such a dispute. His mistake was to pick the wrong saint and the wrong branch of Christianity. Twenty years later and one hundred miles to the northeast of London, in the town of Norfolk, county Norwich, another cranioklept would have more luck.

SUCH WAS THE fate that befell Sir Thomas Browne, whose head had lain waiting, as if for this moment, for 160 years. Browne, who was born in 1605 and died on his birthday seventy-seven years later, was both a doctor and a theologian but is mostly remembered for a series of amazing books that he published late in life. "Few people love the writings of Sir Thomas Browne," said Virginia Woolf, "but those who do are of the salt of the earth." Browne's works run the gamut of Renaissance preoccu-pations, from the religious-philosophical meditations of *Religio Medici* to the manifold superstitious beliefs he exposed in *Pseudo-doxica Epidemica* to the armchair archaeology of *Urn Burial*. His writing is a kind of esoteric secret, passed from library to library, treasured by each who receives it as if it were a rare jewel made of prose—to quote Woolf, it excels by "bringing the remote and the incongruous astonishingly together. A piece of an old boat is cheek by jowl with the funeral pyre of Patroclus. Vast inquiries sweeping in immense circles of ambiguity and doubt are clenched by short sentences rapped out with solemn authority." To read Browne's works "is always to be filled with astonishment, to re-member the surprises, the despondences, the unlimited curiosi-ties of youth."[121]

Sir Thomas predated Gall by a century, so he had never given a thought to phrenology during his life, but the New Science was in the Norfolk air in 1840: A traveling phrenologist had delivered a lecture in February of that year that was extremely well re-ceived, and the entire community of Norfolk had been hotly debating the tenets and findings of phrenology ever since. Phre-nological thoughts were on the minds of many that August when the doctor's bones came to light once more.

Workers had been digging a grave for the recently deceased wife of the vicar of St. Peter Mancroft and unknowingly had been digging into the vault of Sir Thomas Browne. As was the custom at the time, the vault that contained Browne's coffin had earlier been filled in with dirt so as to keep the ground above level, and as a result it was sometimes difficult to tell where one plot ended

[121] Virginia Woolf, "Sir Thomas Browne," in *The Essays of Virginia Woolf, Volume Three,* edited by Andrew McNeillie (San Diego: Harcourt, Brace, Jovanovich, 1988) pp. 368–371.

and the next began. When the diggers struck something hard in the dirt, it was at first unclear what they had hit. Digging further, they found the two halves of a brass plaque that they had inadvertently shattered, and only when they read the plaque did they realize it was Browne's coffin they had broken into.

Whether this disturbance was intentional has long been a subject of debate, though it seems likely that it was an accident. Either way, the news spread quickly, and people from all over Norfolk gathered to see the sudden reappearance of their local saint. The workmen had to cover the remains quickly to keep away the curious, but they did not fill in the grave right away, and the remains of Browne were accessible to the churchwardens as well as to George Potter, the sexton.

Closer inspection revealed a skull in good condition. The brain had long ago liquefied by a process called "apidocere," where the chemical decomposition of biomass is converted to soap; a contemporary report of the remains described the contents of the skull as resembling an "ointment of a dark brown hue."[122]

Then there was his hair—it was also found to be in good condition among the remains, and witnesses described it as "of a fine auburn colour." How had the hair survived in such good condition? Over the decades there was a good deal of speculation about this. In 1894 a surgeon named Charles Williams (who would become somewhat of an expert on the subject of Thomas Browne) would argue that it was not actually Browne's hair but a

[122] Quoted in Tildesley, p. 34.

wig. "It is difficult to believe that a man of seventy-seven," Williams surmised, "who must have suffered much anxiety and worry in an arduous practice of over forty years, and who had lost all his teeth, could have possessed a large amount of hair 'of a fine auburn colour.'"[123] More likely, it seems (since Browne's letters show him castigating others for wearing wigs) that it was indeed genuine, albeit from his beard, and that it had turned the reddish color through the leaching of iron from the soil into the hair.

In any case, Browne's hair had fared better than his coffin, the lead of which had almost completely decomposed into a carbonite substance that crumbled to the touch, the chalky soil having been responsible for its disintegration.

The condition of the coffin and remains was recorded by Dr. Robert Fitch, a chemist, druggist, and amateur antiquarian and collector, who presented his findings to the Society of Antiquaries later that year. Given the excitement surrounding phrenology at the time, it is not surprising that the sexton George Potter had asked Fitch, a parishioner at St. Peter Mancroft who was appointed churchwarden in 1845, to examine the skull to see what information it might provide about the long-dead doctor.

Fitch shared little of the mysticism that had made Browne's writings sparkle. The epitaph written on the brass plaque—the one that had been broken in half—had read, *"Hoc Loculo indormiens, Corporis Spagyrici pulvere plumbum in aurum Convertit"*: "sleeping in this coffin, by the dust of his alchemical body, he

---

[123] Charles Williams, in *Notes and Queries*, October 6, 1894, pp. 269-270.

converts the lead into gold." However, Fitch, in his original report, commented that "whether the last two lines of the original
latinity were meant to predict an alchemic transmutation, or to
express a hyperbolic compliment, we leave to the learned, with
this remark that the coffin is *still a leaden one.*"[124]

While the coffin was being repaired and Fitch was examining
the remains, he ordered a cast of the skull so that it could be
studied after it was reinterred. For this he turned to a fellow
parishioner, Charles Muskett, who was not destined to go down
in history as a virtuoso caster of skulls. The cast he produced was
marginal at best; a twentieth-century anthropologist noted that
"to-day we should class it contemptuously as a miserable specimen of a skull-cast."[125] Most significantly, Muskett's cast didn't
include Browne's face: it replicated only the cranial cavity. Muskett's interest, after all, was phrenology, and what he wanted was
only a record of the bumps of the skull. No physiognomist, he
wasn't the least interested in the face.

The cast being completed and the grave repaired, Fitch in-
structed George Potter to return the skull for reinterment. But
Potter—or "Skull George," as he would come to be known by
his descendents—had other ideas. Apparently he did not take the
inscription on Browne's coffin as literally as Fitch had. With the

---

[124] Quoted in Tildesley, "Sir Thomas Browne," p. 35.
[125] Ibid., p. 46.

skull in his possession, he thought surely there had to be some way to turn the good doctor's leaden bones into gold.

Thus it was that Skull George hid the skull and reburied the rest of Browne's body, then began to look for a buyer. The first person he approached, G. W. W. Frith, turned him down, but Potter soon struck gold. His crass opportunism would later come to be seen as somewhat of an embarrassment; writing in 1905, Edmund Gosse noted that the sexton "offered it for sale, and it was bought by a collector over whose name, in my opinion, it is best to shed the poppy of oblivion."[126] This last line was a reference to the final chapters in *Urn Burial*, where Browne wrote that "the iniquity of oblivion blindly scattereth her poppy, and deals with the memory of men without distinction to the merit of perpetuity."[127] But such poppies could not shield the name of the man who purchased the skull because he ultimately left it, quite publicly, to the Norwich and Norfolk Hospital Museum. Entered into the museum's records for the year 1848 is item No. 641, N. 5: "Cranium of the celebrated Sir Thomas Browne." Under the column "Whence derived" is written "Dr. Lubbock."

Not much is known about Edward Lubbock (for this we can blame the poppies) except that he was, like Fitch—and, for that matter, Browne—both a doctor and an antiquarian, and he apparently enjoyed the same lack of scruples about purchasing

[126] Edmund Gosse, *Sir Thomas Browne* (London: MacMillan and Company, 1905), p. 116.
[127] Thomas Browne, *Religio Medici, Hydrotaphia, and the Garden of Cyrus*, p. 129.

heads. He kept the skull in his collection until his death in 1848, when it was left to the museum. The museum displayed it proudly, along with a lock of the doctor's "fine auburn hair" (which was later lost). Thus "gnaw'd from his grave," Browne took up his residence in the hospital museum's pathological section, as if a way with words was somehow a pathology unto itself.

NOT EVERY UNEARTHED corpse was so unfortunate. The great Scottish hero Robert the Bruce was disturbed in 1819 in a similar manner, and while a cast was taken of his skull, it was promptly reinterred afterward. Likewise, in 1835 workers inadvertently broke open Jonathan Swift's grave, which bore the inscription *"Ubi Saeva Indignatio Ulterius Cor Lacerare Nequit"*— "Where savage indignation can lacerate his heart no more." The skull was taken out and examined; the physician William Wilde described it as resembling "in a most extraordinary manner those skulls of the so-called Celtic aborigines of North-Western Europe," while the phrenologist who examined it pronounced its owner as having "amativeness large and wit small." But as with Bruce, once a cast was made, the skull was returned to its grave, sparing Swift any possible savage indignations.[128]

They were among the lucky ones, but it was clear that a new era of relic theft had begun, one to which Browne himself could

[128] Shane Leslie, *The Skull of Swift: An Extempore Exhumation* (Indianapolis: The Bobbs-Merrille Company, 1928), pp. 4–5.

have related. "The Egyptian mummies, which Cambyses or time hath spared, avarice now consumeth," he wrote at the end of *Urn Burial*. "Mummy is become merchandise, Misraim cures wounds, and Pharaoh is sold for basalms."[129] No longer just the Egyptian mummies of antiquity, now the great minds of Europe had also become merchandise.

[129] Browne, *Religio Medici, Hydrotaphia, and the Garden of Cyrus*, pp. 130–131.

THE BRAINOWNER
AND HIS SKULL

The same year that Skull George absconded with Sir Thomas Browne's head, Anton Schindler published his infamous biography of Beethoven. Schindler was careful to put in a note for his phrenological audience, including the autopsy's description of the numerous convolutions of the brain and the thick skull, since "it would not be uninteresting to many admirers of Beethoven to learn the conformation of his skull."[130] Certainly Beethoven was one of those figures whose genius was not only legendary but highly specific, and no doubt a thorough study of his skull could afford much insight to the phrenologically inclined. As it happened, in 1863 they got their chance.

While Stephan von Breuning's attempts to keep thieves away from Beethoven's grave had worked, he couldn't keep out nature, and by 1863 Beethoven's grave was in disrepair. That year the

---

[130] Quoted in Meredith, "The History of Beethoven's Skull Fragments," p. 4.

Gessellschaft der Musikfreunde—the Society for the Friends of Music—decided to exhume and rebury two bodies to "save the earthly remains of Beethoven and Schubert from further decay and, at the same time, to establish their resting places in a deserving manner."[131]

The Society for the Friends of Music was founded in 1812 in an attempt to stem the decline of music appreciation and attendance in the wake of the Napoleonic Wars. In its nearly two hundred–year history it has established itself as one of the preeminent classical music organizations and has counted in its ranks dozens of notable composers and conductors. In 1870 construction would be complete on the Society's Musikverien, a concert hall that still ranks among the finest in the world, but even by 1863 it had become the preeminent musical institution in Vienna, and as such its authority in matters concerning the city's beloved composers was relatively unquestioned.

The exhumation was paid for by a special concert "playing exclusively compositions by the deceased, in order to erect a monument with the proceeds," and it was decided that the exhumations of Beethoven and Schubert would happen simultaneously.[132] There was a certain poetic quality to this decision since Schubert's death was itself connected to Beethoven's. According

---

[131] Bauer et. al., "The Official Report on the First Exhumation of the Graves of Beethoven and Schubert by the Gessellshcaft der Musikfreunde in 1863," translated by Hannah Leibmann, *The Beethoven Journal*, Vol. 20, Nos. 1 & 2 (Summer & Winter 2005), p. 47.
[132] Ibid.

to a possibly apocryphal story, on the evening of Beethoven's funeral a number of his friends and fellow composers had gathered at a local inn to celebrate their deceased friend. "To the memory of our immortal Beethoven!" Schubert is supposed to have said, and after the first toast was drunk, he lifted his glass once more and said, "And now to the first of us to follow Beethoven!" He was toasting himself; of those assembled, he was the first to die, on November 19, 1828.[133]

Linked in death, they were now to be linked in exhumation. The Society for the Friends of Music could count in its ranks a fair number of doctors, and the society's board appointed a committee that would be present to handle the treatment of the remains while their new coffins were prepared. In charge of Schubert was a doctor named Joseph Standthartner. In charge of Beethoven was "Trouserbutton" himself, Gerhard von Breuning.

In the years after his father died Gerhard trained as a doctor, attending the Josephinian Military Academy, from which he graduated in 1837. He began his career as a military doctor and for a time was the chief physician at the Imperial Royal Invalids Home before switching to private practice in 1852. His early friendship with Beethoven had cemented a lifelong love of music, and he had long since become a member of the board of the Society of the Friends of Music. Even as he established himself as a surgeon of some repute, it's fair to say that Beethoven never left him. Like Rosenbaum, he lived a dual life: one of empirical facts,

[133] Breuning, *From the House of the Black-Robed Spaniards*, p. 112.

Gerhard von Breuning.

rational logic, knowable information; the other the ineffable world of music.

So he was the immediate and obvious choice to oversee the exhumation of Beethoven: It was in many ways a culmination of his two lifelong obsessions. Breuning was the perfect man for this job—a capable doctor who had a passion for music and who had known Beethoven personally.

ASIDE FROM RESCUING the two graves from decay, the committee members all hoped for a chance to get another look at the composers' remains, particularly Beethoven's. Wagner and Rokitansky's work during the original autopsy had left many questions unanswered, and the butchered condition in which they had left the corpse—not to mention the sparse details afforded by the autopsy report—suggested that a more serious, detailed, and reverential examination should take place.

Chief among all the questions that remained unanswered was the problem of Beethoven's deafness. Wagner had noted "wrinkled" acoustic nerves and "cartilaginous" arteries dilated to "beyond the size of the lumen of a raven's quill." But what had caused this condition? Breuning and the others were particularly eager to examine the temporal bones, the small parts of the skull that connect the temples to the ears and would have the most to say about the composer's auditory canals. But they hoped that the skull would hold other secrets as well, and they were eager to get to it.

THE EXHUMATION BEGAN on October 13, 1863, during a slow, drizzling rain. Schubert's coffin was unearthed quickly, but the excavation of Beethoven's grave took over eight hours because workers had to break through the layer of bricks that

Stephan von Breuning had placed over the coffin. They were unable to finish that day, and once again an armed guard was posted at Beethoven's grave until the next morning.

The wood of the coffin itself, they found, had disintegrated into white-yellowish chunks. The remains were likewise not in the greatest shape; bones were missing—some carpal bones from the wrists and tarsal bones from the ankles as well as a few ribs.

Beethoven's bones were still a light color, but Schubert's bones were a deep brownish-black as a result of the damp soil and water leakage where he'd been buried. In addition, they noted that around Schubert's skull was a "rather dense covering of his—as everybody knows—very luxuriant hair," which unfortunately was now "mixed with a lot of damp soil, half rotten wood shavings, and many hundreds of insect larvae."[134] At the exhumation Schubert's hair—presumably cleaned of wood shavings and maggots—was presented reverentially to his brother.

The committee also found numerous decayed pieces of clothing, the sole of a shoe, and two pieces of a comb that had been used to hold back the aforementioned "luxurious amount of hair." The committee's official exhumation report stated, "All these objects were carefully collected; the members of the administration took individual parts of the remnants of clothing and the wood of the coffin of Beethoven as well as of Schubert," and while Breuning kept safeguard over most of them, "parts were

---

[134] Bauer et. al., "Official Report," p. 49.

given over to the few persons present at this serious act who were visibly moved by strong emotions."[135]

The hair and clothing were important, to be sure, but, as Breuning later wrote, "the main goal was, of course, the retrieval of the skull."[136] In that age of skull-stealing, all sorts of rumors were circulating about Beethoven's head. Numerous men on the committee believed that the head would be missing, that someone would have bested Stephan von Breuning and removed the head before it had gone into the coffin. Others assumed it would be there, and the committee had heard another, perhaps more reliable rumor that only part of the skull would be missing.

This last rumor turned out to be true. Beethoven's skull was found to be in pieces; it had been broken into approximately nine different fragments by Wagner, and in decay they had not held their shape but lay in a pile at the bottom of the coffin. As some had feared, a few important fragments were missing. Specifically, the petrous segments of the temporal bones—the small pyramid-shaped pieces of the skull that contain all the organs of hearing—had been removed "by having been sawed off vertically."[137] In other words, when Wagner had segmented the head into numerous pieces he had deliberately cut out the single most crucial part of the skull for understanding Beethoven's deafness, and now it seemed that he had never returned them to the body. This also

[135] Ibid., p. 50.
[136] Ibid., p .49.
[137] Ibid., p. 49.

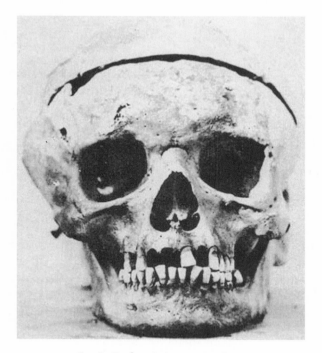

The skull of Ludwig van Beethoven.
REPRODUCED WITH PERMISSION OF THE IRA F. BRILLIANT CENTER
FOR BEETHOVEN STUDIES, SAN JOSE STATE UNIVERSITY.

helped to explain Beethoven's poor appearance while he lay in state because Wagner had patched up the missing bones with clay, further distorting the face.

It was a crushing disappointment. For someone looking for the answer to Beethoven's deafness, the temporal bones were a conspicuous absence. A conclusive diagnosis on the maestro's hearing loss was now all but impossible.

EVEN WITH THE remains in such sad shape, all present under-stood that it was a rare opportunity to study the anatomy of the two composers and learn something vital about their lives and their deaths. The original intention had been to rebury the bodies that same day, but now that they were unearthed, there was a dis-cussion as to whether to keep them aboveground. Casts and pho-tographs, to be sure, could tell a lot, but there was something more to the actual skulls, especially Beethoven's, whose deterio-rated condition meant that, as Breuning argued, "important pro-portions of the skull can only be obtained by comparing repeated measurements of the original skull with its individual parts."[138]

The society's board members agreed with the exhumation committee that, at least for the time being, the skulls need not be immediately reburied. Everyone saw the important scientific op-portunity afforded by the exhumation and agreed that photo-graphs and casts should be taken of the skulls. In addition, the board had to decide whether to rebury the skulls or house them in "a worthy place that would closely reflect the grand activity of the spirits that lived in these bony dwellings."[139]

There was also the problem of the missing temporal bones. "Since two essential components of the skull have never been put

---

[138] Gerhard von Breuning, "The Skulls of Beethoven and Schubert," translated by Hannah Leibmann, *The Beethoven Journal*, Vol. 20, Nos. 1 & 2 (Summer & Winter 2005), p. 60.
[139] Bauer et. al., "Official Report," p. 50.

into the grave," the committee noted, "and in case these components would ever be found, they could only be reconnected with the other components of the skull if the latter is properly kept."[140]

Among those vociferously arguing that the skulls should be kept unburied was Breuning. The skulls, he maintained, had immense scientific value and could not simply be allowed to rot in the ground. Ultimately, though, the society's board decided that the skulls would go back into the ground with the rest of the remains. There would be enough time for plaster casts, photographs, and measurements of the heads, and then they were to return to the coffins—with one exception. The only thing they did not ask to be reinterred was "the hair of Franz Schubert, which was found disconnected from the skull and mixed in with parts of soil, and which was given to the brother of the deceased right at the exhumation."[141]

The composers' remains, minus skulls, were laid out in their new zinc coffins—vertebrae were strung together with twine, and the bones were assembled as best could be accomplished. The coffins were closed and soldered shut and affixed with the seal of the society. Then the doctors turned to the skulls.

The photographer J. B. Rottmayer took a number of photographic studies, while the sculptor Alois Wittman was called in to make plaster casts. A dentist was retained to make records of the composers' teeth. And last was Dr. Romeo Seligmann, who took

---

[140] Ibid.
[141] Ibid., p. 151.

exacting measurements of the skulls for future scientific research. Known by his friends simply by the nickname "Wonderful" for his brilliance and congeniality, Seligmann had taught himself Arabic and Persian while still a high school student and had become one of the foremost scholars of the history of medicine. In his spare time he worked out a philosophical treatise on the relationship between ancient Indian and Greek medicine, and he was building his own skull collection for his anthropological research. In addition to his medical specimens, he was an avid art collector, and through his friendship with Goethe's daughter-in-law, Ottilie (who was a patient and lavished gifts on him), he acquired a massive collection of Goethe portraits and mementoes (which became known as his "Goethiana").

Shepherding the head of Beethoven through the whole process, of course, was Breuning. Indeed, he kept the skull with him at all times; although work on the skulls was done in a secret location, where there had to be at least two people present at all times to prevent tampering or theft, Breuning was allowed to take Beethoven's home with him each night. He was not a phrenologist by profession, nor was he captivated by the New Science, as Joseph Carl Rosenbaum and Johann Peter had been sixty years earlier. But the fact that phrenology had been largely discredited didn't mean it hadn't left its traces on respectable science. As he compared their skulls in the laboratory, Breuning made a pronouncement about the two composers that has since become infamous in classical music studies: He claimed that the skulls "seemed to reflect the characteristics of the composers' works. The walls of Beethoven's skull exhibit strong density and thickness, whereas Schubert's bones show feminine delicateness."[142]

Breuning also claimed that the fragmentation of Beethoven's skull, combined with the dampness of the grave, had caused the bone to warp and that this explained the rather odd shape that the forehead had assumed. Rather than being a high, well-developed forehead, as could be expected of such a genius, it was sloped back and disturbingly low. Warping, due to moisture, seemed the only plausible reason for this.

While the casts were being made, a quick search for the missing temporal bones was also carried out. There had been a published report that a certain unnamed "medical celebrity in Paris" might know their whereabouts and perhaps might even have taken them. But this inquiry came to no avail; the medical celebrity in question replied in a letter, "When I left Vienna, I only had the pleasure to take with me from the Austrian capital the gratitude for my professors and the friendship of my colleagues that I appreciated. I never heard anyone speak about Beethoven's ears."[143]

As for the items of clothing and other fragments, Breuning ordered special zinc cases so that they could be returned to the new coffins without fear of further disintegration.

Despite his work during this time, Breuning was still upset over the board's decision to reinter the skulls, and he would continue to brood over it in coming years. "How important and how

---

[142] Breuning, *From the House of the Black-Robed Spaniards*, p. 116.
[143] Bauer et. al., "Official Report," p. 55.

interesting it would be for science," he wrote twenty years later, "if these skulls remained available for further, more thorough investigation. They should be preserved above the earth and accessible in a museum, art gallery, or library. The two composers would be better honored by such action than by the usual interment of their skulls in tombs." The board's decision reeked of a superstition that Breuning found indefensible when compared to scientific inquiry. "Only highly prejudiced people (who are unfortunately in the majority) would be offended" by putting the skulls in the museum, and "any person with scientific training would certainly not object." Breuning concluded: "I am sure no feelings of piety will be offended if the dry skulls, having long been separated from the rest of the skeletons, should be immortalized in such a way."[144]

But Breuning's attachment to the head of his father's friend had gone beyond simple scientific inquiry. Each night he returned home with the skull, placing it lovingly beside his bed to meditate on while he drifted off to sleep. "What stormy feelings passed through my mind," Breuning later said of those days, "evoking such powerful memories, as I had possession of that head for a few days . . . [and] kept it by my bedside overnight, and in general proudly watched over that head from whose mouth, in years gone by, I had so often heard the living word!"[145]

[144] Breuning, "The Skulls of Beethoven and Schubert," p. 60.
[145] Breuning, *From the House of the Black-Robed Spaniards*, p. 118.

THE COMPOSERS' SKULLS, along with the tin boxes containing the other relics, were reunited with the rest of the remains on October 22. Gerhard von Breuning brought Beethoven's skull fragments, and most likely it was he who reassembled them in the coffin, reconstructing the head of the composer as best he could. It was a solemn, low-key affair, with about twenty people looking on as the coffins were closed and locked; the keys given to Dr. Standthartner; the lids soldered closed; and, finally, seals of the society affixed to the coffins.

The next morning both coffins were interred in newly constructed vaults. The audience for the ceremony was a good deal larger; the chapel was big enough to fit only the doctors and immediate family, while other spectators were obliged to wait outside. After a requiem mass, the coffins were carried to the vault, with Breuning among the Schubert pallbearers and Standthartner among the Beethoven pallbearers.

A blessing and another song were offered, and then the deputy head of the society delivered a homily. He spoke of the way emotions always attach themselves "with heartfelt love" to the remains of the dead, "as to a lock of a friend, as to the letter of a beloved person," even though "cold reason might smile." He said that even though one could honor the dead composers with monuments or by playing their work, "we still like to make a pilgrimage to the places where the earthly part of their being that has been shed rests."[146] After he had finished, the new coffins were sealed in the vault and the crowd dispersed.

But, as these things go, not all of Beethoven had made it back into the vault.

WHAT WAS LEFT of Beethoven remained undisturbed for another quarter of a century, until 1888, when the body was once again exhumed. This time the reason was that the Währing cemetery was in near disintegration and was to be demolished to make way for new buildings. Along with the other coffins to be moved, Beethoven's remains were to be transferred to the "Grove of Honor" of the central cemetery in Vienna.

When Gerhard von Breuning heard the news, he wrote an essay on the skulls of Beethoven and Schubert in which he lamented the dispersal of the cemetery's occupants. "Along with the cemetery's demise, we will likewise have to bury many historical memories that link us to the times and conditions of their lives." He recalled the various composers and friends who had desired to be buried close to Beethoven: Stephan, his father, who had wanted to be buried next to his friend and had been laid to rest "a few graves further down"; Clementi and Ritter von Seyfried, buried on either side of the composer; the playwright Johann Nepomuk Nestroy and the poet Franz Grillparzer; and Schubert, whose "longing to be close to Beethoven, often ex-

[146] Bauer et. al., "Official Report," p. 55.

pressed in his feverish dreams, was fulfilled when he was buried only a few graves up from Beethoven."[147]

Breuning saw the cemetery as a delicate network of old friends and colleagues whose lives had intersected in startling and momentous ways and who now continued their conversations in the grave. A whole history could be unraveled by tracing the connections in the Währing cemetery: "All these memories and reference points connecting us with the past," he wrote, "are now being destroyed and will be forgotten as these 'famous' and 'outstanding' deceased people will be transferred to other cemeteries."[148]

It's odd that a rationalist like Breuning should care about this so much. He was clearly of two minds: He wanted Beethoven's remains transparently available for science for all time; he even complained that the photos taken in 1863 had not been made publicly available. But it was hard for him to maintain scientific objectivity, hard not to see the beauty in a cemetery of old friends lying beside each other, hard not to see the mystery in the skull of a friend by one's bedside, the living word now silent.

As with the 1863 exhumation, when Beethoven was moved in 1888 medical experts were allowed access to the composer, but this time only for a mere twenty minutes—they later complained that the circumstances surrounding this examination "were highly unfavorable." Still, they had enough time to find that the

---

[147] Breuning, "The Skulls of Beethoven and Schubert," p. 58.
[148] Ibid.

plaster casts were accurate enough to be used for future study and that there could be "no real objection to the authenticity of the skull fragments found in the coffin."[149]

The 1863 exhumation had already revealed the strange way in which, over time, underground, bones simply disappear. Decay, bacteria, any number of factors can cause even something as hard as bone to disintegrate. So the 1888 doctors, pressed for time, noted only in passing that a portion of the occipital bone was missing, as was a portion of the left parietal bone. These pieces were substantially larger than the petrous bones taken by Wagner—the occipital bone forms the broad back shelf of the head, and the parietal bones each form half of the roof of the cranial cavity. The missing pieces, each about four inches long, seemed too big to have simply disintegrated, especially considering that the express purpose of the 1863 reburial had been to keep the remains in better condition. The committee continued its cataloging of the bones of the skull, then moved on to its conclusions. Curiously, the members seem to have not found it noteworthy that more of the skull was missing than had been in 1863. Each autopsy, it seemed, led to more bits of Beethoven's head disappearing; perhaps this was just the way of the world.

As in 1863, a speech was given at the 1888 reburial, written by Joseph Weilen and delivered by the actor Joseph Lewinsky. In his praise of Beethoven, Weilen noted that the composer was to be buried next to the cenotaph of Mozart, "whose grave covers not

---

[149] Quoted in Davies, *Beethoven in Person*, p. 115.

his bones but the shameful reproach for his contemporaries who, having received his masterpieces, lacked due regard for preserving his ashes." He then quoted Grillparzer, whose body was also about to be transferred out of the Währing cemetery:

> You who have gathered at this place, step closer to this grave . . . the one who lies here was inspired. Striving for one thing, caring for one thing, suffering for one thing, offering everything for one thing, this is how this man walked through life. . . . If there is still any sense of wholeness in us in this broken time, let us gather together at his grave. This is why there have always been poets, and heroes, singers, and those inspired by God—so that through them poor ruined human beings raise themselves up, ponder their origin and their destination.[150]

IT'S NOT CLEAR whether either Gerhard von Breuning or Romeo Seligmann was present for this second exhumation. It's not clear whether, if they had been, they would have shared what they knew about the newly discovered missing portions of Beethoven's skull, the occipital fragments. As he saw his own death impending, Beethoven had bitterly remarked to Dr. Wawruch that if anyone could save him from the oblivion of

---

[150] Joseph Weilien, "Speech Given at the Reburial of Ludwig van Beethoven," translated by Hannah Leibmann, *The Beethoven Journal*, Vol. 20, Nos. 1 & 2 (Summer & Winter 2005), p. 57.

death "his name would be Wonderful!" He had been referring to the *Messiah*, but in a curious way his prophecy would yet come true: in 1863 persons unknown had kept out a few precious fragments of the composer's skull—to save them from the oblivion of decay and disintegration—and given them to Dr. Romeo Seligmann, known to his friends simply as "Wonderful."

CHAPTER TEN

FRAGMENTS OF A

MYSTERY

Mysteries surround Beethoven's death; perhaps they always will.

With the temporal bones lost, an accurate diagnosis of his deafness may never be made, and even a recent DNA analysis of his hair has raised at least as many questions as it has answered. His ailments may have been caused by lead poisoning, or perhaps by a treatment of mercury for syphilis or some other problem, but in all likelihood the answer will never be known. And then there is the question of the skull fragments, the second set to be removed, extracted, in 1863 during the first exhumation and noted only in the second exhumation. Who gave them to Romeo Seligmann?

Dr. William Meredith, who runs the Ira F. Brilliant Center of Beethoven Studies at San Jose State University has pointed to Gerhard von Breuning. Gerhard had the motive, being perhaps the most vocal proponent of keeping Beethoven's head in a museum rather than having it go back into the ground. And he had the means, since of all those present he was the only one ever to be left alone with the skull. The missing fragments were from the back of the skull and thus would not have been missed when Breuning arranged the fragments face up in the casket for reburial. And the fragments were kept—it would later be discovered—in specially made zinc boxes, the same kind as the ones Breuning ordered for the clothing and other nonhuman remains.

Meredith offered another plausible explanation. "Perhaps Breuning did not lose the argument on October 15, 1863," he suggested, "about the reburial of the skulls. Of all the people involved in the exhumation, he held a unique position, having been Beethoven's friend as a teenager. His word and moral authority in this regard must have carried special weight. Perhaps the Committee agreed to an undocumented compromise. Perhaps Breuning himself was allowed to keep the two large fragments, but the matter was not to be made public."[151]

It may be that the act was on someone else's initiative, but if so, Breuning must at least have been complicit. The same man who watched his father go to such lengths to safeguard the composer and his legacy that it literally killed him, who would later lament the lost memories and reference points from the past as the Währing cemetery was plowed under and the remains of these great men were separated—this same man had a hand in one way or another in the further fragmentation of Beethoven's remains.

[151] Meredith, "The History of Beethoven's Skull Fragments," p. 20.

BREUNING SEEMS TO us now a figure who straddles multiple epochs. He received his medical training at a time when the field of medicine was changing and beginning to assume the shape it has today. Centuries-old practices such as bloodletting were falling out of favor, and others were taking their place. In 1847 Dr. Ignaz Semmelweiss—working in the same hospital in Vienna where Haydn's head had been cleaned in 1809—discovered pathogenic germs after he discovered that doctors attending births directly after performing autopsies were transmitting puerperal fever to their patients. In such a changing medical environment phrenology had little place, but its prevalence as a social phenomenon meant that it continued to influence men like Breuning, who could still claim that thickness of skull could determine the relative "masculinity" or "femininity" of a composer's musical works. With knowledge in this state of flux, men like Breuning were more than capable of seeing in Beethoven's skull both a pathological map and a phrenological map.

Living as he did at a time when phrenology was evolving from a serious scientific pursuit into a disgraceful joke, Breuning also marks the end of another kind of legacy. What seems so shocking about Rosenbaum's theft of Haydn's head is in part the fact that he had known the man in life and that he was capable of seeing the grave robbery as an act of veneration and respect.

Breuning, similarly, had known Beethoven, and in both men's cases this kind of cranial trophy-hunting was an extremely intimate affair. There was nothing ghoulish about it to them; to keep the remains of a loved one in a glass box on a library shelf, or in a zinc box in a drawer, was to them an act that spoke of deep mystery and friendship.

This concept, too, was changing. Until the mid–nineteenth century, it was common for a family to keep the body of a loved one in the house for days, laid out on a table or a bed, as if the corpse's occupant had not yet left them. There was a familiarity to the dead in those days. But in the coming decades burial reformers—spurred in no small part by Semmelweiss's discovery of the corpse's pathogenic possibilities—led a concentrated campaign to remove the dead body more quickly from the sphere of the living and into mortuaries and cemeteries. With our own familiar connection to the dead severed, Rosenbaum's and Breuning's actions may strike us as macabre, but there's no reason to think they would have seen them that way.

Still, others did see their actions as deeply troubling. By the time the term "skulduggery" came into use in 1867 to mean underhandedness and deceit, grave robbing and head-stealing were a fact of life, one more disturbing element of the modern age.

THE 1827 AUTOPSY of Beethoven was hardly an auspicious beginning for Carl von Rokitansky. It was the first autopsy he had attended, and it was nothing short of a disgrace. Wagner was in charge and Rokitansky merely the apprentice, so it's hard to lay any blame on him. Still, it hardly boded well for the young anatomist. Yet, surprisingly, he would go on to pursue one of the most distinguished careers in Viennese medicine.

Rokitansky, a lower-middle-class son of a local District Office clerk, was largely self-taught, chafing under a medical education system that relied on rote memorization through textbooks. While studying under Wagner, he learned a great deal about dissection, but he quickly saw the limitations of his teacher, who could never get beyond the received philosophical theories of the day to see what actually lay before him on the operating table.

In 1833 Rokitansky was appointed prosector for the Vienna General Hospital and worked on literally tens of thousands of corpses in the ensuing years. Unlike similar institutions in other major cities, the Vienna General Hospital acted as a clearinghouse for the whole city, so Rokitansky saw far more bodies than his counterparts in Berlin or Paris. The autopsy of Beethoven was only the first of 59,786 that Rokitansky would perform during his spectacular career.

In this unique position, Rokitansky (by virtue of the sheer volume of bodies at his disposal) saw things no one else had noticed before. His dissections and lectures changed much about the way we see the body, and his teachings ushered in a renaissance of medical knowledge that would come be known as the Second

Vienna Medical School and that was, as one historian recently put it, "centered on the mortuary of the Vienna General Hospital, around Carl von Rokitansky's autopsy table."[152]

Whatever legacy Gall and Spurzheim had bequeathed to Wagner's generation, Rokitansky was singularly influential in demolishing it. Through his insights into the corpse and its pathologies, he opened the study of anatomy to a new generation of gifted doctors ready to be freed of the shackles of superstition and philosophy and to understand what lay before them. Foreign doctors and scholars came from all over to learn from Rokitansky, and by the 1860s nearly every leading clinician and pathologist could say that he had been a student of Rokitansky's at one point or another.

One such illustrious student was the physician Karl Haller, who had studied with Rokitansky in Vienna before setting up his own practice. In 1852 he paid his old teacher a visit, bearing with him two strange gifts that he had received from a patient some number of years back—a certain Johann Nepomuk Peter, who had given the objects to Haller for safekeeping as he was approaching death. That had been in 1839, and now, thirteen years later, Haller could think of no better place for these bizarre specimens than the collection of the "Father of Morbid Anatomy," as Rokitansky had come to be known.

[152] Erna Lesky, *The Vienna Medical School of the 19th Century*, Translated by L. Williams and I. S. Levij (Baltimore: Johns Hopkins University Press, 1976), p. 106.

Rokitansky received them graciously and unwrapped the two parcels, revealing two human skulls. One, Haller explained, had belonged to a little-known and long-forgotten actress, Elizabeth Roose.

The other had belonged to Joseph Haydn.

PART THREE

THE FATE

OF HIS BONES

I hear the skull, at every spurt,

Beg his friend:

"When is this brutal, ridiculous sport

Going to end?

That stuff that from your mouth you scatter

In the air like rain,

You blind murderer, is the matter

Of my blood and brain!"

· Charles Baudelaire, "Love and the Skull"

CHAPTER ELEVEN

A City

of Corpses

Ever since Gerhard von Breuning had discovered that Beethoven's temporal bones were missing, he had kept his eye out for them. About ten years after the 1863 exhumation, a man named Joseph Hyrtl, himself one of the greatest anatomists of his age, told Breuning he had seen the missing hearing organs many years earlier, sealed in a glass vessel in the possession of Vienna's coroner Anton Dotter. How Dotter had come by them, or what had happened to them since, Hyrtl couldn't say, and Breuning's attempts to track them down were ultimately fruitless. But Joseph Hyrtl had something else to show Breuning, perhaps equally interesting: the skull of Wolfgang Amadeus Mozart.

Since Joseph Rothmayer had been seized by an "animated musical enthusiasm" and plucked the skull out of its third-class grave in 1793, it had changed hands a few times. It was given first to Joseph Radschopf, Rothmayer's successor as sexton of St. Marx, who in turn gave Mozart's head to Jakob Hyrtl in 1842. Jakob was a copper engraver and amateur musician, and on his death in 1868 the skull fell to his brother, Joseph, who, of the two Hyrtls, was clearly the one for whom the skull was destined.

Like Joseph Carl Rosenbaum, Joseph Hyrtl had been born in Eisenstadt and had come to Vienna to make his name. Jakob and Joseph's father had been a member of the prince's celebrated orchestra, and like Rosenbaum they had grown up surrounded by music—when Joseph had begun his education, he had put himself through high school by earning money as a choir boy. Like Rokitansky, Joseph Hyrtl had learned under the system of rote memorization of the First Vienna School. It was a miserable, stifling system of education designed to discourage individuality and creative thinking. One teacher in particular Hyrtl would later describe as a "man who idled away 30 years of his lazy life in the desecrated chair of anatomy. As a teacher he made no intellectual bequest to any of his students, among whom I should consider myself one, and his sole function seems to have been to fill the lecture-hall with the size of his belly."[153]

Hyrtl found his calling in the study of comparative anatomy. He began collecting all manner of different animal species, requesting specimens from various Austrian consulates as far away as Beirut and Havana. While George Combe saw phrenology as the key to the manifold mysteries of the universe and the road-map to God's divine plan, Hyrtl sought the same revelations in comparative anatomy, whose purpose was "to establish out of the wealth of facts, and the bare treasures of sporadic experiences . . .

---

[153] Lesky, *The Vienna Medical School of the 19ʰ Century,* p. 69.

the inherent linkage with the unity and universality of the life of Nature." Comparative anatomy was, he claimed, a "philosophical science" in which one could determine "how the same idea of life can manifest itself in the most varied shapes, how the plan and the laws of its structure and functions marked every individual as being relatively perfect, i.e., possessing the highest expediency for his existence."[154] Hyrtl's interest in comparative anatomy, then, went beyond simply lining up the arteries of different animals and looking for differences—it was instead a final flowering of a certain Romantic spirit in an increasingly modern age.

Hyrtl married this passion for the manifold objects of the natural world to a technical brilliance that kept him relevant in the changing landscape of medicine, specifically with scientific preservations, a practice with a long heritage. Frederick Ruysch had been the first to experiment with injecting resins and wax into arteries and veins in the late seventeenth century as a means of preserving specimens. Ruysch, though, was an artist as much as an anatomist, and his mummies were arranged more for aesthetic impact than for scientific taxonomy. It was Joseph Hyrtl who elevated this "Ruyschian art" to a science, unleashing a new "despotism of injections" in his bedroom as a student. The process Hyrtl perfected was known as corrosive anatomy: One identifies the part of the body to be preserved and injects its blood vessels with wax or another preservative. Then the surrounding tissues are corroded away so that a specific tissue or capillary structure can

[154] Ibid., p. 212.

be revealed. Hyrtl became so well known for his preparations that museums from Rio de Janeiro to Stockholm enlisted his services; soon Hyrtl preparations were to be found in museums the world over.

In his cramped, poorly lit rooms at the University of Prague (where he had been made professor at twenty-six), Hyrtl began to build one of the most elaborate collections of anatomical specimens and preparations in the world. It was here that he began giving lectures on anatomy in the back room and established his reputation as a first-rate polymath and teacher, a reputation cemented with the publication of his *Handbook of Topographic Anatomy*, the first applied-anatomy textbook. The book was an instant success, translated into dozens of languages and reaching twenty editions in a few years. It catapulted Hyrtl to medical stardom.

While Hyrtl perfected corrosive preservations, Rokitansky continued to perfect dissection, and under the two of them, Vienna changed from a city of music to a city of corpses. While countries like Britain and America struggled to come up with viable laws to permit dissection, Vienna could boast that it provided over two thousand corpses a year to its anatomists and pathologists. As far back as Emperor Joseph II in the previous century, the Hapsburg Empire had developed a more permissive attitude toward dissection, though Joseph II's burial reforms had stalled during the Napoleonic Wars. Now they leaped forward once again—in the massive General Hospital where Rokitansky worked, unclaimed bodies were turned over to the anatomists as fair repayment for free treatment in the hospital. In the years between 1851 and 1854, the Vienna General Hospital disgorged 11,458 bodies to waiting doctors.

In Vienna you could buy a corpse for 1.5 guldens, a fraction of what Rosenbaum had paid to bribe the grave digger for Haydn's head. Corpses for dissection were known as "study corpses," "free-of-charge corpses," "failed corpses," and "Arimathaea corpses" (so named for the St. Joseph of Arimathaea Society, a benevolent organization devoted to burying the destitute).[155] In such a climate corpses were plentiful, but no one had it easier than Rokitansky himself. As the city's star pathologist and something of a national treasure, Rokitansky had been given secret access to literally any body in Vienna. If he needed a particular corpse, he would simply notify the chief municipal public health officer, who would in turn instruct the appropriate grave digger to bury the body in a shallow grave so it could be easily dug up by one of Rokitansky's assistants later that night. In order to keep the deceased's family from protesting, the grave diggers were sworn to secrecy, and so, in this city of the dead, Carl von Rokitansky claimed dominion over all.[156]

In such a position Rokitansky could have had any famous head stolen—but Haydn's head came to him as a gift. When Rosenbaum had given the skull to Peter, he made him promise to eventually turn it over to the Society for the Friends of Music.

---

[155] Tatjana Buklijas, "Cultures of Death and Politics of Corpse Supply: Anatomy in Vienna 1848-1914," *Bulletin of the History of Medicine*, No. 82 (Fall 2008), pp. 582-583.
[156] Ibid., p. 589.

But after Peter's death his wife had tried to return it to Eisenstadt, only to be informed by the Esterhazy sexton that they already had a head of Joseph Haydn, thanks all the same, and were not in need of another one. So the skull went to Peter's physician, Karl Haller, and then to Rokitansky, both times with the provision that it ultimately get to the society. Rokitansky agreed to this, but like Haller he saw no hurry and would keep the skull for some years in his collection.

Likewise Hyrtl added the skull of Mozart to his other specimens, attaching a note identifying its provenance that included a line from Horace: *"Musa vitat mori!"*—"Inspiration outlives death." By the time the skull of Mozart came into Hyrtl's possession in 1868, Rokitansky had had Haydn's skull in his collection for sixteen years, and Romeo Seligmann had had the Beethoven skull fragments for five years (which he was obliged to keep secret). Thus, the skulls of three of Vienna's greatest composers had found their way, each through different means, into the hands of three of the shining lights of Viennese medicine. It was a changing of the guard, of sorts, an acknowledgment that the soul of Vienna lay in medicine as much as in music—the heads of the city's old masters, in glass cases and zinc boxes, conferring legitimacy on the next generation of thinkers.

And while Rokitansky could proudly display Haydn's head in his cabinet, it wasn't clear that the doctor had much clinical use for it. For Gall the three important categories were the criminal, the insane, and the genius. The heads of the famous had been pilfered, sold, and treasured as representatives of this final category.

They had value to the scientific community as more than simple relics so long as "genius" as a category was still worth studying and so long as one could hope to "fix the organ of imagination" somewhere on the skull. But as the Romantic gave way to the modern, so too did the correlation between mind and body on which Gall had based his insights.

Instead of the criminal or the genius or even the insane, there was now increasingly just one overarching category, the diseased. Rokitansky's *Handbook of Pathological Anatomy* discussed the skull at length, but one is hard-pressed to find any trace whatsoever of Gall. "Increase in the size of the skull, when congenital, involves an excessive development of the brain, or, what is more frequent, hydrocephalus," one passage reads. Exponentially more useful for the treatment of disease, and exponentially less poetic than Gall or Spurzheim, the medical discourse surrounding the bumps on the skull no longer spoke of amativeness or acquisitiveness but of anomalies: "The dimensions of the skull rarely enlarge at any period after birth . . . without some appearance of absorption of the vitreous table, or separation of the sutures; still more rarely does it occur at mature age when the bones are completely formed, and almost never when the sutures are closed."[157]

The difference between Gall's and Rokitansky's regimes of medicine is stunning, a massive paradigm shift of seismic significance. They seem to be of different millennia, not simply forty

---

[157] Carl von Rokitansky, *A Manual of Pathological Anatomy*, in four volumes, translated by William Edward Swaine, Edward Sieveking, Charles Hewitt Moore, and George E. Day (Philadelphia: Blanchard and Lea, 1855), Vols. 3 & 4, p. 162.

years apart. And, in a real sense, they were. Gall's medicine, for all its fidelity to the Enlightenment, proceeded from a belief that metaphysics and anatomy were basically two extensions of the same inquiry: the understanding of humankind. In contrast, Rokitansky understood that even though both might take the human as their starting point, their methodologies were of such different ilk that one had to begin by completely separating them. One could philosophize and one could anatomize, but not at the same time.

THE PASSION FOR pathological anatomy that Rokitansky had helped spark reached all over the globe. Vienna became an essential stop for doctors the world over, particularly from America and England. The Viennese universities held special six-week courses for foreigners, which, while enormously lucrative, were so numerous that they threatened to encroach on the city's supply of bodies. The Irish physician William Wilde—who had examined Jonathan Swift's skull when it had been unearthed and would one day father a son named Oscar—wrote from one such course of "the many opportunities to gain knowledge" in anatomy where "the supply with dissectible bodies is plentiful."[158]

In 1848, the same year that Vienna burned with revolution, the Norwich Pathological Society was formed. Its members met quarterly in the Norwich and Norfolk Hospital Museum, where

---

[158] Buklijas, "Cultures of Death and Politics of Corpse Supply," p. 586.

they were joined by the museum's newest occupant, Sir Thomas Browne. For the most part, it was a bad time for specimens of suspended animation; in the same chaos that had destroyed Angelo Soliman, Hyrtl's house caught fire and his entire collection of preservations burned, forcing him to start again from scratch.

THE FOLLOWING YEAR Romeo Seligmann petitioned for a chair in the history of medicine. Seligmann's interests had always stretched beyond the medical arts: He had been a regular at the Silver Coffee House, where a circle of artists and philosophers, including Grillparzer and Schubert, habitually talked long into the morning hours. For Seligmann, this was just as fascinating as the study of medicine; he was a renaissance man in the old mode, interested in the vast history of thought and its expressions in science and art through the millennia. In this he was similar to Hyrtl, whose romantic passions for the secrets behind life sometimes fell out of step with the rigid empiricism of the Second Vienna School. But at least Hyrtl had his two great practical achievements—corrosive anatomy and the *Handbook of Topographic Anatomy*—guaranteeing his influence and relevance. Seligmann faced a much harder road.

The history of medicine, as a field, had always been valued in the same way that the history of any discipline was useful, in learning from one's forebears and joining a larger conversation. Such was Seligmann's goal; he sought out obscure medical treatises in Arabic, Persian, and Greek, tracking these different cultures through the eons, looking for traces of modern knowledge in ancient wisdom. But Rokitansky and the men who followed him had changed Viennese medicine to such a degree that it was no longer clear that this archaic history had any use. The revelations of the autopsy's knife swept away thousands of years of medical knowledge in a stroke.

So when Seligmann applied for the establishment of a professorship in medical history in 1849, he knew he might have an unreceptive audience. His application to the collegium of professors was for the establishment of a chair of history of medicine *and* epidemiology, this last term added because it was still believed, at least by some, that "the history of mass diseases must be regarded as an inseparable part of the cultural history of mankind."[159]

Despite help from his many friends, the majority of the board was not impressed, and his application was turned down by a vote of eight to three. "The history of medicine is no necessity," stated Joseph Skoda, who was in many ways equal to Rokitansky in terms of fame and impact. "With regard to epidemiology it must be stated that the students receive information on epidemics in the lectures on pathology."[160] A chair in the history of medicine would ultimately come about, but Seligmann would be appointed only at the lower rank of associate professor, so it would be clear where this pursuit stood in the hierarchy of knowledge.

---

[159] Lesky, *The Vienna Medical School of the 19th Century,* p. 569.
[160] Ibid.

Seligmann's troubles revealed the depth of change that Viennese medicine had undergone. He was easily the intellectual equal of Hyrtl, if not Rokitansky, yet he didn't flourish. He was a polymath, not unlike Thomas Browne, and was as interested in the obscure bits of Sanskrit on the humors as he was in modern pathology. But the era had little use for such knowledge. Those who advanced did so through specialization and by careful attention not to the past but to what lay before them on the operating table.

CHAPTER TWELVE

SCIENTIFIC GOLGOTHAS

I n 1851 the Norfolk and Norwich Hospital Museum formally put on display its hundreds of calculi. The calculi (the general term for calcium deposits that form in the body, most notoriously in the kidneys and urinary tract) were its prized possessions: Since the hospital had opened in 1771 the doctors had made a habit of collecting passed stones from their patients as part of an ongoing project. By 1796 there were already nearly a hundred, and the collection had outgrown the cabinet designed for it. Until 1844 it had been kept in the operating rooms, but when the new hospital museum opened they were transferred and in 1851 finally placed in display cases "where, for the first time, the real value and beauty of this unmatched collection may be appreciated."[161] The museum also contained one former board member's skull, of course, but from the present board's point of view his

---

[161] Peter Eade, *The Norfolk and Norwich Hospital, 1770 to 1900* (London: Jarrold and Sons, 1900) p. 91.

head was far less exciting than the ever-growing collection of stones and other detritus spit out by the body.

That same year, in Philadelphia, Samuel George Morton died, bringing to an end a long, distinguished career that spawned an increasingly problematic legacy. Morton wasn't the first to suggest that intelligence was associated with cranial volume, or that some human races were more advanced than others. But he was to become iconically associated with the branch of science known as craniometry, partly because he came of age at a particular moment in history and partly because he had more skulls than anyone else.

If Gall had taught science anything, it was that if you wanted to say something about a skull, you first needed lots of them. And the second half of the nineteenth century saw a proliferation of skull collections that would have made Gall envious. But it wasn't just phrenologists like the Fowlers who collected skulls—all manner of scientists began collections, taking heads from anywhere they could find them.

Everyone wanted skulls. Joseph Barnard Davis had begun building a collection in Britain, and in Vienna Joseph Hyrtl collected them for his ongoing project of comparative anatomy. There was of course the collection of Franz Joseph Gall himself, who had died in Paris in 1828. Gall's collection was subsequently acquired by the natural historian and zoologist Georges Cuvier on behalf of France's Museum of Natural History. Cuvier had been extremely doubtful of Gall's methods, believing cranioscopy to be utterly baseless. But when Gall died in 1828 and his possessions went up for sale, Cuvier saw that there were any number of things one could learn from Gall's specimens beyond locating the supposed organs of personality. And so he fought hard to purchase the collection for the museum where he worked. Phrenology's loss would be natural history's gain. As Gertrude Stein might have said, a skull is a skull is a skull.

In this growing frenzy for crania, no one's collection was greater than that of Samuel George Morton. For years Morton had been developing a collection that would rival the Fowlers' store on 308 Broadway for the title of "American Golgotha." Skulls were Morton's overriding obsession. His friends and colleagues sent him heads from all over the world. A particularly rich supply came from his friend George Gliddon, who was the U.S. consul for Cairo and who sent Morton over a hundred skulls and heads of mummies that he had plundered from Egyptian tombs. In addition to such gifts, Morton spent somewhere between ten and fifteen thousand dollars acquiring specimens for his collection, an astronomical sum in the years before the Civil War.

A French admirer of Morton's collection, Louis Agassiz, wrote to his mother in 1846, "Imagine a series of 600 skulls, most of Indians from all tribes who inhabit or once inhabited all of America. Nothing like it exists anywhere else. This collection, by itself, is worth a trip to America."[162] At the time of Morton's

---

[162] Quoted in Stephen J. Gould, *The Mismeasure of Man* (New York: W. W. Norton, 1981) p. 50

death that number had reached over a thousand, and a fellow scientist remarked of the collection that, "at this moment, it forms one of the greatest boasts of our country in relation to natural science."[163]

Morton's collection was an astounding scientific record, a wonder of the modern world if ever there was one. Everyone marveled at its sheer volume. Possessed with such a vast set of data, Morton had been in a unique position to make substantive claims about racial differences in skull size and relative intelligence. Because of this he was taken seriously, as if he alone were in a position to make pronouncements on the human head. Oliver Wendell Holmes, who had ridiculed "Professors Bumpus and Crane," singled out Morton's skulls, which "from their very nature are permanent data for all future students of ethnology," for praise.[164]

The debate raging at the time was between monogenism and polygenism. Monogenists argued that all the various human races—the European, the African, the American Indian, and so on—were descended from Adam and Eve and that the differences in characteristics could be explained by the "degeneration" of certain races, most notably Africans. Polygenists, in contrast, held that there was simply no way to suggest that the variety of human specimens descended from the same source and held that the "inferior" races were entirely different species. Morton was a

---

[163] George B. Wood, *A Biographical Memoir of Samuel George Morton* (Philadelphia: T. K. and P. G. Collins, 1853) p. 13.
[164] Quoted in Gould, *The Mismeasure of Man*, p. 51

polygenist, a belief he arrived at in part because the Great Deluge, by his reckoning, had happened only four thousand years earlier, which did not leave enough time to create the diversity he saw before him.

Morton saw in his skull collection the measure of all humanity. It was clear enough that cranial capacity distinguished humans from other species. If one could show that different races had definitively different brain sizes, one might be able to prove beyond the shadow of a doubt that they belonged to different species. The question was one of method, that is, how to measure intelligence.

The German physician Rudolph Wagner had devised one method of measuring brain size: He cut up paper into tiny squares, which he then inserted into the convolutions of the brain, measuring how far into the brain each slip of paper went. From there he calculated the entire surface area of a brain, taking into account its folds and fissures. It was, needless to say, not the most efficient process.

The system used by Morton and others was a great deal simpler, and certainly cruder, but it caught on. He simply filled the cranial cavity of each of his heads with mustard seed, then calculated its volume and entered the measure according to his categories of ethnicity. Eventually he discovered that mustard seed produced wildly inconsistent results, so he switched to lead shot, which was apparently more reliable. Plaster casts were of little use to craniometry because they could not give an accurate sense of brain volume. Skull thickness, hair, and other anomalies could all contribute to an unreliable measurement. So for Morton there remained only one true means of calculating brain size—the skull itself.

Morton's findings, published in his *Crania Americana* (1839) and *Crania Aegyptiaca* (1844), were enormously influential in appearing to demonstrate, by means of his system, that there was a clear hierarchy in brain size between different peoples. At the top of his scheme was the European, followed by the American Indian, and then the African, just one short step above the ape. Morton's findings seemed to show, through the cold, objective truth of math and statistics, that the European brain was conclusively larger than that of other ethnic groups.

But there are lies, damned lies, and then there are statistics. In his book *The Mismeasure of Man*, Stephen Jay Gould cited the numerous methodological errors that Morton made in his calculations. For one, he failed to account for differences in sex and body size when calculating brain volume. He tended to include small-bodied Incas in his American Indian sample so as to bring down that average but excluded small-bodied Hindus from his Caucasian sample so as to keep that number higher. His a priori assumptions repeatedly led him to false conclusions— demonstrably false from his own data. On top of this, Morton made elementary computational and methodological errors, all of which coincidentally favored his preexisting beliefs and assumptions.

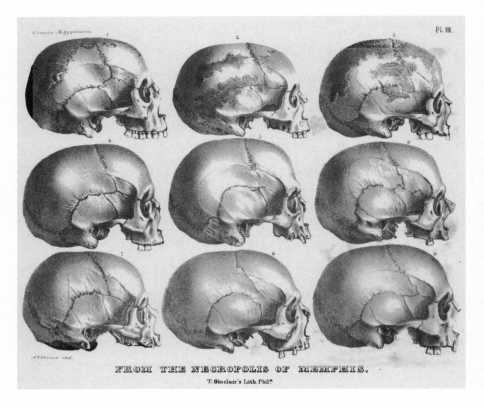

Skulls from Samuel George Morton's Crania Aegyptiaca

And yet, Gould concluded, "through all this juggling, I detect no sign of fraud or conscious manipulation. Morton made no attempt to cover his tracks and I must presume that he was unaware he had left them. He explained all his procedures and published all his raw data. All I can discern is an a priori conviction about racial ranking so powerful that it directed his tabulations along preestablished lines." This in and of itself might not be so lamentable, Gould noted, if Morton hadn't been "widely hailed as the objectivist of his age, the man who would rescue American science from the mire of unsupported speculation."[165]

As Rokitansky was developing pathological anatomy into a major field of modern medicine, Morton was working to provide an empirical basis for racism, giving it a scientific justification and laying out a flawed methodological roadmap for others to follow. Morton adapted to the scientific climate that was blossoming around him—one that relied on direct measurement—and used it erroneously to confirm a long-held belief in racial difference and hierarchy. As with phrenology, at the heart of this scientific field was the skull, which once again came to be the locus of classification.

But there was a crucial difference between the way phrenology and craniometry treated the skull. The phrenologist looked to the skull to find a hidden map of the character and the history of its owner, laid out in physical form just as a seismograph records an earthquake. Craniometrists like Morton were looking for something grander: the history not of an individual but of the entire human race. Each skull, they believed, was a fragment of a grand epic that stretched back to Adam and Eve. One needed only to collect enough fragments to discern the larger picture.

And in this sense they were right: Modern anthropology, now purged of the legacy of racial superiority, still relies on the skulls of our ancestors, and of the different tribes of the world, to fill in the story of human creation and evolution. But what Mor-

---

[165] Ibid., p. 69.

ton failed to understand was that even his massive collection—a thousand skulls—was infinitesimal within hundreds of millions of human lives. And as is the case when one has such a small portion of the puzzle, those fragments could be assembled as the basis of many projected pictures.

Morton didn't live long enough to see the Civil War or the emancipation of those who had been kept in bondage in no small part because of the racist science he helped to pioneer. But his legacy continued well after his death, and it struck a chord in European scientists looking for conclusive evidence that they lay at the pinnacle of human development.

With so much invested in a proof of European intellectual superiority, the heads of those great men whose creativity had defined an age—men like Browne—would seem particularly important. If Morton's theories were to hold up, it seemed necessary to prove that just as Europeans had bigger brains than their African or Indian counterparts, European geniuses must have even bigger brains than regular Europeans.

Across the Atlantic, in Paris, a landmark dispute took place with the goal of settling this very question.

THE AVERAGE EUROPEAN brain was said to weigh around 1,400 grams. Numerous examples had been found of great artists and thinkers who had heavier brains—the brain of Georges Cuvier, the naturalist who had bought Gall's skull collection, had been recorded as weighing an astonishing 1,830 grams. The

Russian novelist Ivan Turgenev's brain weighed a mighty 2,012 grams, and Lord Byron's brain had been placed somewhere between 1,800 grams and a massive 2,238 grams. The question of whether there was a reliable correlation between genius and large brain size was one that consumed two famous craniometrists in the middle of the nineteenth century—the battle between Paul Broca and Louis Pierre Gratiolet would go down in history as a landmark in the evolution of scientific thinking.[166]

Paul Broca was a French anatomist and anthropologist—and Morton's most ardent and capable follower. Broca, who had founded the Anthropological Society of Paris in 1859, refined many of Morton's methodologies while keeping the aim much the same. After Morton's death it was Broca who assumed the mantle of spokesman for craniometry and defended it vociferously against the few scientists who dared to assert that there was no measurable difference in brain size between Europeans and Africans. Friedrich Tiedemann published one such critique, and Broca's response was savage. He thoroughly denounced the German doctor, conclusively demonstrating that Tiedemann had made systematic errors in his calculations and thus invalidating his findings. Of course Morton had made the exact same kinds of misstep, albeit in the other direction, but Broca, who had exten-

---

[166] My account of Broca and Gratiolet follows Gould, *The Mismeasure of Man*, pp. 83-102, and *The Panda's Thumb: More Reflections in Natural History* (New York: W. W. Norton, 1980) pp. 145-151, Francis Schiller, *Paul Broca: Founder of French Anthropology, Explorer of the Brain* (New York: Oxford University Press, 1992), pp. 165-211, and Russell Shorto, *Descartes' Bones: A Skeletal History of the Conflict Between Faith and Reason* (New York: Doubleday, 2008), pp. 167-206.

sively reviewed Morton's work, did not see fit to comment on Morton's irregularities.

An even more radical threat was to come in a theory advocated by Louis Pierre Gratiolet, a rival anatomist whose claim to fame lay in understanding the different hemispheres of the brain and identifying its four lobes. Gratiolet went so far as to argue that brain size simply bears no correlation to intelligence whatsoever, effectively declaring that the whole project of craniometry was fallacious.

In a meeting held on June 6, 1961, which would go down in the annals of craniometry as one of the study's most famous days, Gratiolet attempted to disprove the prevailing hypothesis that skull size could be a useful metric for intelligence. He reviewed the data on the brain of the mathematician Carl Friedrich Gauss and concluded, "This is not an enormous brain; this is not an exceptional weight." The same was true of the famous mineralogist Johann Hausman. Most famously, Gratiolet set out to challenge the notion that Georges Cuvier's brain had been exceptionally large. But this time, in true theatrical fashion (and lacking the zoologist's actual skull), Gratiolet brandished Cuvier's hat. He had taken it to the most renowned hatter in Paris, M. Puriau, who had told him that it was a large hat (21.8 by 16 centimeters), to be sure, but not exceptionally so—Puriau estimated that 30 percent of his customers bought hats of that size. Furthermore, Gratiolet reasoned, Cuvier was known for his "extremely abundant mass of hair," which could—could it not?—account for a larger hat size. "The measurements that I have just pointed out," he said, "seem to prove rather obviously that if the skull of Cuvier had a considerable size, this size is not absolutely exceptional and unique."[167]

For Broca, this conclusion was intolerable. Tiedemann may have been blinded by his preconceived notions that all races are innately equal, but at least he had understood the fundamental importance of the skull in science. Gratiolet wanted to end the skull's supremacy altogether. Broca began his riposte to Gratiolet by stating the obvious: If there is really no correlation between head size and intelligence, then "the study of the brains of human races would lose most of its interest and utility."[168]

What Gratiolet was proposing, Broca pointed out, was not just a differing opinion but an attack on the foundation of an entire branch of science. If one were really to take his ludicrous ideas seriously, Broca went on, whole careers, perhaps even lives, would be ruined: "The great importance of craniology has struck anthropologists with such force that many among us have neglected the other parts of our science in order to devote ourselves almost exclusively to the study of skulls." It was a noble goal, central to science, and far more important than Gratiolet's nonsensical conclusions about a hat. Broca concluded by noting that with "such data, we hoped to find some information relevant to the intellectual value of the various human races."[169]

[167] Quoted in Shorto, *Descartes' Bones*, pp. 195-196.
[168] Quoted in Gould, *The Mismeasure of Man*, p. 83.
[169] Ibid.

As an object, the skull had maintained a religious and symbolic weight since the earliest days of humanity: It was the image of death par excellence, the most singular relic of one's mortal remains. It was the sole bone amid a pile of such bones that could definitively identify remains as belonging to a human. But what Broca's comments reinforce is how quickly it had also become the preeminent object of scientific discourse and inquiry. In less than one hundred years the skull had become the founding and central document of not just phrenology and craniometry but psychology and anthropology, criminology and psychiatry. For that matter, it was essential to the programs of slavery and segregation, colonialism and imperialism, patriarchy and misogyny. Next to perhaps the Bible itself, the human skull was *the* inalienable proof of the unchallenged suitability of the white male for dominion over the entire world.

CHAPTER THIRTEEN

A MEASURE
OF FAME

The early 1870s marked a number of important changes for Rokitansky and for Hyrtl, for Paul Broca back in Paris, for the Norwich surgeon Charles Williams—but nothing, as it turned out, lay in store for the head that had once produced the *Religio Medici*.

In Vienna, long-awaited reforms were under way: Since 1848 Rokitansky had been considered an intellectual leader, and his revolutionary scientific approach seemed to mirror the age. Accordingly, he pushed for educational reforms at all levels of Austrian medicine. He argued that the medical establishment should be severed from its long-standing ties to the emperor and the aristocracy, and that the church should likewise be excluded. He finally achieved these reforms in 1872–1873, effectively liberating medical practice from its centuries-old dependence on aristocratic privilege.

It wasn't that Rokitansky was immune to the same Romanticism that burned in Hyrtl and Seligmann. While his professional goal had always been (in one historian's words) to "arouse German medicine from its natural-philosophical dream," his personal philosophy was more nuanced.[170] He had come of age reading Kant (as had been required for medical school when he was a student), and he had never lost that part of his personality that friends referred to as his "poetical side" and he himself called "that bent towards speculation." For the most part he had been able to keep a line of separation between his empirical studies and his personal faith, though in the English preface to Rokitansky's manual, the editor noted that it had been necessary to abridge "somewhat the author's general introduction, partly because, totally unlike the general tendency of the work, it is of too 'transcendental' a character to suit the English language or to harmonize with English ideas; but more particularly because it is interwoven with a train of speculative reasoning upon the relation between power and matter, which might, in this country, very possibly give rise to misinterpretation and rebuke."[171]

Rokitansky's colleague Joseph Hyrtl, meanwhile, had retired out of sight. While he had enjoyed early fame with his *Handbook of Topographic Anatomy*, his life had been filled with more disappointments than Rokitansky's. A long-running and bitter feud with a rival anatomist had cost him dearly in prestige; he had been on the faculty at the University of Vienna for thirty years, yet was never appointed dean. "Disturbed and disappointed," he had

---

[170] Quoted in Lesky, *The Vienna Medical School of the 19th Century*, p. 107.
[171] Rokitansky, *Manual of Pathological Anatomy*, p. viii.

written in 1869, "I withdrew into my professional work, spent my life between my workroom and my lecture hall, became taciturn and therefore disliked by my colleagues, as I still am." In a city where anatomy was given such prominence, the virtuoso Hyrtl, whose preparations were sought the world over, was never given an adequate workspace either at the hospital or at the university. Since 1854 he had worked out of a building that had been built as a stable and had previously been used as a rifle factory. "Slowly," he wrote, "I also learned to put up with these conditions. Only he who knows how and where anatomy is attended to here, will be able to understand how difficult it was for me to bear these conditions."[172]

The same year Rokitansky's reforms were finally passed, Hyrtl relocated to Leipzig, claiming his weakening eyesight as his official reason for retirement. There he established a small room and laboratory in a ruin near a cemetery. In his tiny quarters he kept his rarest and most perfect anatomical specimens. In his bedroom, which was barely big enough to admit a bed, the only decoration was his collection of skulls, which adorned the walls and looked down on him while he slept.

Hyrtl had built his collection during the same era as Broca and Morton, but he was fundamentally opposed to craniometry. A devout Catholic, he had come to believe in Darwin's theory of evolution, but only to a point. He did not believe that the brain was subject to evolution; it was instead, he thought, divinely inserted into the body by the hand of God Himself.

---

[172] Quoted in Lesky, *The Vienna Medical School of the 19th Century*, p. 215.

AROUND THE SAME time the Norwich and Norfolk Hospital celebrated its centenary, and as a tribute, Charles Williams—who had been appointed house-surgeon in 1858 and promoted to assistant surgeon in 1869—presented to the hospital a collection of portraits of past board members. A gathering of lithographs, photographs, and paintings, it told the hospital's hundred-year history through a line of eminent men, each conferring great dignity on the boardroom where their portraits were hung. In addition to past presidents, surgeons, and distinguished benefactors were three portraits of Sir Thomas Browne, the patron saint of Norwich medicine. Hanging next to him was the portrait of Dr. Edward Lubbock, the Norwich physician who had purchased his head in 1840 and left it to the hospital after his death in 1848.

AND LAST, IN Paris, Paul Broca was running into problems with his craniometrics.

In their famous debate in 1861 Gratiolet had been so thoroughly defeated by Broca that at the subsequent meeting he had gone so far as to apologize for having brought up "the little spark that caused a philosophical explosion." But in a way Gratiolet had won the war, even after losing the battle. Less and less was said in those years about the great heads of famous men. While the hefty brain of Turgenev could always be singled out as proof of genius and brain size, such a metric inevitably produced embarrassments, such as Walt Whitman, the poet of phrenology, whose brain weighed a meager 1,282 grams. Leigh Hunt later commented of John Keats that his "head was a particular puzzle for the phrenologist, being remarkably small in the skull; a singularity he has in common with Lord Byron and Mr. Shelley, none of whose hats I could get on."[173] Most embarrassingly, Franz Joseph Gall's own brain was found to only weigh 1,198 grams (though this was a transcription error; the actual weight was 1,312—better, but still not great). Whether you judged by hat size, skull volume, or brain weight, great thinkers and artists were inevitably going to crop up whose measures were below average.

Other anomalies appeared: Broca had measured an African brain that weighed a problematic 1,500 grams, over 200 grams more than the "average" African brain was supposed to weigh. One of his students, Paul Topinard, thoughtfully explained this away by pointing out that the man in question had lived his life in Europe. Topinard went on to inquire, "May it not be asked whether the free negro living among Europeans has not a heavier brain than if he had remained in his own country, far removed from great intellectual excitement?"[174]

But as more and more of these "anomalies" came to light, craniometry had a harder time reconciling them with the general

---

[173] Leigh Hunt, *Selected Writings*, edited by David Jesson-Dibley (New York: Routledge, 2003), p. 105.
[174] Paul Topinard, *Anthropology*, translated by Robert T. H. Bartley (Philadelphia: J. B. Lippincot and Co., 1878) p. 311.

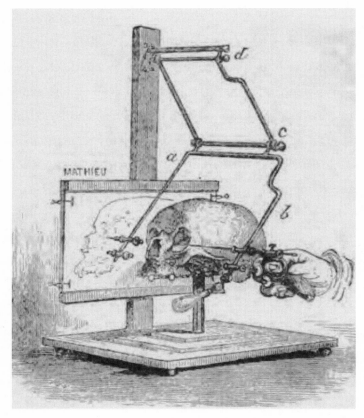

Craniometric Devices, from Paul Topinard's Anthropology

theory. Whereas a phrenologist, as Mark Twain had famously demonstrated, could find some indication of superlative genius on *any* head, determining the size of a particular brain was a bit more of an objective process (though obviously not entirely so). When it came to truly small-brained geniuses, there was little that could be done by way of fudging the data. Both, it turned out, were self-fulfilling hypotheses, each using the skull as a

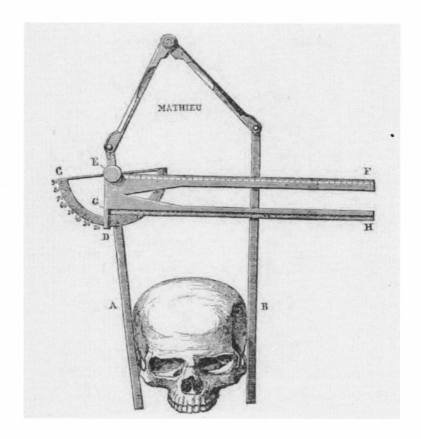

means to verify what was already believed, but whereas phrenology excelled at specifics, craniometry worked best as a science of averages.

Small-headed geniuses were a problem, to be sure, although they could conceivably be swept under the rug. But soon enough Broca began to find some even more problematic statistics with regard to certain ethnic groups. The more data he collected, the

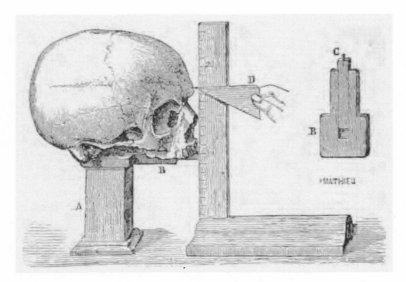

Craniometric Devices, from Paul Topinard's Anthropology

more apparent it became—even to someone with a knack for un-conscious manipulation of data—that certain "inferior" races had disturbingly large heads. In particular, a number of indige-nous peoples—Eskimos, Mongolians, and so on—had an aver-age head size greater than that of Europeans. Broca found himself in the unenviable position of reaching conclusions similar to those of Friedrich Tiedemann, whom he had lambasted decades earlier.

Craniometry's goal had always been a perfect statistical distri-bution, with Africans at the low end, indigenous populations of Asia and America slightly above that, and the European male at the top end. But by the early 1870s, Broca could no longer deny that this distribution was a myth.

Still, with his characteristic obtuseness, Broca did not dare admit that other races might be equal in intelligence to whites, as his data and methodology would have demanded. Nor did he abandon craniometry in favor of some other method of proving racial superiority. His attack on Gratiolet had revealed how much of his life he had already invested in the science. And so he did what anyone but a true scientist might have done: He selectively reinterpreted his data so that it would conform to his prejudices: "A table on which races were arranged by order of their cranial capacity would not represent the degrees of their superiority or inferiority, because size represents only one element of the problem. On such a table, Eskimos, Lapps, Malays, Tartars and several other peoples of the Mongolian type would surpass the most civilized people of Europe. A lowly race may therefore have a big brain."

In other words, the high end of the craniometric distribution was unreliable. But there was no need to dispense with the whole project. "This does not destroy the value of small brain size as a mark of inferiority," Broca wrote. "The table shows that West African blacks have a cranial capacity about 100 cc less than that of European races. To this figure, we may add the following: Caffirs, Nubians, Tasmanians, Hottentots, Australians. These examples are sufficient to prove that if the volume of the brain does not play a decisive role in the intellectual ranking of races, it nevertheless has a very real importance."[175]

---

[175] Quoted in Gould, *The Mismeasure of Man*, p. 87.

Under the weight of its own comprehensiveness, Broca's craniometry was becoming ever more convoluted in the quest for the justification of racism.

IN 1875, THREE years before his death, Rokitansky entrusted the Haydn skull to his sons, instructing them to turn it over to the Society for the Friends of Music, per Rosenbaum's and Peter's wishes. A year earlier Joseph Hyrtl had put his skulls up for sale. He had been in contact with Thomas Hewson Bache of Philadelphia about them for some time. He had already done an extensive series of preparations for Bache on the organs of hearing, but with the acquisition of the Hyrtl skulls Bache's collection went from being a private collection to what is now the Mütter Museum.

Joseph Hyrtl's collection of eighty-two skulls (meager compared to Morton's but still captivating) now occupies an entire wall of the museum's main gallery. Behind glass, dozens of skulls are arrayed in perfect geometric order, each one accompanied by a three-by-five card that lists nationality, name, and cause of death, with an occasional notation of cranial anomaly:

Moravia
Anton Mikschik, Age 17
Shoemaker's Apprentice
Suicide, because of discovered theft

Magyar (Hungarian) from Transylvania

Ladislaus Pal

Reformist, guerilla, and deserter

Executed by hanging

(bilateral flare of gonial angles)

Russia

Kasimir Ostrowsczynski, Age 30

For crime of grave insubordination, died under the most cruel scourging

Russia

Andrejew Sokoloff

Skopzi (Russian sect that believes in castration)

Died of self-inflicted removal of testicles

(dual left of supra-orbital formation)

Among these names is that of Francisca Seycora, who died at age nineteen of meningitis in the Vienna General Hospital and who is listed as a "famous Viennese prostitute." However well known Seycora might have been in her day, her fame was ephemeral—if anything, it was a fame passed from client to client, of which no written record now exists. It was certainly not enough to distinguish her from Mikschik, the distraught shoemaker's apprentice, or Sokoloff, dead from a botched castration. In the end she was just one of many, only another item in Hyrtl's collection.

Mozart's fame, of course, was of a different nature altogether; his skull, held aloft from the rest of the collection, was in a glass case and labeled with a line from Horace. Seycora's bears the inscription "Prominent temporal lines continue onto frontal bones."

It was an age when sample size and sheer volume meant far more than any single relic and thus an age when Seycora, paradoxically, as one of eighty-two meant more to collectors than did Mozart in his sample size of one. By the second half of the nineteenth century it was already abundantly clear that the heads of great men had no real scientific value. With the decline of phrenology as a viable scientific discipline, the heads of the famous, in their glass cases on velvet cushions, threatened to become once more nothing but elegant, secular relics.

CHAPTER FOURTEEN

SOME LAST PATHETIC QUIBBLING

Craniometry, with its averages and distributions, largely rendered the individual skull scientifically useless. But in his retort to Gratiolet, Broca had perhaps inadvertently heralded the end of the skull as the singular object of study altogether. Gratiolet, in his litany of examples, had drawn on the skull of Descartes, which he argued was not exceptionally large. In his response, Broca had commented, almost as an aside, that "the study of a skull, however complete, merely gives an approximate idea of the volume and above all the weight of the brain."[176] Lord Byron, if Leigh Hunt was to be believed, was a perfect case in point: Even with the second-heaviest brain ever measured, he still had a small hat, and thus his skull would hardly have been a useful indicator of his intelligence. The skull, in other words, was not always the most reliable metric, even in Broca's mind.

---

[176] Quoted in Shorto, *Descartes' Bones*, pp. 198-199.

Brains were soon to be the order of the day over skulls, since they held so much more information about the human mind and its secrets. And by the 1860s they could be preserved far better than they could in Gall's day. The German anatomist Johann Christian Reil had first discovered a way to preserve the brain in alcohol in 1809, though it took a few more decades before the process caught on. Alcohol was not ideal, as it had a difficult time penetrating tissue as dense as the human brain—the external surface of the brain tended to dry out and crack, while the interior turned to mush. But Reil's alcohol solution offered a much more promising method of studying the minds of the dead than simply referring to their skulls, and over the course of the nineteenth century it was gradually refined as it became more and more frequently used. Finally the preservative properties of formaldehyde were discovered and became the gold standard for wet preservation. Indeed, after Broca's death in 1880, it was his brain, not his skull, that was preserved and onto which his name was etched.

As brains replaced skulls as the measure of humanity, the legend of Sir Thomas Browne's skull continued to grow, passing in and out of reality like some half-remembered myth. In January 1886, Mr. C. A. Ward wrote to the long-running *Notes and Queries*, the scholarly clearinghouse of ephemeral knowledge and odd questions. "In what museum," he asked, "is the skull of Sir Thomas Browne to be seen, since the desecration of 1840?"[177] It

[177] C. A. Ward, in *Notes and Queries*, January 23, 1886, p. 68.

was almost as if such a thing couldn't be real. Surely that kind of grave robbing belonged to some other era.

In the next issue the surgeon Charles Williams replied that Browne's skull was indeed still to be found in the Norfolk and Norwich Hospital Museum. Williams had been promoted to full surgeon in 1878, upon the death of G. W. W. Frith, the first person to whom Skull George had tried to sell the head. In his reply Williams quoted his favorite passage from Browne's *Urn Burial*: "Truly the good knight may say, 'But who knows the fate of his bones, or how often he is to be buried? Who hath the oracles of his ashes, or whither they are to be scattered?" Then Williams ended with a flourish, "Since I began to write this note, *mirabile dictu*, some veritable hair from the head of our great physician has been deposited in my hands."[178]

In 1883, twelve years after the centenary, the new Norfolk and Norwich Hospital was opened. The museum was greatly expanded, and Browne found a new home in these enlarged dwellings, though he was still a marginal figure among the calculi and other preparations and was kept company by "a remarkable specimen of the skeleton of a rickety dwarf, executed many years ago in Norwich for a murder."[179] Sir Thomas's skull remained, almost like the mascot of a rival school held for ransom—the church and the hospital each laying claim to it as symbolic property.

---

[178] Charles Williams, in *Notes and Queries*, February 20, 1886, p. 165.
[179] Eade, *The Norfolk and Norwich Hospital*, p. 159.

IN 1888 BEETHOVEN'S remains were exhumed for the second time, and the small committee of scientists was given twenty minutes to examine the skull fragments. Though they barely remarked on the missing pieces (still in Seligmann's possession), their report did make one oddly emphatic point: Even taking into account Wagner's hatchet job and the subsequent treatment of the skull, one fact was beyond question: Beethoven's head was ugly. "It is an undeniable fact that Beethoven's skull agrees in no way with our concepts of beauty and harmony of form," they wrote in an uncharacteristically strident conclusion. "The hitherto quite pathetic quibbling and fault finding which we have seen from time to time lack any basis in fact."[180]

At issue was the forehead, which seemed too low and too sloped back to match the image of the composer with his lion's mane of hair. As discussed above, Breuning had suggested that because Beethoven's skull had been segmented and kept in such damp conditions prior to 1863, moisture had caused it to warp. The image of Beethoven in life had already become iconic: wild, disheveled hair, unkempt but with a burning look in his eyes. Not beautiful, perhaps, but a powerful appearance nonetheless. Based on the figure he cut in life, it was generally assumed that his skull would be equally stately, and if it didn't conform to our notions of what a beautiful skull should look like, if it didn't

[180] Quoted in Davies, *Beethoven in Person*, p. 115.

seem to fit the mold of all those paintings of Jerome and Mary Magdalene—well, Wagner and his botched autopsy were to blame. The 1888 committee asserted that this was nonsense, though they didn't mention Breuning by name: "The pronounced slope of the forehead," they wrote, "cannot be attributed either to prior loosening of the suture lines or post-mortem changes in the bones."[181]

Similar speculation had long dogged Browne's head, which also had a low, sloping forehead hardly becoming a European male of great renown. Some simply believed it could not be his skull. There were those who argued, against all other prevailing evidence, that it was the skull of a woman. And then there was the American surgeon who was shown the skull of Sir Thomas Browne, whereupon he "laughed heartily and replied that for his part he should class it as that of a Peruvian!"[182]

The inability of these skulls to conform to the notion of what a genius's head should look like would lead to continual disputes about their authenticity. As with Browne, the gender of Swedenborg's head had been repeatedly called into question. The sculptor John Flaxman had examined it in Charles Tulk's phrenological cabinet and declared, "How beautiful the form, how undulating the line here; here's no deficiency. . . . Why I should almost take it for a female head, were it not for the peculiar character of the forehead." The phrenologist Anna Fredrika Ehrenborg was even

---

[181] Ibid.
[182] Quoted in Tildesley, "Sir Thomas Browne," p. 41.

more emphatic when she visited the tomb in 1853. Ehrenborg was a close friend of the famous John Didrik Holm and was widely respected in phrenological circles. "One needs very little knowledge of phrenology," she later wrote, "to see that the skull could not have belonged to an excellent scientist, who, for 80 years, had preoccupied his brain in mental tasks from the lower and uttermost to the highest and innermost. It looked most like that of a woman, with fine harmonious organs."[183]

The doctors who looked at Beethoven's skull in 1888 had no patience for this type of unfounded speculation and wanted to make one thing clear: As the craniometry wars of polygenism versus monogenism and Broca versus Gratiolet receded into the distant past, it was absolutely clear that the shape of one's skull was no measure of genius.

THE PATHETIC QUIBBLING was to go on a bit longer. In the early 1890s controversy erupted surrounding the head of Charlotte Corday. Corday was not so much famous as infamous: During the French Revolution, she had come to the Jacobin radical Jean-Paul Marat's home and stabbed him while he was taking a bath (an image shortly immortalized by the painter Jacques-Louis David). Corday was a noteworthy specimen not because she was a representative of genius but because she was utterly unrepentant about her act, even as she ascended the scaffolding to the

[183] Quoted in Henschen, *Emanuel Swedenborg's Cranium*, p. 11.

guillotine, and was a virgin, a fact conclusively proven by a rather barbarous autopsy.[184]

In the inaugural issue of *L'Anthropologie*, Paul Topinard, Paul Broca's talented student and inheritor of his methods, published a craniometric analysis of Charlotte Corday's skull, which had been kept by Napoleon Bonaparte's descendents since 1815. "The skull, before my eyes," he wrote, "is yellow like dirty ivory; it is shiny, smooth, as, in a word, those skulls that have been neither buried in the bosom of the earth, nor exposed to the open air, but which have been prepared by maceration, then carefully placed and kept for a long time in a drawer of a cupboard, sheltered from atmospheric vicissitudes." While he offered a detailed analysis of the skull, he wasn't out to prove anything about it—no attempt was made to demonstrate any particular facet of Corday's character through her head. "Our project is not to describe the skull as if it were that of a known person," he explained, "with the objective of comparing craniological characteristics with the moral characteristics historically attributed to this person. We merely wish to take the opportunity for a study which could be carried out on any other skull."[185] Craniometry had reached the point where it recognized that individual skulls were useless for scientific study and could have meaning only in large samples.

But the Italian criminologist Cesare Lombroso was aghast at the sloppiness of Topinard's thinking. Of course, he argued, one

---

[184] Further information on the skull of Charlotte Corday can be found in Leslie Dick, *The Skull of Charlotte Corday and Other Stories* (New York: Scribner, 1995), pp. 1-32.
[185] Quoted in ibid., p. 7.

could make connections between skull shape and the subject's moral characteristics. Lombroso had discovered this revelation some twenty years earlier while working on the notorious criminal Vihella: "At the sight of that skull, I seemed to see all of a sudden, lighted up as a vast plain under a flaming sky, the problem of the nature of the criminal—an atavistic being who reproduces in his person the ferocious instincts of primitive humanity and the inferior animals." This animalistic tendency that gives rise to criminal behavior, Lombroso asserted, was particularly problematic in women: "If female born criminals are fewer in number than the males, they are often much more ferocious." Lombroso's explanation was simple: Atavistic tendencies in women are normally held in check by "piety, maternity, want of passion, sexual coldness, by weakness and in undeveloped intelligence."[186] But when these checks are absent, the inherent criminality of woman is unleashed.

Corday was a prime specimen for Lombroso, since her virginity and lack of repentance seemed completely to exemplify his theories. "Not even the purest political crime, that which springs from passion, is exempt from the law which we have laid down," he wrote in *The Female Offender*. "In the skull of Charlotte Corday herself, after a rapid inspection, I affirmed the presence of an extra-ordinary number of anomalies," Lombroso proclaimed, singling out "Topinard's very confused monograph" for the in-

[186] Cesare Lombroso, *The Female Offender* (New York: D. Appleton and Company, 1897), pp. 150–151.

ability to see what was plainly obvious.[187] Lombroso argued that had Corday been married and raised children, as she ought to have done, she would never have become an assassin. It took some work to make Topinard seem enlightened—Topinard who, not much earlier, had argued that African brains might grow larger in the intellectually exciting climate of Europe. But Lombroso's claims were yet one more version of the story that stretched as far back as Gall and even earlier: Biology is destiny, and it can and should be used to maintain social, sexual, and racial hierarchies.

Such an argument was anathema to Rokitansky, who had presided over massive changes in the medical industry and been responsible for countless breakthroughs and advances—today half-a-dozen conditions are named after him. Rokitansky had hoped that this age of scientific discovery would bring with it an equal advance in freedom and progress. And in 1848 the brief and intense flowering of democratic movements throughout Europe seemed to promise such great things.

But in the years since, the august doctor had seen the high tide ebb. Rokitansky believed firmly that all animal life was driven by the same "protoplasmic hunger" that led to a constant war of all against all in the animal kingdom, and that humanity alone was capable of transcending this. But humanity had proved, time and time again, unwilling or unable to do so, and when Rokitansky looked around him he largely saw the squandering of a great

[187] Ibid., pp. 3-4.

legacy. By way of a valediction to future generations of scientists, Rokitansky summed up his life of achievements with the phrase "Sorrow is knowledge," a quotation from the heavy-brained, small-hatted poet, Lord Byron.

ROMEO SELIGMANN DIED in 1892, and his vast collection of treasures passed on to his son Albert. Albert, who was born in 1862, grew up not so much in a house as in a museum. "My elderly father," he wrote in his memoirs, "even though he loved me, was for me primarily an authority figure whose presence was enough to dampen my childish doings. I hardly saw him except for meals and then only through the open door of his study working in mysterious candle light among tomes, papers and skulls."[188] Albert, who would go on to be both a painter and an art collector, inherited his father's "Goethiana," the expansive collection of Goethe treasures. Among this invaluable art were two small zinc boxes in which were some small pieces of bone. They looked like they might be from someone's skull, but it was not clear to Albert where they had come from or what their significance was.

[188] Quoted in Meredith, "The History of Beethoven's Skull Fragments," p. 8.

CHAPTER FIFTEEN

HOMO RENAISSANCUS

By the end of the nineteenth century Sir Thomas Browne's skull had sat for over fifty years in its case in the Norfolk and Norwich Hospital Museum and had presided over enormous changes. "Gnawed" from the ground in the name of phrenology, it had seen that so-called New Science pass into nothing but a sideshow, just as it had stood mute when the great men of science had first changed the world and then retired and died. While it stood steadfast, one of Joseph Hyrtl's former students, a young doctor named Sigmund Freud, began fundamentally to alter the study of the mind. By the time Freud was done, hardly any vestige of Gall's legacy would remain.

In the 1890s Haydn's skull was given to the Society for the Friends of Music, and shortly thereafter Mozart's skull would find its way to the Mozarteum. Still unburied, these two were at least given some respect, which their owners certainly deserved. But Sir Thomas's head remained sorely out of place amid the kidney stones, beside the rickety, murderous dwarf. Finally, in

1893, the clergy at St. Peter Mancroft decided to do something about it.

That year the vicar of the church, Reverend Pelham Burn, who had gone to Oxford (Browne's alma mater) and had himself been on the hospital's board of management for a time, was traveling in London when a friend pointed out the disgraceful treatment of Browne's skull. The vicar's friend was especially animated about how poorly the situation reflected on the church, and he succeeded in goading Burn into taking some kind of action. Given his association with the hospital, Burn hoped his opinion would hold some weight, and so he wrote a lengthy request to the board. He argued that the skull's theft had been an act of wanton sacrilege, something the board members—themselves, he was sure, good Christian men—should find disturbing. Furthermore, Burn pointed out what had become increasingly clear in the fifty years since the theft had taken place: that Browne's skull held no scientific interest, that it was a perfectly ordinary skull with nothing to distinguish it. Considering all this, the vicar asked in conclusion, would the board consent to returning the skull so that Browne's head might be reunited with the rest of his remains and his soul allowed to repose in peace?

The hospital board spent a long time considering the request and then sent back its reply. Its decision was unanimous: absolutely not. After a "prolonged and careful consideration of all the circumstances pertaining to the request," the board gave the following reasons:

That as there is no legal title to, or property in, any such relic, so there can be no question that this and all other specimens in the Hospital Museum belong inalienably to the Governors. That no instance is known of such a claim for restitution having been made after nearly half a century on any museum, and were the Governors to yield to this request they might be unable to resist similar claims. That the presence in a museum of such a relic, reverently preserved and protected, cannot be viewed as merely an object of idle curiosity; rather it will usefully serve to direct attention to, and remind visitors of, the works of the great scholar and physician.[189]

The hospital board's response sums up the status of Browne's skull at the dawn of a new century. The board provided no real reason for keeping the skull other than some rather pathetic legal quibbling and a claim that its usefulness lay in its ability to remind people of Browne. But the board members saw no legal reason to give it back, so this thin rationale carried the day. And thus the skull hung in a state of limbo, somehow still valuable even as it had lost its scientific usefulness.

THUS REBUFFED, PELHAM Burn took the issue back to the vestry, who decided by a vote of eight to six to let the matter rest.

---

[189] Charles Williams, in *Notes and Queries*, October 6, 1894, pp. 269-270.

And that would have seemed to be the end of it—at least as far as the skull was concerned, though there were other loose ends surrounding Browne and the "desecration of 1840." There was still the question of the missing coffin plate, the one with the inscription about turning lead to gold that had been broken in half in 1840. It had been missing for decades.

Charles Williams took it upon himself to try to locate it. No one had been able to figure out when it had disappeared, or where, but Williams knew where to start: Robert Fitch, the same Fitch who had reported on the skull when it had first been discovered. Fitch was now ninety-one years old but still an active member of the church. And, as everyone knew, he still had some rubbings he had done of the plaque. Williams thought he might have a lead on where the plaque had ended up.

When the good doctor asked him about it, Fitch was terse. The old man stated only that he had returned it to George Potter, the sexton at the time, who had probably locked it away in some church chest somewhere. Williams returned to Burn, and the two of them decided to search the church premises in an effort to find it. But nothing came of the search.

It was another fruitless attempt to right the injustice done to Browne, or so Burn thought of the search, though this story would end more quickly than his dispute with the board. Two years later Fitch died, leaving his papers and effects behind in his church office. As the church staff was cleaning out his massive desk, they found a hidden compartment behind a false wall in the back of a drawer. Inside they found the two halves of Browne's broken coffin plate.

Fitch had warned Skull George not to take the head, but he'd had no qualms about keeping the coffin plate for himself, even going so far as to devise a means to keep it hidden and secret. Later commentators would note that Fitch's "antiquarian zeal" had perhaps made him unsuitable for church office; it was, at any rate, just one more indignity that Sir Thomas Browne was made to suffer in his afterlife.

THE YEAR 1896 saw another edition of Browne's works, edited by William Alexander Greenhill. Charles Williams, who was gradually becoming the authority on the Norwich doctor's head, provided a craniometric reading at the request of Greenhill, who wanted "to make the account more complete by giving the measurements of that great man's skull." Regarding the fracas with Reverend Burn and the church, Williams commented only that the skull "has recently been claimed by the vicar of St. Peter Mancroft, but unsuccessfully," before noting that the skull "is in a state of excellent preservation."[190]

"The forehead is remarkably low and depressed," he went on, "the head is unusually long, the back part exhibiting a

---

[190] Charles Williams, "The Measurements of the Skull of Sir Thomas Browne," in *Hydriotaphia and the Garden of Cyrus*. Edited by W. A. Greenhill (London: MacMillan and Company, 1896), p. xxvi.

singular appearance of depth and capaciousness." Browne's "low, depressed forehead" had once been scandalous, as had Beethoven's—now Williams passed over it without comment.

A few years later another campaign was mounted to have the skull returned. This time the campaign occurred in the court of public opinion. One writer commented in *Notes and Queries* that "a movement was on foot for the return of Sir Thos. Browne's skull to its original resting place" and that it had always seemed to the writer that "this step should have been taken long ago by its present custodians, and I very much hope that a record of its re-interment will soon appear in the pages of 'N & Q.'"[191] Another writer published an editorial in the *Times* of London arguing that "now is the proper time, late though it be, to undo the sad act of vandalism" that was responsible for this "tragical abomination" by hands that had "knav'd" away the skull so many years ear-lier.[192] By now the "tragical abomination" line was becoming somewhat of a cliché, with commentators endlessly citing it either as a reason to have Browne's head returned or as an ironic prediction that made Browne's current predicament almost noble.

On the other hand, there were some who weren't exactly sure that Sir Thomas would have found it such a tragical abomination; one James Hooper, also writing in *Notes and Queries*, suggested that Browne, were he to be consulted on the matter, might well have sided with the hospital board, of which he had been a mem-

[191] John T. Page, in *Notes and Queries*, May 19, 1906, p. 397.
[192] Edmund Owen, "The Skull of Sir Thomas Browne," *Times*, October 24, 1905.

ber in life, rather than with the church that purported to be acting in his interests.[193]

Hooper had a point. In Browne's time there had been no contradiction between being a man of science and a man of religion. They provided different means to the same goal: understanding the works of God. But by the turn of the twentieth century, of course, these pursuits were completely separate. There were fewer and fewer men like Hyrtl and Rokitansky, who were able to inhabit both spheres independently. Had Browne been born in the nineteenth century, which half of his mind would have won out: his zeal for scientific inquiry or his spiritual longing?

The war over Browne's bones brought the church of St. Peter Mancroft a good deal of notoriety as the not-quite-last resting place of the Norwich doctor, while among the vestry members themselves, the inability to recover Browne's skull became something of a grim joke. In 1898 the *New York Times* ran a short dispatch on the church's remodel, including a lowering of the floor that was sure to disturb the remains of Browne. The *Times* reporter, oblivious to the generations-old saga, asked Burn if "he did not feel some respect for the last resting place of Sir Thomas Browne," and Burn replied, somewhat facetiously, "Yes, he is buried there. We shall probably see him again." The American reporter was incredulous. "The words the rector used were so delightfully comic, this idea of raking up Sir Thomas Browne's bones, that all hands present indulged in a loud and side-splitting

---

[193] James Hooper, in *Notes and Queries*, September 22, 1894, p. 234.

guffaw. Certainly the rector's reply was flippant and in the worst possible taste. Let us hope that the higher English Church authorities will resent any such desecration."[194] But what Burn and the others knew, of course, was that when it came to matters like these the church authorities seemed utterly powerless. The only thing one could do, it seemed, was laugh.

IF BROWNE'S HAD become the example of a skull that could not get *out* of a museum, back in America the paleontologist Edward Drinker Cope was trying to get his head *into* a museum. Cope had been a pioneering paleontologist who had become embroiled in a legendary battle with his rival Othniel Charles Marsh in the 1860s and '70s.[195] What had started out as a friendship had quickly turned ugly after Marsh had quietly bribed men working for Cope to send Marsh any fossils they found. As a result the two became bitter enemies, each trying to outdo the other in discovering and naming new prehistoric species—in the process they identified more than 130 of the 287 known species of dinosaur. Things came to a head—literally—when Cope published his findings on a new species of aquatic dinosaur, which he named *Elasmosaurus*. Marsh quickly pointed out that Cope had not discovered anything new—he had just put together the bones of a preexisting species in the reverse order, putting the head at the tip of the tail.

[194] *New York Times*, February 26, 1898.
[195] My account of this rivalry follows Louie Psihoyos, *Hunting Dinosaurs*, with John Knoebber (New York: Random House, 1994), pp. 15-29.

Humiliated, Cope conceded the point, but he hoped to yet get the last laugh. What he and Marsh coveted most, as taxonomists, was the discovery of a "type specimen"—the first appearance of a new species of animal and the fossil by which all future such animals are judged. Cope realized that in paleontologists' zeal to identify type specimens for the hundreds of dinosaurs they had discovered, they had forgotten to name a type specimen for the most central animal of all—*Homo sapiens*. And so in his will Cope directed that his bones be cleaned and prepared for display as the type specimen for the entire human race. But upon his death in 1897, his request was rejected—his bones already in bad decay from syphilis, Cope's skull was deemed unworthy of type status and was ingloriously shelved in an anatomical warehouse in Philadelphia.

BUT BACK TO the skull of Sir Thomas. In addition to his craniometric report on that skull, Charles Williams would yet be known for one other contribution to Browne's afterlife. At some point during the skull's tenure at the hospital, Williams took what has since become the iconic photograph of the specimen: in profile, resting atop three of Browne's books. The photo has since displaced even the portraits made of the scholar during his lifetime. When the antiquarian and bibliographer Charles Sayle published an edition of Browne's works in 1804 to commemorate the three hundredth year of his birth, he used Williams's photograph as a frontispiece.

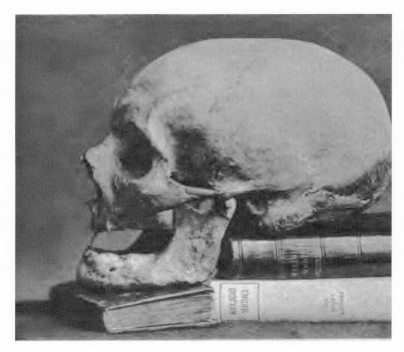

The skull of Sir Thomas Browne.

By placing Browne's head on books, Williams had symboli-
cally moved him out of the pathology museum and back into
the library, connecting Browne to the same legacy as Schiller,
seventy-five years earlier, when Duke Carl August had placed the
writer's head in his personal library. Of all the photographs of
skulls taken during this time, Williams's seems the most digni-
fied. Beethoven's skull is ghastly, already cut up and badly man-
gled. Haydn's leers up out of its ornate cabinet, gothic as any
death's-head. But in the Williams photograph Browne's head
manages to preserve something like poise. Of fundamental im-

portance are the copies of the books on which the head rests. Browne's head, emblematic of the secular saint, rests not in the crypt or altar but in the library.

But who is really qualified to interpret what these skulls say? Who can speak on their behalf? Lombroso tried, as did Topinard and Broca and Morton before him, as had Gall and Spurzheim before them. In each case what they asserted were not truths but self-reflective prophecies. The only truth to be found was that no one is in any real position to speak for these skulls—not the living and certainly not their owners. They sit, mute, endless ciphers, and reflect our minds back to ourselves.

NEARLY THIRTY YEARS after the iconic photo was taken, Virginia Woolf published a novel about a curious figure named Orlando, who ages a scant thirty years over the course of four centuries, changing from male to female somewhere along the way. Early in the novel Orlando (still a young man at that point) descends into his family's crypt to contemplate the bones of his ancestors: "'Nothing remains of all these Princes,' Orlando would say, indulging in some pardonable exaggeration of their rank, 'except one digit,' and he would take a skeleton hand in his and bend the joints this way and that. 'Whose hand was that?' he went on to ask." Echoing Hamlet, Orlando contrasts the mortal works of these long-dead men and women with the immortal word of literature, which solidifies his desire to be a writer: "What remained? A skull; a finger," he muses, turning to the writings of Thomas

Browne, "and Orlando, comparing that achievement with those of his ancestors, cried out that they and their deeds were dust and ashes, but this man and his words were immortal."[196]

Why did Woolf choose Browne as the figure for immortality? In life Browne had been a quintessential renaissance man: doctor, philosopher, amateur anthropologist, and theologian. Now he was becoming something like Renaissance Man—*Homo Renaissancus*—the archaeological specimen that told the story of an entire age.

The joke is that Orlando is, by virtue of Woolf's imagination, already immortal. But then again, so was Browne, whose time on earth continued to lengthen with each rebuffed entreaty from the church. In 1814 Sigismund Neukomm had placed a stone tablet above Haydn's grave with the inscription *"Non omnis moriar"*—"Not all of me shall die." Hyrtl, also quoting Horace, had added another line referring to immortality to Mozart. The belief that one is made immortal through one's art is certainly as old as art itself. But for this bizarre handful of cases, a kind of immortality had been achieved literally as well as metaphorically.

THE BATTLE WAS to go on, as Browne's fate lay in limbo. The march of scientific progress moved inextricably forward, with new advances and breakthroughs every day. Forlorn and forgotten, Browne's skull gathered dust as its uselessness became more

[196] Virginia Woolf, *Orlando* (San Diego: Harvest, 1956), p. 81.

and more absolute. He was to receive his glass case, belatedly, in 1902, but the hospital museum allowed the tercentenary of his birth to come and go with no movement on his return.

One hundred years earlier Angelo Soliman's daughter had learned a bitter lesson as she had made endless entreaties to have her father's taxidermied remains removed from the emperor's wonder cabinet and finally buried. Entreaties to Christian virtue or common decency, she learned, inevitably fell on deaf ears, a lesson Pelham Burn gathered a century later. It is hard to relinquish something so precious, even if the relic is ultimately useless. With no higher authority to which to appeal, Browne's status had become an endless source of frustration for Burn and for others who continued their attempts to reclaim the great man's skull so that he might rest in peace.

But for every skull belonging to a great man like Browne, for whom the church and other learned men would fight, there were thousands of others—those of Peruvians, Eskimos, Egyptians, Mongolians—with no one to argue on their behalf. The cobbler's apprentice, dead by suicide after his crime had been discovered, or the young girl dead from meningitis at age nineteen, her luminous body cut apart on the autopsy slab, or the reformist guerilla executed by hanging—who would speak for them?

PART FOUR

REPATRIATIONS

The relics of many lie, like the ruins of Pompey's,

in all parts of the earth; and, when they arrive at

your hands, these may seem to have wandered far, who,

in a direct and meridian travel, have but few miles

of known earth between yourself and the Pole.

· Sir Thomas Browne, *Urn Burial*

CHAPTER SIXTEEN

HOMECOMINGS

B ones cannot travel by themselves—they need labels, they need identifying marks, and most of all they need stories. Medieval saints' relics were usually accompanied by a reliquary or other identifying feature—an inscription or an image that could testify to the owner or the power of the remains. The history of bones, transmitted through oral and written stories, is central to their significance. Especially when a saint's relic moved from one community to another, or when it was passed down from one generation to the next, the story attesting to its power mattered as much as—if not more than—the bone itself.

Increasingly this became an issue with the skulls of these great men as well; as generations passed and their collectors passed on, it wasn't always clear how authentic the skulls were. Saints were lucky enough to have reliquaries and narratives accompanying them, but when a skull was taken under deliberately obscure or illegal circumstances, it was likely to lack reliable documentation.

Such was the situation in which a group of French scientists found themselves in 1821 when a curious artifact came their way. Jacques Berzelius, a Swedish naturalist, had been working with Georges Cuvier in the Museum of Natural History in Paris since 1819 and had recently returned to Sweden. There he came across a notice in a newspaper concerning Rene Descartes's skull. The French philosopher and mathematician, founder of much of modern science and philosophy, had died in Sweden in 1650, and now, over 170 years later, it seemed that a rather disreputable entrepreneur in Sweden had bought the head of Cartesius at an auction, to be used as decoration in his casino.[197]

Fortunately Berzelius was able to buy back the skull, and he shipped it off to Cuvier and his colleagues in Paris for analysis. In May 1821 they met to consider whether the skull really belonged to Descartes. The rest of the philosopher's remains had been sent back to France in 1666 and had been celebrated as the relics of a secular saint during the French Revolution. So why had his skull now shown up in Sweden? And was it authentic?

It certainly claimed to be the skull of Descartes. On the forehead were a few lines written in Latin, which read:

> *This small skull once belonged to the great Cartesius,*
> *The rest of his remains are hidden far away in the land of France,*
> *But all around the circle of the globe his genius is praised,*
> *And his spirit still rejoices in the sphere of heaven.*

[197] My account follows Shorto, *Descartes' Bones*, pp. 129-165.

Not only that, the skull had inscribed on it a record of its travels through the years. The names Isaak Planström, Stiernman, Celsius, and Ahlgren could be made out written on various parts of the head. They seemed to speak of a chain of ownership through the years.

But as Cuvier's colleague Jean-Baptiste Delambre pointed out, what proof did these names offer? During the discussion surrounding the skull, Delambre asked his colleagues, "What proof have we from elsewhere regarding its authenticity? Some inscriptions, more or less effaced, that one makes out on the convexity, which are the names of the successive owners, with some dates and nothing more."[198] Delambre argued that there was no conclusive evidence that the skull belonged to Descartes, and certainly the words on the bone couldn't be taken as reliable testimony.

To complicate the matter, while this discussion was taking place one of Berzelius's colleagues wrote to tell him that there was a different skull, in Lund, Sweden, that was also believed to be Descartes's. In addition, a third candidate for Descartes's head was announced by a man named Johan Arckenholtz, who claimed that the French philosopher's head had been split in two—Arckenholtz had kept half, and the other half had ended up with another Swede named Hägerflycht. The longer Descartes had been dead, it seemed, the more heads he had managed to grow.

It took months to untangle the histories of the separate heads, and while the Planström skull was ultimately judged to be the

[198] Quoted in Ibid., p. 148.

philosopher's actual head, there would never be anything like definitive proof. You could trace the owners, you could match the bone structure to known portraits, but beyond that you could only hope for the best. Even in the twentieth century, as forensic techniques became more and more advanced, there would never be anything like 100 percent certainty, particularly if anyone voiced any doubt about the provenance of a skull. And there was always doubt about skulls stolen under the cover of night.

The skulls stolen throughout the early nineteenth century now sat mostly in libraries and museums, some with inscriptions bearing the names of their owners. But who could say for sure where they had really come from? Joseph Carl Rosenbaum, Skull George Potter, Ludvig Granholm, even Gerhard von Breuning— they had all followed their quarries to the grave, as had those who had inherited the skulls. But as the chains of ownership grew longer and memories grew dimmer, questions about the skulls' origins became increasingly important.

In the beginning of the twentieth century, studies were carried out on the heads of both Haydn and Mozart. Both had been traveling through the world long enough that questions about their origins had become unavoidable. Besides, there was already a head supposed to be Haydn's buried with the rest of his remains—the one turned over by Rosenbaum in 1820. Both skulls couldn't belong to Haydn. And as for Mozart, well, any head that was picked out of a mass grave several years after the burial was bound to raise some suspicion.

Skull identification was far from an exact science. Prior to the development of DNA testing in the 1980s, there was no definitive means of matching a set of remains to its owner. One could perform any number of tests that involved matching the skull to known portraits and descriptions, but in the end it came down to educated guessing, such as when Julius Tandler published an exhaustive study of the Haydn skull in the Society for the Friends of Music's possession in 1909.[199] He compared the bone structure of the skull to that evident in the available busts and portraits of Haydn as well as the death mask made of the composer. This last was the most reliable method, since it most closely mapped the form and contours of the skull at the time of death. Tandler found that the skull in the society's possession seemed much more genuine than the one currently entombed with the rest of Haydn's remains, given the available evidence. But in this conclusion he relied heavily on the testimony of Rosenbaum and Peter, which he attached to his own findings. Without this written record, his measurements—whatever their exactness—would not have held the same weight.

Mozart's skull had traveled a somewhat different route than the other skulls in Hyrtl's possession, the ones that had ended up in the Mütter Museum. After Joseph Hyrtl's death in 1894 the skull had changed hands a number of times, and, according to

---

[199] Julius Tandler, "Über den Schädel Haydns," *Mitteilungen der anthropologischen Gesellschaft*, Vienna, XXXIX (1909).

Notes and Queries, at least one attempt had been made to substitute another skull for Mozart's, "but the fraud was discovered; upon which, in some mysterious way, the spurious skull disappeared and the genuine one was restored to its place."[200] The skull still had the accompanying verse from Horace, verifying that it was the same one that Hyrtl had owned. But there was still no way of knowing if it was actually the composer's head— because it had been unearthed from a mass grave, doubts would linger for decades.

Even more unclear was the case of the painter Francisco Goya, which remains unsolved to this day. At the height of his career Goya had been appointed court painter to Charles IV in 1789 but had left Spain for Bordeaux after the ascension of Charles's reactionary son, Ferdinand VII, in 1813. Goya died in 1828, still estranged from his homeland, but as the politics of his own lifetime receded into the past he joined the ranks of Cervantes and Velázquez as a Spanish cultural treasure, which meant that his body ultimately had to return to Spanish soil. In 1901 the Spanish consul to France was tasked with repatriating the painter's remains, but upon exhumation he discovered a problem and immediately dispatched a telegram to Madrid: "Goya skeleton without a head. Please instruct me."[201]

But the consul's telegram didn't tell the whole story. There was, in fact, a skull with the remains. It just wasn't clear whose

---

[200] *Notes and Queries*, October 19, 1901, p. 322
[201] See Sarah Symmons, *Goya* (London: Phaidon, 1998), p. 328.

skull it was. What they found in the grave was not one but two almost complete sets of remains, lying together as if in an embrace, with only one skull between them. The two bodies dovetailed neatly into the head, as if it were a secret shared between them. There was no clear indication as to the identity of the other skeleton, how it had found its way into Goya's grave, or which of the two was the owner of the head.

Unsure what belonged to whom, the Spanish consul took both sets of remains back to Madrid and reburied everything in the church of San Antonio de la Florida. Upon further investigation, it seemed likely that the skull belonged to the second set of remains that had somehow found its way into Goya's grave. Perhaps the soil in the Bordeaux graveyard had settled in some uneven manner, or perhaps the grave robbers who had taken Goya's skull had inadvertently disturbed another grave in their haste to fill in the painter's plot.

"THE LITTLE GREEN oasis known as Princes-square," the *Times* reported on April 8, 1908, "in the desert of bricks and poverty lying between Whitechapel and the river, was the scene yesterday of a strange ceremony, the beginning of Emanuel Swedenborg's last journey to his first home."[202] Goya's remains went home because he had become a national symbol, and his countrymen felt he belonged with them. For Swedenborg, it

---

[202] "The Removal of Swedenborg's Body," *Times*, April 8, 1908.

was his repatriation that in turn guaranteed his reputation as a Swedish national treasure. Having lain undisturbed since 1823, Swedenborg's remains were being moved because the Swedish Church was to be demolished. Two of Swedenborg's followers had approached the Swedish secretary of state to suggest that the remains might be moved to Sweden, a proposal that had also been made by the Swedish Royal Academy of Sciences, which was in the process of publishing a new edition of the philosopher's works.

He was booked on the Swedish destroyer *Fulgia* for passage back to Sweden in what was hoped to be his final voyage. In Uppsala 3,500 schoolchildren were lined up along the road to witness the procession as it made its way to the church. Inside, a lavish service welcomed him home, and a chorus sang the following song:

> *So when late spring sings its song,*
> *You call out from your grave to our youth*
> *That in light and dark times*
> *Think nobly and do great deeds!*[203]

Swedenborg now had a new oak coffin to replace the disintegrated one that had held him in London, but there was immediately talk of providing something more suitable. A grand sarcophagus was proposed, but the government's finance committee balked at spending that much money on a private citizen.

---

[203] Quoted in Harry Lenhammer, "Swedenborg in Uppsala's Cathedral," *The New Philosophy*, January-June 2003, p. 399.

But was he just a private citizen? In addition to his religious teachings, Swedenborg had been a pioneer in math and science, and many saw him as one of Sweden's great scientific leaders. In a 1909 Parliament meeting, the conservative John Fredrik Nyström began a campaign to appropriate Swedenborg as a national icon. The money for the sarcophagus could easily be raised by Swedenborgians abroad, he pointed out, but then "the memorial therefore primarily would honor a religious writer and not a scientist." In addition, the money would be coming primarily from America and England, not from Swedenborg's home country. "Should the simple wooden coffin stand there," Nyström offered plaintively, "and witness how Sweden values her great men's memories?"[204]

His words touched a nerve, and a month later the money was appropriated for a granite monument—decorated with images representing the four faculties of learning: an owl for philosophy, a snake for medicine, scales for law, and a cherub for theology—to house Swedenborg's remains. Much was made of the Swedish granite from Gylsboda and Vånga, as if to reflect the very Swedish origins of the dust and bone inside. Nyström's words echo something of what Adolfo Frederick had said to Nicholas II about Haydn so many years earlier: "How fortunate was the man who employed this Haydn in his lifetime and now possesses his mortal remains." To own the remains of a great artist or genius, it would seem, is to own that man's legacy as well. In the twentieth cen-

[204] Quoted in ibid., pp. 412-413.

tury it was not the phrenologists or even the museums who owned these heads, but their countries of origin.

THE REPATRIATION OF Swedenborg's remains in 1908 received a great deal of attention, not just in the Swedish press but also in the English papers. Given the still relatively small following he had, it seems odd that so much ink was devoted to it. Perhaps it was the singularity of the event, the easy cooperation between two countries at a time when national alliances were increasingly fraught, or the pomp and reverence it received, but the repatriation made all the papers. And none of the newspapers could avoid making comparisons between this exhumation and the earlier, extralegal one that had separated Swedenborg's head from his body for a half-dozen years. In July 1908 *Notes and Queries* ran a short note on the repatriation of the philosopher-scientist's remains, including a short reference to the matter of his skull.[205] Just above it, completely unrelated, was a short notice about some odd riddles a certain scholar used to put to grammarians, such as "Who was Hecuba's mother? What name did Achilles assume among the virgins? What was it that the Sirens used to sing?" The scholar's name was Sir Thomas Browne.

[205] *Notes and Queries,* June 18, 1908, p. 56.

CHAPTER SEVENTEEN

RIVAL SKULLS

After reading a newspaper description of the destroyer *Fulgia* and its precious cargo, a man named William Rutherford sat down and composed a quick letter, which he sent to the "Swedish Envoy Extraordinary and Minister Plenipotentiary" on April 1.

> Sir,
>
> I have noticed with interest the announcements in the press that the remains of Emanuel Swedenborg are to be transferred from St. George's in the East to Sweden.
>
> Some forty years ago I knew a man in the East End of London who boasted of the possession of a human skull, said to have been taken from the broken coffin containing Swedenborg's remains during some excavations of the old church.
>
> I am not aware whether an examination of the remains is intended now, but it would interest me to know

whether the man (generally a very veracious old gentleman) spoke the truth or not. The matter may also be of
interest to the Swedish government, hence my main
reason for calling your attention to the matter & my
apology for addressing you.
I am, Sir,
Yours most obediently,
(signed) William Rutherford[206]

Rutherford's letter was certainly odd—its randomness, his
apologetic tone, the utter lack of particulars. It didn't present
much to go on other than a vague notion that he intended to label
the head now in transit to Sweden as inauthentic. More out of
courtesy than curiosity, the pastor of the Swedish Church wrote
back. "We would," he wrote, "of course, be very interested to know
all particulars you may know of. Have you any idea where the
skull which the old man talked about is now? When the coffin has
been brought to Stockholm there may be an examination of the
remains by an expert."[207] Rutherford's reply came the next day.

Rev:d & Dear Sir,
Please accept my thanks for Your letter of yesterday.
    It was early in the "seventies" that the skull was
being exhibited, but doubtless it could be traced in case

---

[206] Quoted in Henschen, *Emanuel Swedenborg's Cranium*, p. 18.
[207] Ibid.

of need. Would it not be well, before taking any steps, to await the examination of the remains? If the coffin contains a skull & the experts accept it as authentic, there is no more to be said, but my impression is that the old antiquary in question *did* possess the one taken out of the coffin, i.e., the actual skull of Emanuel Swedenborg.

In any case I shall be glad to do what I can when occasion arises.

I am,

Rev-d & Dear Sir,

Yours truly,

(signed) W:m Rutherford[208]

Who was William Rutherford? What was his interest in Swedenborg, or his skull? His letter didn't even mention that he had seen the skull, only that he had heard someone boasting of it forty years earlier. He certainly didn't profess to be a member of the New Church himself.

Still, there had been enough rumors over the years about the skull's authenticity that Rutherford's letter was passed along to the Royal Academy of Science. In May, when Swedenborg arrived in his homeland, the academy decided to open the casket and examine the remains to settle the matter once and for all regarding the provenance of the skull.

[208] Ibid.

THE TEAM OF scientists put in charge of the examination was made up of six members of the academy's Faculty of Medicine, including Johan V. Hultkrantz, who took the lead. None of them were forensic specialists, but Hultkrantz's research was incredibly thorough. Like Tandler, Hultkrantz knew there was no one test that would confirm the origin of the skull beyond a shadow of a doubt, so he subjected it to a battery of tests, hoping to build a solid case through the accumulation of circumstantial evidence.

Hultkrantz was meticulous throughout. First of all there was the cast that had been made of the skull in 1823, just before it had been reinterred. The skull and cast matched perfectly, and there could be no doubt whatsoever that it was the same head that Granholm had given to Wåhlin, which had been displayed in Tulk's phrenological cabinet before going back into the vault.

Hultkrantz characterized it as a "well-shaped skull, of medium size," and noted that there was no doubt that "the cranium in question is masculine and is that of a person of advanced years." For the age, he relied on an examination of the sutures of the individual bones (which continue to grow closed over the course of one's life) and the teeth to conclude that "the skull is that of man over 50 years of age, and in no wise in disagreement with the assumption of an age of 84 years."[209]

The skull was not as decayed as the rest of the body, but this

[209] Hultkrantz, *The Mortal Remains of Emanuel Swedenborg*, pp. 45-46.

was only to be expected since it had been out of the crypt from 1816 to 1823 and thus not subject as long to damp air and other unfavorable conditions. Hultkrantz also found pieces of the jawbone which had not been extracted with the rest of the skull and thus were in the same condition as the rest of the body. The jaw fragments, he surmised, could be used to match the head with the rest of the body. He was able to fit them together without difficulty, shellacking them so as to re-form the jaw. "To enable me to judge of the matter more exactly," he explained, "I made a reconstruction of the missing parts on a plaster cast of the fragment of the lower jaw. The modeling was done free handed and with the guidance of a number of lower jawbones of older individuals from the collections of the Anatomical Museum." Based on his reconstruction, Hultkrantz found that the close match of the jaw and skull suggested that they had once belonged to the same individual. "When the reconstruction was completed it was found to fit together surprisingly well with the cranium, only a very slight correction in the position of the articular processes being necessary."[210]

But Hultkrantz wanted to go beyond this; he did his best to achieve absolute certainty, to make sure that the head could only be Swedenborg's. He consulted the collection of "108 male crania" from "old burial places" around Uppsala, which dated from the eighteenth century and thus were likely contemporaries of Swedenborg, to make sure that the skull in question conformed to prevailing anthropological trends—it did. He then estimated

[210] Ibid., p. 53.

that the brain would have been between 1,350 and 1,450 grams, keeping within the average of 1,400 grams for European males. "This appears," he wrote, "perhaps, at first glance, to diminish the probability of the cranium in question having been Sweden-borg's," since a genius's brain could be expected to greatly exceed the average. But Hultkrantz—quite rightly—dismissed this question immediately. While explaining that it was "not the place for an exhaustive critical review of the theory regarding dependence of intelligence upon brain-volume," he did point out that "strong protests have been made against such hasty conclusions, which neither rest on sufficiently comprehensive material nor have been arrived at with the proper criticism and necessary regard to sources of error, which are in such investigations just as difficult to avoid as they are easy to point out."[211] That Hultkrantz spent so little time on this question suggests its fading importance, and as the twentieth century progressed the argument that intelligence did not strictly correlate to brain volume would become more and more obvious and accepted.

Hultkrantz's description of his work runs close to a hundred pages, indicating the range of tests to which he subjected the skull. He next made a bust of the philosopher, using the skull as a basis, to see whether or not, in a rough sense, the skull could hold a reasonable facsimile of Swedenborg. "The purpose of the reconstruction was not the production of an artistic piece of sculpture," he felt the need to disclaim, "but only to scientifically

[211] Ibid., p. 49.

test whether the man whose cranium was the basis for the bust could have had an appearance which agreed in its essential characters with Swedenborg's, as we know him from his portraits."[212]

He did not have a death mask of Swedenborg, so to match the skull to the head he had to rely on portraits. Like Browne, Swedenborg had had a relatively low forehead, and various painters had felt the need to correct this supposed defect in their portraits of him, resorting to a fair amount of *"poetica licencia"* when it came to his forehead and other elements of the face. "According to the esthetic conceptions of former times," Hultkrantz noted, "the Greek nose was supposed to give the impression of 'freedom from the passions,' of 'equilibrium between intelligence and sensuality,' traits of character which an artist might well desire to introduce into his likeness of Swedenborg."[213] Hultkrantz, unlike many who had come before him, recognized these ideas as so much nonsense and was unfortunately forced to compensate with his own studies. He saw that he could rely on the portraits only to a limited extent and that any divergences between the skull's forehead and the one depicted in the paintings meant not that the skull didn't fit but rather that the paintings were to be distrusted.

To map the skull onto the portraits, he placed a transparency of the painting over a camera lens, then lined up the skull on the other end so that the lines of the skull showed through the painting. The images he produced offer a strange *memento mori*: a ghostly

[212] Ibid., p. 66.
[213] Ibid., p. 59.

*Portrait of Emanuel Swedenborg superimposed on
Swedenborg's skull, by Johann V. Hultkrantz*

image of a skull creeping through from beneath the stately visage
of the philosopher. Hultkrantz's bust of Swedenborg may not
have had an artistic goal, but the superimposition of the skull on
the portraits echoes a fundamental theme that has long obsessed
artists—the presence of death in the full flowering of life. *"Et in
Arcadia ego,"* the skull in Guernico's painting famously told the two
young shepherds: "Even in idyllic Arcadia I exist." Behind every
proud portrait and testament to human genius, find this skull.

After such exhaustive study, Hultkrantz felt confident of his
conclusion. Having dispensed with the faulty methods of the last
century and all its ideological biases, Hultkrantz produced a rig-

orous and thorough analysis of the head of Emanuel Swedenborg, but even so, he did not want to rule out other possibilities.

In the preceding pages I have already pointed out the difficulty, not to say impossibility, of arriving, in a question of
this sort, at an absolutely infallible result in a positive direction. To prove that a given cranium cannot be that of a
specified person may at times be a relatively easy task,
while the demonstration of the true identity of a skull must
be, almost without exception, limited to a calculation of
probabilities, a proving that there exist no invalidating reasons, and a collecting of a number of arguments, each of
which by itself has only a rather modest value as proof, but

all of which, when taken together, by their number and unanimity, carry conviction to the mind.

This was the best that could be hoped for when it came to the authenticating of a disputed head. But for Hultkrantz it was enough—by way of conclusion he pronounced that the skull "which now lies in Emanuel Swedenborg's coffin may, with the greatest degree of probability, be regarded as genuine."[214]

THIS ENTIRE UNDERTAKING had been brought about by William Rutherford's letters, and Hultkrantz had felt obliged to address him; he didn't conclude that Rutherford's recollection was wrong, per se—it may very well have been the case that an antiquarian had told Rutherford he had Swedenborg's skull and may even have believed it himself. But based on the apparent authenticity of the skull now in Sweden, it appeared "much more probable," Hultkrantz concluded, "that the grave-digger had deluded the old antiquary into buying a false skull."[215]

Hultkrantz's paper was delivered as part of the jubilee celebration surrounding the unveiling of Swedenborg's granite sarcophagus and was extremely well received by the Royal Academy of Sciences. Thus the matter seemed to be closed.

[214] Ibid., pp. 68-69.
[215] Ibid., p. 26.

In London, members of the Swedenborg Society, perhaps out of a desire for closure, still felt a need to resolve Rutherford's claims. His account seemed so far-fetched, so full of half remembrances and gaps, that it was dubious in the extreme. But in February 1909 a representative of the society sought him out, just to be sure they had gotten the whole story and could dispel any nagging doubts. Rutherford was delighted that someone was finally taking an interest in his tale. As his letter had promised, he was all too willing to assist when the occasion arose, and he offered to track down the "very veracious old gentleman," a herbalist and antiquarian, who had claimed to have the skull and see what he could find out. Rutherford spent the spring and part of the summer in pursuit of the skull. The antiquarian had long since died, but Rutherford was able to track down his children. Although most of these leads turned out to be dead ends, he did succeed finally in finding one descendant who knew what had happened to the old man's skull collection and who gave Rutherford the name of the inheritor of the skulls.

Shortly thereafter Rutherford sent a letter to the Swedenborg Society. He had found the antiquarian's collection, he wrote, and while the labels identifying each individual skull had long been lost, he believed he knew which one had been Swedenborg's. Because it was a particularly noteworthy skull, it had been kept in good condition, and besides, someone had pricked a number of dots into the bone that spelled out the letters "E. S'Borg."

Rutherford's tale was becoming increasingly bizarre, but perhaps he was actually on to something. In August another representative of the Swedenborg Society came to Rutherford to see the skull he had uncovered. In the meantime, though, Rutherford had moved—since supposedly discovering the skull he had been institutionalized in an insane asylum. It's not clear what Rutherford suffered from, only that he was described as having a "periodical mental disease" and was at times "almost completely normal."[216] Regardless, his mental condition did not bode well for his tale. Unsure what to make of this, the Swedenborg Society representative asked to see the skull, but Rutherford didn't have it, and he refused, under any condition, to divulge the name of the gentleman who did have it or to reveal his location. He instead told the representative that if he wanted to see the skull Rutherford would have to travel with him to London, in the company of two wardens, and locate it himself. Exasperated, the Swedenborgian consulted Rutherford's physician as to his condition. The doctor found the whole thing dubious; he doubted there even was a skull and thought that Rutherford's strategy was only to get himself freed from the asylum.

The story turned out to have been a complete waste of time. In high-profile murder cases, there are always false confessions by those seeking publicity and attention, and Rutherford's story appeared to be something similar—Swedenborg's was by then a high enough profile that it was only a matter of time before a crazy like Rutherford tried to write himself into the philosopher's story.

[216] Ibid., p. 25.

The matter thus seemingly resolved, the Swedenborg Society followed the example of the Royal Academy of Science in moving on. But Rutherford, motivated by whatever unknown reason, did not. Eventually released from the asylum, he returned to London and once more tracked down the skull. In October 1911 he sent another letter, claiming that he now had the skull and inquiring again whether Hultkrantz or anyone else would be interested in analyzing it.

Patiently Hultkrantz responded, noting that since there was now at least an actual skull, it was "most correct to probe quite without bias the import of Mr. R.'s suggestion and its actual basis."[217] He agreed to take a look at the skull Rutherford possessed, but Rutherford refused to send it, perhaps fearing that Hultkrantz would not return it. Instead he sent a lengthy written description of the skull. There was nothing Hultkrantz could do with just a description of a specimen he had never seen, so Rutherford agreed to send tracings and some photographs. These were hardly sufficient either. Finally Rutherford sent a cast of the skull, but under no conditions would he send the thing itself. Hultkrantz would just have to make do with the documentation and the cast.

Hultkrantz's second monograph, "Additional Note on the Mortal Remains of Emanuel Swedenborg," is a good deal shorter than the first, reflecting his increasing impatience with the sometimes insane "Mr. R." Rutherford offered two indications that

---

[217] Johan Vilh. Hultkrantz, *Additional Note to the Mortal Remains of Emanuel Swedenborg* (Uppsala: Nova Acta Regiae Societatis Scientiarum Upsaliensis, Ser. IV, Vol. 3, No. 2. 1912), p. 1.

might aid Hultkrantz in identifying the skull. First, there was a scar on the right temple "that might have been caused by a sabre or cutlass and that should form a mark of identification if it could be proved that he had received such in his lifetime."[218] And second, there were the pinpricks, the dots that spelled out "E. S'borg."

Hultkrantz was unimpressed with both of these: "They were not sufficiently well produced on the photos and the cast to enable us to form a decided opinion as to their nature and origin." Hultkrantz added that even if the scar was genuine and had not been made postmortem, that would argue *against* the skull being Swedenborg's, since no record of such an injury existed in his journals or biographies. And as Delambre had with Descartes's skull, Hultkrantz found the name written on the skull of no importance at all: "Even if there were a quite distinct, unabridged name instead of the rather dubious 'tiny dots,' it would be of no consequence since we do not know at all who has written it, at what time, and for what reasons."[219]

Without any reliable positive indications of the skull's owner, Hultkrantz turned to the skull itself. Its chief characteristic was that it was scaphocephalic, a pathological deformity that was somewhat rare. The main features were "a ridge-like vertex and (at least in the majority of the cases) a more or less complete fusion of the parietal bones with an alteration of the growth of the

---

[218] Ibid., p. 2.
[219] Ibid.

skull, so that it becomes extraordinarily long and narrow, often with an overhanging front and a prolonged back of the head."[220] In other words, this long, narrow skull gave the head a pronounced shape that was not likely to have gone unnoticed or unremarked on by Swedenborg's contemporaries. Hultkrantz thought it extremely doubtful that so prominently deformed a skull could belong to the great philosopher and scientist. Not only would it have been noticed by his contemporaries and commented on somewhere in some document, it was unlikely in the extreme that great creativity or intelligence could flower in such a deformed head.

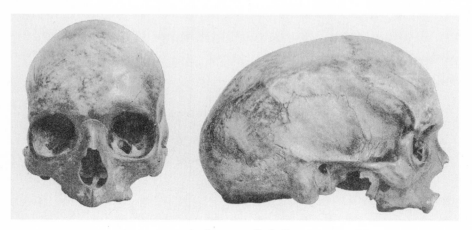

The "Swansea" skull.

[220] Ibid., p. 4

Hultkrantz happened to have access to another scaphoce-phalic skull from the Anatomical Institute of Uppsala, belonging to a tinsmith who had suffered from dementia and died poor. In addition, a death mask had been made of this individual, owing to the peculiar shape of his head. Based on this cast, Hultkrantz claimed, scaphocephaly indicated an abject physical appearance and a high degree of mental deficiency; thus he felt confident in ruling out the scaphocephalic skull from Rutherford as even re-motely likely to have belonged to Swedenborg.

Finally there was a question of gender. When John Flaxman had examined the Swedenborg skull, then in Charles Tulk's phre-nological cabinet, he had stated, "Why I should almost take it for a female head, were it not for the peculiar character of the fore-head." Hultkrantz took this as one more piece of corroborating evidence: "Everyone who is acquainted with the sexual differ-ences of human crania must admit that this skull is of a decided masculine type, and that if it in any point at all approaches the fe-male type, it is just in regard to the forehead!"[221] Once again it seemed impossible that the skull that had been in Tulk's phreno-logical cabinet was the same as Rutherford's.

Hultkrantz ended, perhaps now long tired of Rutherford's antics, with a fairly dismissive note: "With regard to the consid-erable value that a collector of curios may attach to such a rarity as a skull of Emanuel Swedenborg, I should be very much sur-prised if not more than one 'genuine' skull of the great mystic

[221] Ibid., p. 7.

should make its appearance in the future. Still, judging from the present case, it will probably be fairly awkward to find any real proofs countervailing those on which the opinion expressed in my account is based."[222]

Hultkrantz had now publicly disproven Rutherford twice, this time in far more detail. He had the weight of science behind him, and Rutherford, in addition to being a sometime lunatic, had only the word of a long-dead antiquarian and some dots that seemed to spell out a name.

HOWEVER, RUTHERFORD, STUBBORN to the end, refused to concede. Instead he realized only that he could not count on the scientific establishment for support. He took matters into his own hands, publishing a note in the local *East London Observer* titled "A Swedenborg Mystery: The Rival Skulls," which compared the heads and laid out his admittedly thin reasoning for the importance of the skull in his possession. In response to Hultkrantz's argument about scaphocephaly, one of the editors of the journal feebly noted that there "is absolutely no evidence that this cranial deformity (scaphocephaly) is accompanied with any type of mental or moral development. The two I have known during life were essentially commonplace persons."[223]

If he had hoped to draw Hultkrantz back into the dispute

---

[222] Ibid.
[223] Quoted in Henschen, *Emanuel Swedenborg's Cranium*, p. 20.

once more, it didn't work. Nothing else was forthcoming from Sweden about Rutherford and his skull. He did, however, manage to convince at least one person, selling it to one William A. Williams on the premise that it was the authentic head of Emanuel Swedenborg. Williams was a phrenologist in the old mold, arguing not just for the relatively uncontroversial localization aspects of Gall's theory, but also for the highly dubious aspects of cranioscopy—not long before buying the head from Rutherford he had argued that "the skull is as much a living tissue as the brain," and thus that accurate readings of the mind's activities could be traced through the skull.[224] Williams was also a student of Swedenborg and understood phrenology as the first science to be developed since the Second Coming that Swedenborg had identified in 1758.

And so the matter might have ended—the true skull in Sweden with the body, Rutherford's diseased head in the possession of a quack phrenologist, and all best left forgotten—if not for a young Swede named Folke Henschen, living in London studying anthropology, who read Rutherford's article in the *East London Observer* and took notice.

---

[224] William A. Williams, *A Reply to Our Critics* (London: L. N. Fowler and Company, 1890), p. 13.

CHAPTER EIGHTEEN

THE RUINED BRIDGES
TO THE PAST

B y 1922 St. Peter Mancroft had a new vicar, Reverend F. J. Meyrick, and among his named duties he inherited the task of endlessly badgering the Norfolk and Norwich Hospital Museum for the return of a certain skull. But where Pelham Burn had had to rely on appeals to decency and common sense, Meyrick had the help of a medical celebrity. The Canadian physician Sir William Osler had pioneered the practice of residencies for medical students and had helped to establish Johns Hopkins in Baltimore as a preeminent hospital when he had become chief physician in 1889. As a sixteen-year-old theology student at Trinity University in Toronto, Osler had fallen in love with Browne's work—*Religio Medici* was the second book he had ever bought, and it would end up buried with him. It was Browne's book that convinced him to become a doctor; he found it to be "full of counsels of perfection which appeal to the mind of youth, still plastic and unhardened by contact with the world."[225]

Osler had first visited Browne's skull in 1873. To be in the presence of his idol stirred him deeply; as he wrote to a friend, "Say what people will about pictures, emblems, relics & the like, they have been and ever will be the most delightful & I think reasonable means of raising the thoughts to higher and holier hopes."[226] In 1902 Osler had donated a glass case to hold the skull of his idol, the base of which was inscribed with the Norwich doctor's thoughts on the body and death: "At my death I mean to take a total adieu of the world, not caring for a monument, history or epitaph, not so much as the bare memory of my name to be found anywhere but in the universal register of God."

But only a few years later Osler had changed his mind about the fate of Browne's bones. In an address on Browne in 1906, he noted that the "tender sympathy with the poor relics of humanity which Browne expresses so beautifully . . . has not been meted out to his own." Osler began to use his fame to influence the hospital board, asking it to reconsider its 1893 decision in response to Pelham Burn.

That year the board agreed unanimously that the skull, should eventually be returned, provided that members of the board were present when the grave was opened and that the skull

---

[225] Quoted in Harvey Cushing, *The Life of Sir William Osler* (London: Oxford University Press, 1940), p. 709.
[226] Ibid., p. 102.

would not be displayed by the church as a "relic" before it went back into the ground. In retrospect, these do not seem particularly complicated conditions, but the negotiations between the hospital and church over Browne's skull would take another sixteen years. Osler (who sometimes published under the pseudonym "Egerton Yorrick Davis") died in 1919, with the repatriation of Browne still unresolved, the actual reinterment taking place finally in 1922.

As with other notable skulls, there was a rush to take some final measurements of Browne's. Sir Anthony Keith was asked to take measurements of the skull, supervise the making of casts, and determine its authenticity. A prominent anthropologist, Sir Anthony had lately become something of a one-man jury when it came to cranial mysteries. Around the same time he had been asked to identify the remains of a small skeleton found buried in a shallow grave in Rosherville Gardens. It was originally thought to have been that of a chimpanzee or other primate, but when Keith pronounced the remains to be human, an inquiry was launched on "suspicion that here was evidence of some dark crime of bygone years." Only by chance was the matter mentioned to one of Keith's colleagues, who suddenly recalled a display in the gardens some seventy years earlier that had included a Peruvian mummy.[227]

Keith had been the director of the Hunterian Museum at the

---

[227] A. A. Campbell Swinton, "The Strange Story of a Skeleton," *Times*, April 21, 1925.

Royal College of Surgeons since 1894, but his reputation had been greatly enhanced in the previous ten years as the result of a series of events that became known as the "Piltdown Affair."[228]

ARCHAEOLOGY AND PALEONTOLOGY had changed fundamentally. The notion of a single Great Flood, as described in Genesis, had long given way to a slowly forming picture of epochs and eras, Ice Ages and extinctions, rising out of gravel beds and bits of bone. As the fossil record began to yield its story, the missing links that would establish the evolution of apes to humans became of crucial importance. Hominoid remains such as the Neanderthal *Pithecanthropus erectus* ("Java Man") had begun to appear in the previous decades, but it was not yet clear whether they were the direct ancestors of *Homo sapiens* or if both races had descended from an as yet undetermined common ancestor. The meaning of these bones remained tantalizingly elusive; they were what Sir Arthur Keith called the pieces of a "ruined bridge" that "connected the kingdom of man with the rest of the animal world."[229]

In 1912 the lawyer and amateur geologist Charles Dawson found a fossil that seemed to shed light on the question. Discovered in Piltdown, England, the find consisted of multiple fragments of a hominoid skull—notably, the jaw pieces resembled

---

[228] My account of the Piltdown affairs comes from Frank Spencer, *Piltdown: A Scientific Forgery* (London: Oxford University Press, 1990).

[229] Quoted in ibid., p. 58.

those of an ape while the brain case was almost as large as that of a human. Given the genus name *Eoanthropus* ("man of the dawn"), the Piltdown skull changed how anthropologists had come to view human evolution.

First, though, the skull had to be put together. Only large fragments of the cranial case and some smaller jaw fragments were extant, so Dawson's friend Arthur Woodward, the keeper of geology at the British Museum, put together a complete reconstruction of what the head might have looked like. There was nothing unusual in this—complete specimens were rarely found—but it did mean that one had to reconstruct the skull based on these fragments and that some amount of imagination was involved. The front of the jaw was missing, so Woodward had to extrapolate from ape anatomy, building a jutting mandible and pronounced lower canines.

In December 1912 Sir Arthur Keith and a dozen other scientists gathered to discuss the Piltdown skull and argue over its significance. While Woodward was cautious about the meaning of the find, Keith led a contingency of scientists who believed the elusive common ancestor to both human and Neanderthal had been found. Claiming that Dawson and Woodward were not aware of the significance of what they had uncovered, Keith took issue with Woodward's reconstruction of the skull fragments. He proposed another version of the Piltdown remains, one in which the brain case was significantly larger and the jaw closer to that of modern humans. The missing link that scientists the world over had been searching for, he believed, had been found in England.

This was the other major reason the Piltdown Man was important. In these years before World War I, nationalism was at its height and anthropology had its own share of chauvinistic rivalries. Various countries were vying for the claim to be the cradle of civilization. In 1907 the so-called Heidelburg Man became a coveted trophy for Germany, and a few years later the paleontologist Florentino Ameghino had claimed that humanity's earliest ancestors were to be found in his home country of Argentina. Anthropologists had gone from asserting that their respective cultures were the height of civilization to bragging that they held the birth of civilization.

Battles continued to rage between Keith and others over Piltdown for a decade. To settle the question of the skull's reconstruction, Keith's colleagues broke a skull into pieces and challenged him to reconstruct it, which he was able to do flawlessly. As the debate attracted worldwide attention, Keith's fame continued to rise, and when it was announced that he would investigate the head of Sir Thomas Browne, it was big news indeed.

As IT HAPPENED, Keith didn't have the time to carry out the investigation himself, so it fell instead to Miss Miriam Tildesley. Like Tandler with Haydn and Hultkrantz with Swedenborg, Tildesley made extensive, detailed comparisons of known portraits and other extant data relevant to Browne. The skull's authenticity was much clearer because it had had fewer owners, but again Tildesley relied primarily on written documents and testimony—

ultimately the provenance of the skull was nothing more than the collected stories of Robert Fitch, Skull George Potter, and Charles Williams.

Tildesley also weighed in one last time on the question of Browne's forehead. Since it was very nearly undeniable that this low-sloped head had belonged to Browne, she offered two possible explanations to resolve the discrepancy. First, she noted that phrenologists had connected the forebrain to concentration and discrimination and suggested that "Sir Thomas Browne is undoubtedly a characteristic writer who has charmed many generations of English readers; but after all do his writings suggest great powers of concentration or discrimination? . . . We should rather anticipate that the sense of rhythm, the appreciation of sound and music, the artistic rather than the logical side of mind would be markedly developed in him. Hence it is possibly not reasonable to demand that Sir Thomas Browne must have been 'high browed.'"

The other solution of the problem she offered was "to take the results of this memoir as confirming earlier investigations which indicate that there is very little correlation between the shape of the head or indeed of the brain cavity and the mentality of the individual. . . . The present investigation seems to indicate that the skull of another man of genius can depart from general mediocrity in a few isolated characters, and in some of these reach a form which current opinion describes as a 'low type' of skull."

Unsurprisingly, she noted that this second possibility was "to us the more reasonable one" and concluded that "Sir Thomas

Browne's skull supports the conclusion that the correlation of superficial head and brain characters with mentality is so low as to provide no basis for any prognosis of value."[230]

IT WAS COMMONLY accepted that Tildesley had proved that the skull was indeed Browne's. When Keith got around to presenting his own findings on Browne two years later, the question he asked—in a speech that bore the oddly anachronistic title "Phrenological Studies of the Skull and Brain Cast of Sir Thomas Browne of Norwich"—was whether one might learn anything else from it beyond merely its provenance.

Keith had been attracted to phrenology as a child and had felt that "Nature had dealt rather meanly by myself as regards to size and form of head." By the time Keith entered college he had all but abandoned Gall's science, but he argued that nonetheless phrenology might one day be salvageable. He cited human evolution, with its attendant growth in cranial capacity, as well as the localization of brain functions as indications that someday, "when our knowledge of the human nervous system is perfected, it will be possible by a mere inspection of a brain to assess the mental potentialities of its owner. This is the ultimate goal of a scientific phrenologist."[231] In many ways Keith's program maps onto much of current psychology and neuroscience, though no one would be

---

[230] Tildesley, "Sir Thomas Browne," p. 68.
[231] Arthur Keith, *Phrenological Studies of the Skull and Brain Cast of Sir Thomas Browne of Norwich* (Edinburgh: Oliver and Boyd, 1924) p. 4.

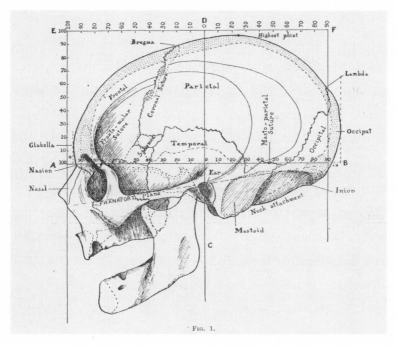

Fig. 1.

Drawing of Sir Thomas Browne's skull, by Sir Arthur Keith.

so gauche as to use the term "phrenology" anymore. "The goal the phrenologist has in mind is a knowledge which will make it possible for him to examine the head of a living child, by sight, touch, and X-ray transillumination, and to thus form an accurate estimate of the development of its brain as a whole and of its various parts, and from this knowledge of the brain infer the abilities of the child."[232]

But it was a dream whose time had not yet come. "It was my

[232] Ibid., p. 30.

ambition," Keith wrote in what had become a well-worn meta-phor, particularly since Williams's photo of Browne on his books, "to make the skull of Sir Thomas Browne a text from which I might preach a sermon concerning the forces which mould the skull and brain into their several forms, and to illustrate the meth-ods I had devised to measure and elucidate the nature of the forces which are involved."[233] Instead his appraisal was notably lacking in anything like a conclusion. After meticulously comparing Browne's skull and its measurements to those of Robert the Bruce, Jonathan Swift, and Robert Burns, Keith's report ended on a flat, anticlimactic note: "Even if I had dealt fully with all of these matters, we should not, in our present knowledge of the brain, have been any nearer to an explanation of the peculiar abil-ities of the author of *Religio Medici*."[234]

So the text of Browne's skull was to remain undeciphered, leaving us with only his books.

BROWNE'S HEAD WAS already back in the ground by the time Keith delivered his lecture. Whether or not his repatriation had any influence on the Society of the Friends of Music in Vienna is hard to say. But not long after Browne's return to earth, talks be-gan about bringing Haydn home to Eisenstadt. Though Tandler had proven in 1909 that the authentic head of Haydn was with the

---

[233] Ibid., p. 2.
[234] Ibid., p. 30.

Society for the Friends of Music and not in his tomb in Eisenstadt, it wasn't until 1932 that there was serious discussion about its repatriation. The society agreed to the transfer, ready to relinquish this most valuable relic, but as negotiations got under way the municipal authorities of the city of Vienna lodged a protest, claiming that the city had a legal right to the skull that trumped Prince Esterhazy's claim. Their reasoning was that the city had a clear title to the head, regardless of how Rosenbaum and Peter had come into possession of it, because Rosenbaum and Peter had willed it to the society, which was ultimately a function of Vienna.

It would seem to be a repetition of the same legal battle that had kept Browne's head out of his tomb for so long. But this dispute was quickly overtaken by other matters—as the 1930s rushed headlong forward, Vienna and the rest of Europe were quickly engulfed in matters much larger than the disposition of a composer's skull.

As World War II unfolded, it became clear that much of Europe's vast cultural and artistic heritage was at risk, from centuries-old monasteries to irreplaceable paintings and sculpture. At least Haydn's head, locked in the society's archives, appeared to be safe. The same could not be said of Beethoven's skull fragments. Thomas Browne's endless saga suggested the dire predicament of a skull in the hands of despotic museum curators, but the story of Beethoven's fragments suggested the even more tenuous nature of those precious relics that were not protected by some kind of museum.

Romeo Seligmann's son Albert kept the skull fragments along with his Goethe treasures (his "Goethiana") until the increasingly dire climate of the 1930s, when he began to ship his prized possessions to his sister Alma Rosenthal in the northern Austrian town of Traunkirchen.[235] He gave her instructions on displaying the objects, in the process transforming her home into a veritable Goethe museum; Albert's remaining collection in Vienna was proclaimed by the Institute for the Preservation of Monuments as having an "artistic and cultural value" that kept it from being requisitioned by the Housing Office during the war.

But because of the Seligmann family's Jewish heritage, the works in Albert and Alma's possession could not be considered safe. Alma was traveling in India when Hitler annexed Austria in March 1938; her thoughts immediately turned to her valuable collection and its safety. She had little help from Albert; he had remained in Vienna throughout the war, declaring himself Roman Catholic to escape detection. He was seventy-six when war broke out and left much of the work of safeguarding the family's collection to his sister.

She immediately wrote her son Tom, then living in Paris, trying to get him to come home and box up the collection— despite the fact that she was worried he did not yet have his

---

[235] My account here follows Meredith, "The History of Beethoven's Skull Fragments," pp. 6-13.

French citizenship, and if he didn't he would surely be conscripted into the German army ("The Germans will not want to do without him as canon-fodder," she wrote in a letter).[236]

For the next two years Alma would work frantically to safeguard the collection. At the end of 1938 she learned that her house was to be demolished to make way for a new road, which made the need for relocation acute. But Alma's worries went beyond getting the treasures out of the house; because of their nature, they were at special risk. Goethe had always been a national icon in Germany, and he had been appropriated by the Nazis as part of their nationalist propaganda. The treasure trove of Goethiana that the Seligmanns possessed would prove a temptation to the Nazi authorities, especially because the collection belonged to Jews and could be requisitioned with impunity. "The name of Goethe is on no account to be mentioned," she told her son Tom, "or it might easily and probably happen that the Denkmalschutz would prevent it leaving what they consider God's own country."[237]

The Nazis had appropriated not just Goethe but also Beethoven—Hitler and Goebbels cited him, along with Wagner and Bruckner, as singularly embodying the "heroic German spirit." They appropriated much of Beethoven's music, particularly the Ninth Symphony, as part of the aesthetic trappings of the Third Reich. It would seem natural that the notorious art thieves of the

[236] Ibid., p. 11.
[237] Ibid., p. 12.

Nazi regime would take as much interest in the skull fragments of a great German genius as in the portraits of Goethe. But in all her correspondence, Alma seems never to have mentioned the Beethoven fragments. It is unclear whether they were with Alma or Albert during this time, but it seems that whatever status they had as precious relics had greatly diminished. In an age when Browne's head had already been returned to the ground and Haydn's was on its way back, skulls simply had very little of the pull they had once had. This was even more true of these simple fragments, hardly representing anything.

Alma fled to England in June 1939 and continued working from afar to move the collection into friendly hands; she sent a number of important works in the Goethe collection to her son-in-law's parents and contemplated sending them as far away as Hawaii (where a family friend had offered to take them) in order to safeguard them. But she finally decided against Hawaii out of a fear that the tropical insects would eat through the paintings and drawings; instead she shuffled them endlessly around Germany. But the tropical insects and termites were nothing compared to the Nazis, who eventually seized the paintings and drawings and auctioned them off, breaking up the holdings of the Seligmann collection. By the time the war was over the collection was almost entirely lost, and Alma was distraught. "The last link with the old generation is now gone," she wrote. "I feel utterly floating, like a bit of torn seaweed in this ocean of life."[238]

[238] Ibid., p. 13.

But not all, it later turned out, had been lost. Albert died on December 13, 1945, and among his possessions was a small box that contained the fragments of Beethoven's skull. It may be that they had not been mentioned by Albert or Alma through much of the war because their authenticity had only lately been established. In February 1944, sensing the end, Albert had added a codicil to his will that mentioned the small metal box, noting that "proof concerning its provenance and authenticity and thus its not inconsiderable value has only been found very recently." The box had one word written on it—"Beethoven"—and contained "8 fragments of skull bones, 2 larger and 6 smaller ones." Seligmann then explained that he had been going through his father's old letters when he had discovered one from the anthropologist Hermann Welcker that described how Romeo Seligmann had been given the fragments shortly after the 1863 exhumation; he asserted that the contents of the box were "without doubt genuine parts of Beethoven's skull that were given over to my father for his skull collection that was very well known at that time."[239]

Albert Seligmann's will dictated that the bones, along with much of the rest of his possessions, should be put up for sale, with the proceeds going to his relatives. But Albert's friend Emma von Mérey, who helped to settle the estate, chose in this instance not to follow her friend's wishes; she kept the box with the skull fragments and gave them to Alma's son Tom in 1946.

---

[239] Seligmann, "Last Will and Codicil," translated by Hannah Leibmann, *The Beethoven Journal*, Vol. 20, Nos. 1 & 2 (Summer & Winter 2005), p. 64.

Though Tom kept the fragments for most of the rest of his life, he was a bit more cavalier in his treatment of them—he reportedly once blew a handful of bone dust into the air, with a quip about "dust to dust," and gave at least one of the smaller fragments to the pianist Jean-Rodolphe Kars, who kept it as a good-luck charm. Kars mentioned the bit of bone in an interview with the *Daily Telegraph* in 1968 but admitted that while he loved to show off his trophy, he could never convince anyone that this bit of bone had really once been a part of Beethoven.

CHAPTER NINETEEN

HOAXES AND
RINGERS

With the end of the war came a taking of stock and a settling of accounts. Death had come to Arcadia, and now it was time for reappraisals and reassessments. In the coming years one of the greatest scientific hoaxes ever perpetrated would be uncovered, and a minor correction would be made concerning an old skull.

By the 1950s the Piltdown skull had been perplexing geologists and anthropologists for forty years. The fights over its origins and its meanings had given way slowly to a nagging concern that something more fundamental was wrong. The different elements of the skull—the brain case, jaw, and teeth—seemed too disparate to be reconciled with the same animal. In 1953 three men—Joseph Weiner, Le Gros Clark, and Kenneth Oakley—published findings that conclusively proved the skull to be a forgery. The cranium, it turned out, had belonged to a human, probably from the thirteenth century, while the jaw was that of a chimpanzee into which filed-down human teeth had been inserted.

Over the years suspicions turned to Charles Dawson, the original discoverer of the skull, who had died unexpectedly in 1916, just a few years after the Piltdown Affair had begun. The picture of a jovial amateur gradually gave way to that of a compulsive and notorious forger. The mastodon remains that he had presented to the British Museum, and which had been named for him, were revealed to be fake, as was an iron statuette that he claimed had come from the Roman Empire. Even his well-received monograph *History of Hastings Castle* had been taken almost wholesale from an 1820s manuscript. Ultimately he was responsible for at least thirty-eight archaeological forgeries—it seemed to be something of a hobby of his.[240]

But why forge a hominoid skull? And had Dawson had help? A great number of hypotheses on the motives of the forgers have been offered. One persistent theory is that the skull was designed to embarrass evolutionary theory—indeed, at least one theory posits that Sir Arthur Conan Doyle was the culprit, as a spiritualist attempting to slow up the materialists. Another possibility for Dawson's collaborator is Sir Arthur Keith himself, perhaps in a misguided attempt to win fame and immortality. But this is also speculation.

Kenneth Oakley was only a year old when the Piltdown skull

---

[240] See Miles Russell, *Piltdown Man: The Secret Life of Charles Dawson* (Stroud: Tempus Publishing, 2003).

was discovered, and he had spent his whole career believing it to be genuine. Later that decade he would find himself involved in another major skull dispute.

IN 1955 THE anthropologist Folke Henschen had paid a visit to the Swedenborg Society. He had never forgotten the dispute he had read about in the *East London Observer* and Rutherford's adamant insistence that he had found the real head of Emanuel Swedenborg. Henschen, now a well-respected anthropologist, was convinced that "it would be worthwhile to analyse the problems involved."[241]

The Swedenborg Society was by this time also receptive. In the society there had long persisted a story from an old former secretary named Elliott that the skull that had lain with the remains wasn't the correct one. In 1930, learning that Rutherford's skull was now with William Williams, the society had sent a representative to investigate and had found a particular element that was suggestive: a tooth. Late in his life Swedenborg had reported to a friend that his teeth had begun to grow again. In Williams's skull was what appeared to be a "young tooth, white and bright as a child's."[242] It was enough of an indication that there might be some value to the Rutherford skull. It was impossible to verify the age of the tooth from the cast Rutherford had sent Hultkrantz,

[241] Henschen, *Emanuel Swedenborg's Cranium*, p. 4.
[242] Swedenborg Society Confidential Report, May, 1930.

but nevertheless Henschen couldn't believe that the "mediocre cranium" was really the right one. The Swedenborg Society gave Henschen full access to its files as well as relating its suspicions about the tooth.[243]

The main problem with Rutherford's claim, of course, was the cast that had been made in 1823. It was a perfect match to the skull now in Sweden, so the provenance from 1823 onward was clear—the skull Wåhlin and the others had buried was indeed the same skull they had recovered from Tulk. Tulk had been at the reinterment ceremony, so certainly he would have noticed if another skull had been substituted for the one from his phrenological cabinet. Tulk's skull had come from Wåhlin, who in turn had received it directly from the culprit Granholm; thus, there was a direct chain of succession from Granholm to the Sweden skull, and it seemed highly unlikely that the skull could somehow have ended up an antiquarian's cabinet in the 1870s, as Rutherford had claimed.

But Henschen wanted to investigate the possibility anyway. He received permission from the Swedish government to take another look at the skull in Sweden, and he sent a letter to William Williams to see if he could borrow the skull in his possession (now referred to as the "Swansea skull" after the town where Williams lived). Williams, unfortunately, died only a week before the letter arrived, but his daughter managed to recover the skull from his stock and lent it to Henschen for analysis.

---

[243] Unpublished correspondence, Folke Henschen to Freda Griffith, November 22, 1955

HENSCHEN ASSEMBLED TWO teams to work on the skulls—one in Sweden and one in London, at the British Museum. No fewer than fifteen different specialists worked on the specimens, including forensic scientists, anthropologists, a mining engineer, a dentist, and an antiquarian. Henschen headed the Swedish team, while the group in England was headed by his friend and colleague Kenneth Oakley.

It quickly became apparent that, whatever else one might think, the Swedish skull had *not* belonged to Swedenborg. For all Hultkrantz's rigor, Henschen began to see that his predecessor's process had had numerous problems and that Hultkrantz had introduced his own set of biases even as he was dispelling others'. Fluorescence analysis revealed distinctly different colors between the head and the rest of the bone, and other forensic evidence strongly suggested that the head had come from a different set of remains altogether.

Henschen took particular issue with the reconstruction of the jaw—Hultkrantz had admitted he'd done the job free-handed, an approach Henschen recognized as highly dubious. The battle over the Piltdown reconstructions was sufficient to show how easy it was to allow one's own biases to enter into a job. "Obviously, such a joining together of strongly disintegrated bone fragments as these by free-hand," one of Henschen's team noted, "cannot be regarded as satisfactory. Merely a glance at the reconstructed mandible evokes doubts about the exact joining together of the fragments. Such an acute angle between the shanks of the mandible may belong to rareties, and there is little to see of the parable shape, described on p. 53 of his book."[244]

In addition, there was the problem of the portraits Hultkrantz had used. True, some painters had certainly used *"licencia poetica,"* in Hultkrantz's words, and could not be relied on. But if there were discrepancies, it wasn't clear why he had chosen some portraits and not others. Why not compare the skull to *all* the known portraits of Swedenborg and let the images speak for themselves? Henschen also noted that the bust Hultkrantz had produced revealed the facial structure not of an eighty-four-year-old man but of a young man in his prime. What did this prove? For all his rigor, Hultkrantz had failed to keep his own biases from filtering in.

By the time the Sweden team was done, there was enough evidence to suggest that Hultkrantz had been wrong and that the Sweden skull didn't match what was known of Swedenborg or the rest of his remains. But as Hultkrantz himself had written forty years before, it was easier to prove a negative than a positive, and the fact that the Sweden skull was wrong didn't make the Swansea skull right.

But the fact that the Sweden skull was wrong raised all sorts of questions since its provenance had seemed so clear. If it wasn't Swedenborg's, whose head was it, and who had tried to pass it off as the philosopher's? Tulk, the owner of the phrenological cabi-

---

[244] Henschen, *Emanuel Swedenborg's Cranium*, p. 24.

net, may have substituted another skull for Swedenborg's. Even Wåhlin, who had been offered 500 pounds for it, may have been tempted. But there was nothing in the record to suggest that either of these men had had anything to do with the ruse.

There was one thing Henschen couldn't quite get out of his mind, something that didn't add up. He kept going back to a series of letters in the *Times* beginning in April 1823 from Noble, Hawkins, and Wåhlin, each of whom had written to clarify the original account of Swedenborg's head. They all agreed on the basic story: that the head had been stolen after the casket had been left open, and that it had *not* been stolen by a Swedenborgian. But other than that, they didn't seem to be in agreement about anything. Noble claimed that the skull had been stolen in 1816, during the funeral of Baroness von Nolcken, by a phrenologist who was still living in London. Hawkins claimed it had been stolen at the end of 1817 by Granholm after the funeral of a fellow officer—Granholm, who was dead by 1819 and who had no attachment to phrenology but was instead trying to make a quick buck. Wåhlin, the third to write, sided with Noble: It was a phrenologist, still alive, who had taken the skull. Hultkrantz had dismissed these inconsistencies as just part of the confusing circumstances of the theft, and certainly, with such a shadowy process, there was likely never to be one conclusive version of events. But was that really all there was to the letters?

HENSCHEN MEANWHILE RECEIVED the findings of Oakley's team regarding the Swansea skull. They confirmed the canine tooth, whose presence was of "considerable value," and seemed to suggest that the Swansea skull was genuine.

As with the Sweden skull, portraits were used to verify the facial features. Chief among the problems with verifying the Swansea skull was the lack of profile portraits of Swedenborg. As a scaphocephalic skull, it was most identifiable from the side, and a profile would have made the comparisons much easier. The fact that there were none extant may have been because no one wanted an unflattering portrait, although this was just conjecture. But Rosemary Powers, who conducted the analysis of the skull in relationship to the portraits, did find a particularly striking match and concluded tentatively that "considering how freakish the 'English' skull is, one is tempted to regard this very striking correspondence as conclusive."[245]

Some problems did arise—Kenneth Oakley's examinations suggested that the skull was probably not more than sixty years old. A blood analysis, which involved pulverizing a small section of the bone, was inconclusive. But other clues strongly favored the Swansea skull. Among Swedenborg's remains had been an old pillow on which his head had once lain and which had long since disintegrated badly. But new forensic technologies were able to trace the imprint of the head on the pillow—the Sweden skull did not fit the profile at all, but the Swansea head, with its extremely odd shape, matched it perfectly.

[245] Ibid., p. 36.

If this truly was Swedenborg's skull, then where had it come from? When had it been stolen, and when had it been swapped for the Sweden skull? How had it ended up with Rutherford's "veracious" old antiquarian? Puzzling over these questions, Henschen went back once again to the letters from Noble, Hawkins, and Wåhlin. He didn't believe that their memories could have faded in just a few years to the point where they'd disagree over such basic facts.

Noble and Wåhlin claimed the skull had been as stolen by a phrenologist, still living, in 1816.

Hawkins claimed it had been stolen by Granholm, now dead, in 1817.

Then Henschen saw. All three men were correct. The *Times* had not published two differing accounts of the same robbery. They were accounts of two entirely different robberies.

Swedenborg's head had been stolen twice.

DESPITE THE MYRIAD claims over the years that the Sweden skull was not authentic, Henschen—like Hultkrantz before him—had had no trouble dismissing all of them as baseless, even that of Anna Frederika Ehrenborg, who had visited the tomb in 1853 and proclaimed that one needed "only very little knowledge of phrenology to see that the skull could not have belonged" to Swedenborg and that it "looked most like that of a woman, with fine harmonious organs."

Ehrenborg had likely hoped that her declaration would make more of an impact—she had in fact hoped to be joined by her friend John Didrik Holm. She had visited "Excellent Holm" earlier that day, and they had discussed her upcoming visit to Swedenborg's tomb. "Holm obstinately declares that the skull which lies in the coffin is not the right one," she later recorded, and when she pressed him on the matter, he answered "with sullen certainty": "I know that it is not the right one."[246] He agreed to meet her there to prove that it was fake, but he didn't appear, leaving her to make her best attempt alone. Holm alone was in a position to know that Ludwig Granholm had not stolen Swedenborg's skull—because Holm had stolen it first.

The story, as best Henschen could reconstruct it, was as follows. After Swedenborg's grave had been disturbed in 1790, it was vulnerable to anyone who happened to wander down into the tombs to take a look. But it wasn't until 1816 that John Didrik Holm, there for the funeral of Baroness von Nolcken, found the tomb ajar. A devout phrenologist, he imagined that he could study the skull and add to the store of knowledge surrounding the question of genius, so he quietly purloined the head. It was *this* theft that Noble and Wåhlin later learned about. But Holm had mentioned the theft to friends and been told to return the skull. He agreed to do so but at the last minute substituted a different skull for Swedenborg's.

It was *this second skull*, the ringer, that Ludvig Granholm found a year and a half later while there for the funeral of a friend. Granholm took it for financial gain but died before he could sell it, and *that* skull came back to Wåhlin. It was this version of events that Hawkins, who had known Granholm, later recorded. Wåhlin, meanwhile, conflated Granholm's story with what he already knew about Holm's theft, further obscuring the matter.

After his death in 1856 Holm's collection was broken up. There was no inventory and no way to confirm that Swedenborg's head had been in his possession. But Henschen's report attracted some publicity, and in 1958 Mrs. Stina Christby of Stockholm contacted Henschen. She was a descendant of Holm's sister and told Henschen that Holm's niece had visited him in the 1840s and that he had shown her Swedenborg's skull, swearing her to secrecy. The family had never broken its silence regarding this visit until Christby told the story to Henschen.

And so Henschen was able to conclude that the Swansea skull was, "with the greatest degree of probability . . . Swedenborg's authentic cranium."[247] One hundred seventy years after Swedenborg's death, 140 years after the thefts, and 50 years after the philosopher's reburial in Sweden, Henschen had vindicated the bizarre and dubious tale of William Rutherford, the sometime mental patient who had once overheard a story and had produced a singularly shaped head: that of Emanuel Swedenborg.

[247] Ibid., p. 49

CHAPTER TWENTY

THE END OF THE
END OF THE STORY

In 1978 Sotheby's announced an auction to consist of "Printed Books Relating to Masonry, Science, and Phrenology." In addition to the "Constitutions of the Freemasons" and Einstein's first scientific paper, the auction included a first-edition copy of Gall and Spurzheim's *Anatomie de Systeme Nerveaux*, "an extensive collection of books on phrenology and the New Jerusalem Church," and a human skull. It was the first time in the auction house's history that it had sold a skull, and it had belonged to Emanuel Swedenborg.

The skull had been put up for auction by the descendents of William A. Williams, but the sale was not without controversy. Members of the Swedenborg Society, particularly General Secretary Mrs. G. P. Dawson, launched an extensive letter-writing campaign. "Although I have no objection whatsoever," she wrote to Sotheby's, "to your client wishing to sell books relating to Swedenborg (and I wish him well in this as it is a large and impressive collection), I still feel that his skull is in a *very* different category and should *not* be included with them."[248] Sotheby's reply was brief and to the point: "We are naturally sorry that our proposal to auction Swedenborg's skull has upset you. It would certainly be appropriate if the skull could be returned to Uppsala and we hope that this may be possible as a result of the sale. However, we have a responsibility to our client who also asked us to sell a number of books relating to Swedenborg and we do not feel it would be in his best interest to remove the skull from auction."[249]

Letters were sent to the newspapers, to members of Parliament, and even to the archbishop of Canterbury. "If the sale is allowed to take place and such a precedent is set," Dawson wrote, "the fear of grave robbing could once again return to haunt the loved ones of the famous."[250]

Dawson's protests seemed a far cry from Reverend Noble's feelings on the same subject 150 years earlier. Noble's disdain toward any sentiment at all regarding human remains had given way to an outcry over the desecration of a great man's bones. What might Swedenborg himself have thought? If the body truly didn't matter, then perhaps he might have been uncomfortable with both Noble and Dawson. As a scientist, he had examined human remains for anatomical purposes and certainly had not seemed bothered by their scientific use. Beyond that, the mortal

---

[248] Unpublished Correspondence, G. P Dawson to John Collins, February 15, 1978.
[249] Unpublished correspondence, John Collins to G. P. Dawson, February 21, 1978.
[250] Unpublished Correspondence, G. P. Dawson to the archbishop of Canterbury, February 19, 1978.

remains of a body were something to be neither worshipped nor vilified. They were simply remnants. Certainly for Swedenborg the remains of the famous were no different than anyone else's. He might well have agreed with the archbishop's secretary, who wrote in her reply to Dawson, "Emanuel Swedenborg has been dead for two hundred years and, after that lapse of time, it is difficult to see how his skull differs from any other human remains of archeological or historical interest at present on display in museums and elsewhere, many of which will have been the subject of sale for money."[251]

Despite Dawson's efforts, the auction went as planned. The skull was bought for 1,650 pounds by the Swedish Royal Academy of Sciences, with the express purpose of finally reuniting it with the rest of the philosopher-scientist's remains.

John Collins of Sotheby's, in his final reply to Dawson, expressed hope "now that it has been sold for return to Sweden that you will feel more sanguine about the whole thing. We feel that this is a very happy result."[252]

As it turned out, the seller never requested payment.

ATTEMPTS TO RETURN Haydn's skull to Eisenstadt were resumed again in 1946. Negotiations took another eight years. It wasn't until 1954 that Haydn's remains were made complete.

---

[251] Unpublished Correspondence, H. H. A. Whitworth to G. P. Dawson, February 28, 1978.
[252] Unpublished Correspondence, John Collins to G. P. Dawson, March 7, 1978.

Beethoven's skull fragments were kept by Tom Rosenthal until the 1980s, when increasing dementia overtook him. They were entrusted to Paul Kaufmann, who made their existence public; they are now at the Ira F. Brilliant Center for Beethoven Studies at San Jose State University.

Mozart's head, having no real tomb to which to return, is still at the Mozarteum, though it is no longer on display because too many docents complained of its unnerving presence. Its origins forever in doubt, the skull was subjected to a DNA analysis in 2002 and compared to two extant samples of hair from the composer's aunts. The skull did not match either sample, but the hair samples didn't match each other either, so it's not at all clear what conclusions can be drawn.

Goya's head remains unaccounted for. Over the last hundred years several heads have surfaced with claims that they belonged to the painter, but none has been verified. It's unclear whether the true skull will ever surface from that dark necropolis of skulduggery and resurrectionists that swallowed it so long ago.

Some skulls, it seems, will always hold their secrets.

THE DESIRE FOR the skulls of the famous flourished at a particularly unique moment, when old attitudes toward the body's remains were made new in the light of the Enlightenment and an arriving modern age. Just as quickly attitudes changed again; by the mid–nineteenth century stealing the skulls of the famous had already become passé.

Well, almost. Rumors continue to persist that while at Yale, Prescott Bush (grandfather to George H. W. Bush and great-grandfather to George W. Bush) and some friends stole the head of Geronimo and perhaps that of Pancho Villa for the Skull and Bones Society. Of the two, the Geronimo story is more likely; Alexandra Robbins, who wrote a history of the secret society, states that there is indeed "a skull encased in a glass display when you walk in the door of the Tomb, and they call it Geronimo."[253] The supposed grave robbery was in fact described in the society's internal history:

> The ring of pick on stone and thud of earth on earth alone disturbs the peace of the prairie. An axe pried open the iron door of the tomb, and Pat[riarch] Bush entered and started to dig. We dug in turn, each on relief taking a turn on the road as guards. . . . Finally Pat[riarch] Ellery James turned up a bridle, soon a saddle horn and rotten leathers followed, then wood and then, at the exact bottom of the small round hole, Pat James dug deep and pried out the trophy itself. . . . We quickly closed the grave, shut the door and sped home to Pat Mallon's room, where we cleaned the Bones. Pat Mallon sat on the floor liberally applying carbolic acid. The Skull was fairly clean, having only some flesh in-

[253] James C. McKinley, "Geronimo's Heirs Sue Secret Yale Society over His Skull," *New York Times*, February 19, 2009, p. A14.

side and a little hair. I showered and hit the hay . . . a
happy man.

But is the skull really Geronimo's? In 1986 the Apache representative Ned Anderson met with George Bush's brother Jonathan, who offered to hand over the skull. But Bush stalled, and
when a skull was finally offered more than a week later, it appeared to be that of a young boy. Suspecting a bait-and-switch,
Anderson refused the skull—but did Skull and Bones really have
the right one?[254] The description of skulduggery is certainly colorful, but it mentions a tomb with an iron door, while Geronimo
was buried in a regular grave. Numerous inside sources have suggested that Prescott Bush fabricated the story from whole cloth;
certainly no independent evidence exists that Geronimo's skull is
still housed at Yale. On February 17, 2009, however, descendents
of Geronimo formally filed suit against Skull and Bones for the
repatriation of his remains, hoping that a federal law suit would
help to clarify the matter once and for all.

Prescott Bush notwithstanding, cranioklepty was first and
foremost the work of phrenologists. William Williams had called
phrenology the first new science since the Second Coming (which
Swedenborg claimed had already taken place in 1758). And in
many ways it *was* a new science for a new time—it boldly claimed
to lay bare centuries-old mysteries through a cursory touch of

---

[254] See Alexandra Robbins, *Secrets of the Tomb: Skull and Bones, the Ivy League, and the Hidden Paths of Power* (New York: Little Brown and Company, 2002), pp. 144–146.

the scalp, making visible what had long been hidden. It was a product of the Enlightenment, to be sure, but its popularity was owing in part to its ability to tap into a deep wellspring of anxiety and hope about who we are, why we act the way we do, and why we create art and imagination. In those days of rapid progress and advance, all things seemed possible, and phrenology's claims to explain the human mind and the mystery of genius did not seem at all far-fetched then, as they seem today. As a science and as a social movement, phrenology has long since exhausted itself, but the curiosity and yearning that fed it remain fervently alive.

If phrenology was a New Science for a new age, it also hearkened back to something very ancient, to the mystery of life contained within the bones, an unknowable secret dug up from deep sepulchers and overgrown cemeteries. Those who took it upon themselves to take the heads of famous men such as Haydn, Beethoven, Browne, and Swedenborg looked forward and backward at once—to a future when the meaning of "genius" might yet be revealed and to a past that stretched down a long path of *mementi mori* and saints' relics to the silent truths locked deep in bone.

As phrenology moved from a theory to a science to an art and finally to a sideshow, its practitioners were always careful not to predict genius from the shape of the skulls and instead to confirm only the already established genius in the heads before them. When examining the heads of men such as Haydn or even Browne, phrenologists *assumed* them to be geniuses. What these "scientists" were doing, in essence, was not proving the genius of the skull's owner so much as the validity of their own clinical tenets. The phrenologist could never hope to read something in a genius's head that wasn't already known; it was instead phrenology itself that was under scrutiny. And this is really what the skull represents to science: a proving ground. A breadth of new sciences have been tested against the skull, which has been held up to phrenology, anatomy, craniometry, and anthropology, to name only a few disciplines. The skulls remain the same; it is the science that changes. And in two centuries of endless attempts to identify genius through some objective measure, it's worth noting that the geniuses themselves were never questioned. It would seem possible that at least one true believer might at some point have argued that the skull shape of someone like Browne may in fact have contraindicated that he was the genius others believed him to be. The identification should have worked both ways. But no one ever made such a claim. When it came to a definition of genius, the ultimate measure could never really be the skull—the measure was always the writing, the music, the art itself.

THE SKULLS OF these artists came to light during a time of enormous upheaval and stayed aboveground long enough to witness vast changes, long enough that their postmortem odysseys began to develop lives of their own. In his biography of Haydn, Karl Geiringer referred to Rosenbaum's theft in a brief final chapter titled "An Incongruous Postlude." But were these episodes really all that incongruous? If the hallmark of great artists is that they live on, obtaining immortality through their creative works, then might it not be fitting that their bones, too, have a share of immortality? Maybe we have two halves to our lives—the time we spend on earth and the time afterward, perhaps equally brief, during which our works outlive us. Perhaps the odd, even unfortunate odysseys of these skulls are just the physical traces of those second lives.

Perhaps the vicar of St. Peter Mancroft, F. J. Meyrick, was thinking along these lines when he entered the reinterment of Sir Thomas Browne's skull into the church registry and wrote, in the "age" column, "317 years."

St. Peter Mancroft's burial book.
PHOTO TANYA MCCALLIN, COURTESY NORFOLK RECORD OFFICE
AND *CABINET* MAGAZINE.

BIBLIOGRAPHY

Bauer et. al. "The Official Report on the First Exhumation of the Graves of Beethoven and Schubert by the Gessellshcaft der Musikfreunde in 1863," translated by Hannah Leibmann, *The Beethoven Journal*, Vol. 20, Nos. 1 & 2 (Summer & Winter 2005)

Bierce, Ambrose. *The Unabridged Devil's Dictionary*. Edited David E. Schultz and S. T. Joshi. Athens: University of Georgia Press, 2000.

Blom, Philipp. *To Have and to Hold: An Intimate history of Collectors and Collecting*. Woodstock: Overlook Press, 2003.

Bowditch, Sarah. *Taxidermy: or, the Art of Collecting, Preparing, and Mounting Objects of Natural History*. London: Longman, Hurst, Rees, Orme, and Brown, 1820.

Bradbury, Malcolm. *To the Hermitage*. Woodstock: Overlook Press, 2002.

Breuning, Gerhard von. *From the House of the Black-Robed Spaniards*. Translated by Henry Mins and Maynard Solomon. Cambridge: Cambridge University Press, 1992.

———. "The Skulls of Beethoven and Schubert". *The Beethoven Journal*, Vol. 20, Nos. 1 & 2 (Summer & Winter 2005)

Brown, Raphael (ed.). *The Little Flowers of St. Francis of Assisi*. New York: Doubleday, 1958.

Browne, Thomas. *Religio Medici, Hydriotaphia and The Garden of Cyrus*. Edited by R. H. A. Robbins. Oxford: Clarendon Press, 1972.

———. *Hydriotaphia and the Garden of Cyrus*. Edited by W. A. Greenhill. London: MacMillan and Company, 1896.

Buklija, Tatjana. "Cultures of Death and Politics of Corpse Supply: Anatomy in Vienna 1848-1914". *Bulletin of the History of Medicine*, No. 82 (Fall 2008).

Burke, Edmund. *A Philosophical Enquiry*. Oxford: Oxford University Press, 1990.

Burrell, Brian. *Postcards from the Brain Museum*. New York: Broadway Books, 2004.

Combe, George. *A System of Phrenology*. Boston: Marsh, Capen and Lyon, 1838.

Cushing, Harvey. *The Life of Sir William Osler*. London: Oxford University Press, 1940.

Davies, Peter J. *Beethoven in Person: His Deafness, Illnesses, and Death*. New York: Greenwood Press, 2001.

———. *Mozart in Person: His Character and Health*. New York: Greenwood Press, 1989.

Descartes, René. *Discourse on Method, Optics, Geometry, and Meteorology*. Translated by Paul J. Olscamp. Indianapolis: Hackett, 2001.

Dick, Leslie. *The Skull of Charlotte Corday and Other Stories.* New York: Scribner, 1995.

Eade, Peter. *The Norfolk and Norwich Hospital, 1770 to 1900.* London: Jarrold and Sons, 1900.

Eliot, George. *Adam Bede.* London: Penguin, 2008.

———. *Scenes from Clerical Life.* London: Penguin, 1998.

———. *The George Eliot Letters,* Nine Volumes. Edited by Gordon Sherman Haight. New Haven: Yale University Press, 1954.

Fuentes, Carlos. *The Buried Mirror.* New York: Mariner Books, 1999.

Geary, Patrick J. *Furta Sacra: Thefts of Relics in the Central Middle Ages.* Princeton: Princeton University Press, 1990.

Geiringer, Karl. *Haydn: A Creative Life in Music.* Berkeley: University of California Press, 1982.

Gosse, Edmund. *Sir Thomas Browne.* London: MacMillan and Company, 1905.

Gould, Stephen Jay. *The Mismeasure of Man.* New York: W. W. Norton, 1981.

———. *The Panda's Thumb: More Reflections in Natural History.* New York: W. W. Norton, 1980.

Goyder, David George. *My Battle for Life: The Autobiography of a Phrenologist.* London: Simpkin, Marshall, and Co., 1857.

Gramit, David. *Cultivating Music: The Aspirations, Interests, and Limits of German Musical Culture, 1770-1848.* Berkeley: University of California Press, 2002.

Hagner, Michael. "Skulls, Brains, and Memorial Culture: On Cerebral Biographies of Scientists in the Nineteenth Century." *Science in Context,* Vol. 16, Nos. 1 & 2 (2003).

Hegel, G. W. F. *Phenomenology of Spirit.* Translated by A. V. Miller. Oxford: Oxford University Press, 1977.

Henschen, Folke. *Emanuel Swedenborg's Cranium: A Critical Analysis.* Upsala: Nova Acta Regiae Societatis Scientiarum Upsaliensis, Ser. IV, Vol. 17, No. 9. 1960.

———. *The Human Skull: A Cultural History.* New York: Frederick A. Praeger, 1966.

Hultkrantz, Johan. Vilh. *Additional Note to the Mortal Remains of Emanuel Swedenborg.* Upsala: Nova Acta Regiae Societatis Scientiarum Upsaliensis, Ser. IV, Vol. 3, No. 2. 1912.

———. *The Mortal Remains of Emanuel Swedenborg.* Upsala: Nova Acta Regiae Societatis Scientiarum Upsaliensis, Ser. IV, Vol. 2, No. 9. 1910.

Hunt, Leigh. *Selected Writings.* Edited by David Jesson-Dibley. New York: Routledge, 2003.

Kant, Immanuel. *Critique of Judgement.* Translated James Creed Meredith. Oxford: Oxford University Press, 2007.

Keith, Arthur. *Phrenological Studies of the Skull and Brain Cast of Sir Thomas Browne of Norwich.* Edinburgh: Oliver and Boyd, 1924.

Larson, Erik. *The Devil in the White City: Murder, Magic, and Madness at the Fair that Changed America.* New York: Vintage, 2003.

Lenhammer, Harry. "Swedenborg in Uppsala's Cathedral." Translated by Jane Williams-Hogan. *The New Philosophy,* January-June 2003.

Leopardi, Giacomo. *Operette Morali: Essays and Dialogues.* Translated by Givanni Cecchetti. Berkeley: University of California Press, 1982.

Lesky, Erna. *The Vienna Medical School of the 19ʰ Century.* Translated by L. Williams and I. S. Levij. Baltimore: Johns Hopkins University Press, 1976.

Leslie, Shane. *The Skull of Swift: An Extempore Exhumation*. Indianapolis: The Bobbs-Merrille Company, 1928.

Llosa, Mario Vargas. *The War of the End of the World*. Translated by Helen R. Lane. New York: Farrar Straus Giroux, 1984.

Lombroso, Cesare. *The Female Offender*. New York: D. Appleton and Company, 1897.

Mackey, Nathaniel. *Paracritical Hinge*. Madison: University of Wisconsin, 2005.

Martin, Russell. *Beethoven's Hair*. New York: Broadway Books, 2000.

Meredith, William. "The History of Beethoven's Skull Fragments." *The Beethoven Journal*, Vol. 20, Nos. 1 & 2 (Summer & Winter 2005).

Morton, Samuel George. *Crania Aegyptiaca; or, Observations of Egyptian Ethnography*. Philadelphia: John Penington, 1844.

Noble, Samuel. "Unfounded Tale Respecting the Skull of Swedenborg and Its Refutation." *The Intellectual Repository for the New Church*, No. XLVII (July-September 1823).

Pezzl, Johann. *A Sketch of Vienna*. In *Mozart and Vienna*, edited by H. C. Robbins Landon. New York: Schirmer Books, 1991.

Psihoyos, Louie. *Hunting Dinosaurs*. With John Knoebber. New York: Random House, 1994.

Richardson, Ruth. *Death, Dissection and the Destitute*. London: Phoenix Press, 2001.

Robbins, Alexandra. *Secrets of the Tomb: Skull and Bones, the Ivy League, and the Hidden Paths of Power*. New York: Little Brown and Company, 2002.

H. C. Robbins Landon, *Haydn: The Late Years, 1801–1809* (Bloomington: Indiana University Press, 1977), pp. 379–390.

Robertson, Priscilla Smith. *Revolutions of 1848: A Social History*. Princeton: Princeton University Press, 1968.

Rokitansky, Karl von. *A Manual of Pathological Anatomy*. Four volumes. Translated by William Edward Swaine, Edward Sieveking, Charles Hewitt Moore, and George E. Day. Philadelphia: Blanchard and Lea, 1855.

Rosenbaum, Carl. *The Haydn Yearbook V: The Diaries of Joseph Carl Rosenbaum*. Edited by Else Radant. Translated by Eugene Hartzell. Vienna: Theodore Presser Company, 1968.

Rufus, Anneli. *Magnificent Corpses*. New York: Marlowe & Company, 1999.

Russell, Miles. *Piltdown Man: The Secret Life of Charles Dawson*. Stroud: Tempus Publishing, 2003.

Schiller, Francis. *Paul Broca: Founder of French Anthropology, Explorer of the Brain*. New York: Oxford University Press, 1992.

Shorto, Russell. *Descartes' Bones: A Skeletal History of the Conflict Between Faith and Reason*. New York: Doubleday, 2008.

Spencer, Frank. *Piltdown: A Scientific Forgery*. London: Oxford University Press, 1990.

Starobinski, Jean. *The Invention of Liberty: 1700-1789*. Translated by Bernard C. Swift. Geneva: Skira, 1964.

Stern, Madeleine B. *Heads & Headlines: The Phrenological Fowlers*. Norman: University of Oklahoma Press, 1971.

Swedenborg, Emanuel. *The Spiritual Diary of Emanuel Swedenborg*. In five volumes. Translated by George Bush and John H. Smithson. London: James Speirs, 1883.

Spurzheim, J. G. *Phrenology: In Connexion with the Study of Physiognomy*. Boston: Marsh, Capen & Lyon, 1834.

Symmons, Sarah. *Goya*. London: Phaidon, 1998.

Tandler, Julius. "Über den Schädel Haydns." *Mitteilungen der anthropologischen Gesellschaft*, Vienna, XXXIX (1909).

Thayer, Alexander Wheelock. *Thayer's Life of Beethoven*. Revised and Edited by Elliot Forbes. Princeton: Princeton University Press, 1964.

Tildesley, Miriam. "Sir Thomas Browne: His Skull, Portraits, and Ancestry." *Biometrika*, Vol. 15, No. 1/2 (August 1923).

Tomlinson, Stephen. *Head Masters: Phrenology, Secular Education, and Nineteenth-Century Social Thought*. Tuscaloosa: University of Alabama Press, 2005.

Topinard, Paul. *Anthropology*. Translated by Robert T. H. Bartley. London: Chapman and Hall, 1878.

Twain, Mark. *The Autobiography of Mark Twain*. Edited by Charles Neider. New York: Harper Collins, 1959.

Webster, James. "The *Creation*, Haydn's Late Vocal Music, and the Musical Sublime." In *Haydn and His World*, edited by Elaine Sisman. Princeton: Princeton University Press, 1997.

Weilien, Joseph. "Speech Given at the Reburial of Ludwig van Beethoven." *The Beethoven Journal*, Vol. 20, Nos. 1 & 2 (Summer & Winter 2005).

Witemeyer, Hugh. *George Eliot and the Visual Arts*. New Haven: Yale University Press, 1979.

Williams, William A. *A Reply to Our Critics*. London: L. N. Fowler and Company, 1890.

Wood, George B. *A Biographical Memoir of Samuel George Morton, M. D*. Philadelphia: T. K. and P. G. Collins, 1853.

Woolf, Virginia. *Orlando*. San Diego: : Harcourt, Brace, Jovanovich, 1956.

———. "Sir Thomas Browne." In *The Essays of Virginia Woolf, Vol. 3: 1919-1924*. Edited by Andrew McNeillie. San Diego: Harcourt, Brace, Jovanovich, 1988.

Index of Names

Acknowledgments

Many people helped with the development of this book. Thanks to Bruce Smith for his initial encouragement, to Colby Chamberlain and Sina Najafi at *Cabinet* Magazine, and to Mark Allen and Jason Brown at Machine Project. Thanks also to the following people who provided information, resources, translation assistance and other help: William Meredith, Patricia Stroh, Michael Reeve, Sarah Symmons, James Wilson, Erin Sullivan, Ariane Simard, Seth Sherwood, Anna Dhody, Julie Gardham, and Tia Resleure. Any errors in fact or judgment are mine, not theirs. Special thanks to the wonderful folks at Unbridled Books, in particular Fred Ramey, who nurtured this book from its beginning and without whom it never would have seen the light of day. Above all thanks to Nicole, for reasons too numerous to list.